The
EVERYTHING®
Creative Wedding Ideas Book

Dear Reader:

Unlike many young girls, I never really daydreamed about an elaborate fantasy wedding. Even when I was first engaged, I always considered a wedding a means to an end—the party was pretty much incidental. The important thing was the commitment to spending the rest of our lives together. And while I never lost sight of the latter, I soon also discovered how much fun planning the party could be.

The flowers. The music. The favors. It occurred to me that this was the biggest, most expensive event I'd ever plan. With that fact came responsibility—and opportunity. Responsibility that our guests would be comfortable, well fed, and entertained. And opportunity to free ourselves from the idea of a cookie-cutter wedding, so we could express our own personalities, tastes, and interests. We enjoyed this creative process through every party-day decision we made, from the invitation to the wedding program to the reception location.

My point? The more creative and personal you get when planning your wedding, the more fun it is to plan it—and enjoy it. You *can* free yourself of traditional expectations, even if it's just in small ways. And your guests will appreciate it. A little creativity is a welcome change after a lifetime of attending one similar wedding after another.

My best wishes in planning your big day and your lifetime of days together beyond. A creative, distinctive wedding is the perfect start to a relationship that is also fully and uniquely your own.

Jennifer Lata Rung

The EVERYTHING® Series

Editorial

Publishing Director	Gary M. Krebs
Managing Editor	Kate McBride
Copy Chief	Laura MacLaughlin
Acquisitions Editor	Bethany Brown
Development Editor	Karen Johnson Jacot
Production Editor	Khrysti Nazzaro

Production

Production Director	Susan Beale
Production Manager	Michelle Roy Kelly
Series Designers	Daria Perreault
	Colleen Cunningham
Cover Design	Paul Beatrice
	Frank Rivera
Layout and Graphics	Colleen Cunningham
	Rachael Eiben
	Michelle Roy Kelly
	Daria Perreault
	Erin Ring
Series Cover Designer	Barry Littmann
Cover Illustrator	Dave Winter

Visit the entire Everything® Series at everything.com

THE

EVERYTHING®

CREATIVE WEDDING IDEAS BOOK

Cultural traditions and offbeat themes to
make your day extra-special

Jennifer Lata Rung

Adams Media Corporation
Avon, Massachusetts

To sometimes taking a risk

An Everything® Series Book.
Everything® and everything.com® are registered trademarks of F+W Publications, Inc.

Published by Adams Media, an F+W Publications Company
57 Littlefield Street, Avon, MA 02322 U.S.A.
www.adamsmedia.com

ISBN: 1-58062-863-X
Printed in the United States of America.

J I H G F E D C B

Library of Congress Cataloging-in-Publication Data
Rung, Jennifer Lata.
The everything creative ideas book / Jennifer Lata Rung.
p.   cm.   -- (An everything series book)
ISBN 1-58062-863-X
1. Wedding etiquette. 2. Weddings–Planning.
I. Title. II. Series: Everything series.
BJ2051 .R86   2003
395.2'2–dc21   2002014955

This publication is designed to provide accurate and authoritative information with regard to the subject matter covered. It is sold with the understanding that the publisher is not engaged in rendering legal, accounting, or other professional advice. If legal advice or other expert assistance is required, the services of a competent professional person should be sought.
—From a *Declaration of Principles* jointly adopted by a Committee of the American Bar Association and a Committee of Publishers and Associations

Many of the designations used by manufacturers and sellers to distinguish their products are claimed as trademarks. Where those designations appear in this book and Adams Media was aware of a trademark claim, the designations have been printed with initial capital letters.

This book is available at quantity discounts for bulk purchases.
For information, call 1-800-872-5627.

Contents

Acknowledgments

Thanks to Jessica Faust, agent extraordinaire, for helping me be sure my own risk was not in vain. Also, thanks to everyone who took the time to tell me their own creative wedding stories, including Gertrude Lata, Edna Cabarga, Kim Lata, Christa Hobart, Brian and Jeanne Meissner, Chad and Amy Rataczak, Deb Parnes, Meredith Horowitz, Kate Jayson, Emily Spensieri, and everyone else who helped along the way. Thanks most of all to Mark for his unquestioning support . . . and for inspiring me with his own style of creative thinking.

Top Ten Reasons
to Choose a Creative Wedding

1. You want a ceremony and reception that are as unique as you and your partner are.

2. It allows for nontraditional situations and special circumstances, such as interfaith or same-sex marriages.

3. Adhering to budgetary restraints can be simpler when you incorporate clever variations in your event.

4. You want to be able to include your favorite hobbies (or your favorite pets!) in this very important day.

5. You can keep very traditional relatives happy while still adding a touch of your personality to the day.

6. Your idea of "spiritual" involves a beautiful beach or mountaintop, rather than a church or temple.

7. Your best friends aren't just women, and you don't like the idea of leaving out the guys just because they don't fit into a pink bridesmaid dress.

8. You want wedding vows that are straight from your heart and his.

9. The planning stages of the creative wedding can be as fun as the wedding itself.

10. Your guests will remember your wedding long after they've gone home.

Introduction

▶ SAY GOOD-BYE TO COOKIE-CUTTER WEDDINGS.

Farewell to the generic reception hall, the bland chicken entrée, and the DJ spinning the "Electric Slide."

Adios to traditionalists who claim anything outside this norm to be unacceptable.

Because today's weddings are whatever you want them to be. From tiny budget to carte blanche affairs, there are a wealth of ideas that you can incorporate into your wedding to make it uniquely your own. This book is meant to help you redefine your traditional notions of a wedding by giving old ideas new life—or discarding those old ideas entirely. For instance:

- Your engagement ring doesn't have to be a diamond. Or a ring.
- Your reception budget doesn't have to equal the cost of a new car.
- Your maid of honor doesn't have to be female.
- Your menu doesn't have to consist of "chicken or beef."
- You can create the elaborate fantasy you've always dreamed of, from a traditional Victorian wedding to *Saturday Night Fever* redux.

This is *your* wedding day, which means you can throw exactly the party you want—from traditional with a few distinct flairs—to completely and utterly off the wall.

There are plenty of books that will dictate your wedding day parameters. This book is meant to show you wedding day possibilities. It's full of ideas that you'll love or hate, and that you can embrace or discard. That's the point: pulling out the ideas that make sense to you and incorporating them into the biggest party you'll ever throw (or the smallest—it's all up to you). So if you're looking for ideas ranging from fully themed extravaganzas to traditional weddings with a twist, you've come to the right place. If you're having a "nontraditional" wedding, from same-sex unions to second weddings to pregnant weddings, you'll find plenty of (solid and sensitive) nontraditional ideas. And because it ain't over 'til it's over, there are also some unusual honeymoon destinations as well as ideas for celebrating your first anniversary and beyond. There's even etiquette specific to situations that may arise from throwing a more creative wedding.

Have fun. After all, this is the one time in your life you can get away with believing "it's all about me."

Chapter 1

Deciding on a Creative Wedding

Think of all the weddings you've been to in your lifetime. Most likely, a few pop into your mind immediately. They are probably the ones that offered a new twist on the old traditional wedding—something you'd never seen or experienced before. Now ask yourself: Do you want people to remember *your* wedding in ten years?

Why a Creative Wedding?

If you answered "yes"—you *do* want people to remember your wedding ten years from now—you're the perfect candidate for throwing a creative wedding. And whether you infuse the occasion with a little creativity or a lot, you'll pretty much guarantee an unforgettable event. After all, the majority of us are used to going to pretty standard events—ceremonies we can recite from memory, receptions that move like clockwork from cocktails to dinner to dancing with no surprises. That's because historically all but the really courageous were fearful of taking a risk on something new and different.

FACT

A "creative" wedding can range from a full-blown theme wedding— like a Renaissance wedding or a disco-themed wedding—to a more traditional wedding with creative touches your guests will never forget.

Fortunately, the idea of a wedding that conforms to one ideal is changing. Today's weddings are becoming much more unique, with brides and grooms putting their individual touches on everything from the ceremony to the last dance. Wedding vendors are becoming more amenable and accommodating to these special requests. And with theme weddings growing in popularity, you're free to put your own personal stamp on your special day.

Before you decide to throw a creative wedding, however, you may want to make a quick list of pros and cons to determine if it's really for you.

Pros

The following list outlines some of the positives to throwing a creative wedding:

- Your guests will enjoy a new experience.
- You can turn your longtime fantasy into reality.
- Your day can truly reflect your personal interests.
- You'll enjoy planning it.

- You won't have to participate in traditions you don't care for.
- You can break the old conformist mold.
- You can make your wedding as unique as your relationship.
- Your wedding will be an event talked about for years to come.
- It's one time in your life you're expected to be self-indulgent.
- You're spending lots of money already—why not spend it on exactly what you've dreamed of?

Even if you've never considered yourself a "creative" person, you *can* throw a creative wedding. The ideas in this book are meant to inspire your imagination and bring out your creative spirit—feel free to use them as they appear or to put your own unique spin on them. Or use the creativity exercises at the end of this chapter to develop creative ideas of your own.

Cons

And here are some of the challenges you may want to consider as you plan a "creative" wedding:

- Planning a theme wedding is time-consuming and detail-oriented (though so is planning a traditional wedding).
- Your vision? Your decision. You will be involved in every step of the process and can't assume the florist or musicians or photographer will understand your vision until it's well explained . . . or well supervised.
- You may encounter the occasional party pooper or critic.
- Not every vendor will be willing—or have the capability—to carry out your plan.

What Is Your "Creative Comfort Level"?

So, you've weighed the pros and cons and are venturing ahead. Congratulations on your decision to get creative! The next step is determining just how creative you want to be. Again, your affair can range from the completely and utterly outrageous to the traditional with a few special touches.

The following quiz will help you figure out just how creative you want to get . . . and will help you determine some of the creative ideas that best suit you:

- Have you always longed for a special wedding, such as a holiday wedding, a costumed affair, or a romantic fantasy?
- Do you have special interests or hobbies that you feel passionate about?
- Do you and your fiancé share any hobbies or interests that you feel passionate about?
- Are your family and friends open to new ideas?
- Can you easily brush off criticism?
- Are you comfortable going against the grain?
- Do you enjoy attention and standing out in a crowd?
- Do you feel comfortable breaking tradition?
- Do you have patience to deal with the unexpected?
- Will your parents be supportive of ideas that are "outside the box"?

Count up how many times you answered "no" and refer to the following scale to determine your Creative Comfort Level.

Scale:

0 No's: You are extremely comfortable asserting your own personal style. Get as outrageous and wild as you want on your wedding day—you're the ideal candidate for the most creative of weddings.

1–2 No's: You are also comfortable with creativity, with just one or two factors that could complicate your plans. If you deal with these from the beginning—say, convincing your parents or tuning out critics—you'll be in a perfect position to be as creative as you like.

3–4 No's: If yours is an extremely conservative social group, plus you hate being the center of attention, plus you don't feel comfortable breaking tradition, you may not want to throw that disco wedding with all the trappings. But you don't need to give up creativity entirely. You can certainly still incorporate your favorite elements—say a decorative disco ball—without asking all your guests to don leisure suits.

5–6 No's: You've got some creative adversity, both internally and externally. This is certainly no reason, however, to give up on being creative. Your best bet might be a traditional wedding with as many creative touches as you feel comfortable with. (See Chapters 13–16 for creative ideas for each of the elements of your wedding, from the invitation to the reception.) Or you can opt to express your creative spirit through a more intimate event, such as a shower or at the rehearsal dinner. (See Chapter 4 for Uncommon Pre-parties.)

Soliciting Support

Family politics are a part of every wedding, from the most creative to the most traditional. With so many people involved, it is inevitable that you may have different ideas from your parents, that your parents may have different ideas from *his* parents, and that no one readily agrees with anyone. With this kind of conflict, it's no wonder the groom often avoids all the wedding trappings.

Obviously, if you and your groom are paying for the entire affair, you will have free reign in making wedding day decisions. If there are others sharing in the costs, things can get a bit more complicated. But with a little diplomacy and compromise, you can get through it. It may take some time and diplomatic maneuvering to convince your parents that a mountaintop wedding is what you've always dreamed of—and what they should, in turn, finance. The end result will, of course, be worth the work. If your future in-laws are involved, you may have a second hurdle to cross, with another set of people to please. Deal with each of these issues as they arise.

Just as you've always fantasized about your wedding, so, probably, has your mother. If your parents aren't immediately convinced that your idea to have a hot air balloon wedding is the greatest ever, it may take some work to get them to agree. Broach the topic carefully, and don't make any demands right off the bat. Give your parents some time to get used to the idea. Solicit the support of your siblings or grandparents (always an easier sell). Tell them why it means so much to you. And *don't* throw a temper tantrum. Eventually you'll win them over, or you'll find an acceptable compromise you can all agree on.

Unleash Your Creativity

As you begin to plan your creative wedding, it's important to remember that creativity is an attitude, a state of mind. When you drop all of your preconceived notions of right and wrong, it will open your mind to new ideas. The key to creativity is to challenge your habitual responses—in this case to how a wedding *should* be—to design a wedding exactly as you *want* it to be.

QUESTION?

What is creativity?
The American Heritage Dictionary defines "creative" as "characterized by originality and expressiveness; imaginative." Creativity is simply putting these characteristics into action.

In addition to being open to ideas that you learn about through this book, magazines, and Web sites, you'll probably want to tap into your own creative thoughts and personal ideas. The following are some tips to help you get into a creative state of mind. These are tips that can be applied to planning your wedding, or to any other task that requires a creative thought process.

Brainstorm. Get together with friends or family, set aside a predetermined amount of time, and write down every stream-of-consciousness idea your group has about a specific issue. For instance, if the topic is wedding favors, create a long list of everyone's ideas. During your brainstorming session, accept each idea and suggestion with equal weight, without rejection or ridicule. Once you're finished, you can decide on the best ideas while weeding out the not-so-great ones . . . or modify the ideas to fit your personal style. By accepting all ideas equally during brainstorming, you create an environment where participants are not afraid to make contributions, which will result in more numerous and better ideas.

ALERT!

During brainstorming, no idea should be rejected. If participants are afraid that their ideas may be laughed at or frowned upon, it inhibits the creative process and will limit your results.

Carry a pen and paper. You never know when a good idea will hit. Whether you're in line at the grocery store, at your gynecologist's office, or at Thanksgiving dinner, a creative thought can sneak up—then be forgotten as quickly as it arrived. Carry a pen and small pad of paper—or, even better, a Palm Pilot with all of your other wedding to-do information—to jot down your great ideas as you have them.

Exercise. There's nothing like physical exercise to relax your body, free your mind, and open you up to new ideas.

Get a good night's sleep. Hitting a creative brick wall? Save your task for the next day. A good night's sleep can do wonders to rejuvenate your thinking and energy level.

Research. Be a sponge. The more magazines, books, and Web sites you check out, the more things you'll learn—and the more your own personal creative process will flourish. Whether you take the ideas you see as verbatim or reinterpret them to fit your own situation, keeping your eyes and ears open is a great way to generate creativity.

Delay judgment. Tonight, you may think the N'Sync themed wedding cake is a fab idea. Tomorrow you may see the situation a bit more clearly. By letting an idea marinate before you take action, you will discover whether it's got staying power—or whether it should be dumped as quickly as boy-toy Justin.

Discover Your Passion

If you have a passion, you obviously don't have to discover it. But it may not be completely obvious at first how it fits into your wedding. For instance, an artist could hand paint invitations, or create individual and unique wedding favors for each guest. An avid romance reader might have a romance-novel-theme wedding. Or a horse lover may want to incorporate something of the sport into her special day.

Weaving a favorite hobby, talent, or interest into your wedding plans can be a highly personal, unique exercise that guests will thoroughly enjoy. It's simple but often overlooked—and all you need to do for inspiration is think about what you like to do most. Then use it as a springboard to develop an entire wedding theme, or include it within a smaller aspect of your wedding, such as the cake design, wedding favors, or centerpieces.

Breaking the Rules

Even if you plan the most traditional wedding, you will inevitably experience some conflict with those who have their own ideas. Everyone has his or her own opinion of what is proper, or expected, or fun. Your best friend may pressure you to follow one course of action, while your mother-in-law insists on the opposite. When planning a creative wedding, these challenges can become exacerbated, due to plans that may fall outside the traditional expectations of friends and family.

If conflict erupts, weigh each battle according to its importance to you, rather than fighting every issue to its bitter end. If you display some flexibility, your parents or fiancé's parents will likely follow suit.

Remember, this is your wedding day. That doesn't mean you get to throw a fit demanding everything go your way. What it does mean, however, is that with a little diplomacy, you can remind all the relevant players—your parents, your future in-laws, your sister, your best friend—that this is your vision for one of the most important days of *your* life. If you and your groom feel passionate about a theme wedding, or certain creative touches, your enthusiasm and excitement are bound to be infectious. Ⓔ

Chapter 2

E Proposals with Panache

An expensive meal, champagne, and the one-knee proposal followed by a huge diamond set in platinum—while this may be the dream of many a bride-to-be, *your* proposal fantasy might be quite different. Maybe you don't care much for jewelry, or you think three months' salary would be better spent on a racing bike. Here you'll find tips and advice on getting engaged . . . creatively.

The Engagement Ring

Today's engagement rings are the ultimate symbol of commitment. For most young men, the idea of spending three months' salary on anything but a big-screen TV is a travesty. That's why the engagement ring means so much, and why you know a man means business when he buys one. It also explains why there are still people—like radio psychologist Dr. Laura Schlesinger, for instance—who do not consider a couple to be truly engaged until she wears a ring on her finger (and, preferably, a diamond one).

FACT

While most consider it a harmless—and, in fact, welcome—tradition, some women feel the engagement ring symbolizes "ownership," particularly because only she (and not the groom-to-be) wears a ring prior to the wedding date.

Symbolism

Across religions and cultures, the symbolism of the engagement ring—and wedding ring—lies in its simple, circular design, which has no beginning and no end. It is considered to symbolize perfection, eternity, and unity. Some associate the ring's circular design with bodies of the solar system, including the sun and moon.

History

There is much speculation on the origination of the engagement ring. Some theories indicate that a ring given in B.C. times indicated a woman's slavery to the man who gave it to her, with the ring serving as a "slave band" (a theory some women would agree still rings true today). Other theories point to the fact that engagement rings may have been part of dowries given by the groom to the bride's family. There is evidence of rings being exchanged in ancient Greek culture, in ancient Roman culture, and in various other cultures and times leading up to the present.

The first recorded gift of a diamond ring dates back to the fifteenth century. It was given as a promise of marriage by the Archduke Maximillian of Austria to Mary of Burgundy in 1477. Thus began the royal tradition of giving a diamond engagement ring, a tradition spanning hundreds of years, eventually trickling down to us plebeians of today.

FACT

The "Claddagh" ring is believed to have originated in seventeenth-century Ireland. Designed of metal (usually gold), with two hands clasping a crowned heart, it's sort of like a mood ring for Irish women. Worn on the right hand with the crown turned inward, it indicates the woman is open to suitors. Worn with the crown turned outward, it shows there's someone in her life. Worn on the left hand with the crown turned outward, it means she's married—lay off.

Nontraditional Engagement Rings

Of course, times have changed. And while for many the perfect engagement ring is still a diamond set in simple gold or platinum, other women prefer alternative gems or atypical settings. In addition, some feel the financial investment of a diamond is money better spent elsewhere. After all, no one actually *needs* a diamond ring (though you may hear some pretty convincing arguments to the contrary).

There are plenty of ways to "seal the deal"—or, more nicely put, express one's commitment—that involve an untraditional piece of jewelry or no jewelry at all.

Unconventional Stones

There's no steadfast rule that says an engagement ring has to be a diamond. It's only since the 1930s that the diamond has become so dominant, probably for a number of reasons:

- They are the hardest known substance on earth, thus very durable.
- They are universally valued as a luxury item.
- They are part of a long tradition.

- They have been extremely well marketed.
- They are, simply, beautiful.

There's no rule that says an engagement ring has to have a diamond—or any gemstone, for that matter. Other engagement ring possibilities include metals like silver, gold, or platinum, designed as simply or elaborately as you like. Tap into your own style to choose a ring you'll love and want to wear forever.

There is no doubt that a well-cut, clear diamond is a stunning thing to behold. But there are other options, especially for those who care to express their own individual style. With the availability of everything from birthstones to crystals to precious minerals, there are countless options to create the perfect ring. And though the majority of engagement rings still consist of the classic diamond solitaire, trends from Hollywood to Hackensack show an upswing in individuality:

- Actress Debra Messing wears a ruby eternity band.
- Actress Mena Suvari wears a band covered with amethysts and citrines, her birthstones.
- Princess Di wore an engagement ring comprising of an 18-carat sapphire surrounded by diamonds.
- When presented with a very large diamond from current husband James Brolin, Barbra Streisand reportedly told him she preferred something a bit more "subtle."

The growing popularity of colored gemstones—from emeralds to sapphires to rubies and even pearls—allow today's couples stylish, creative alternatives to the traditional diamond. And whether you choose to forgo the diamond completely in favor of another gemstone, or add gemstones to a diamond setting, the following is a guide to popular gemstone's symbolism.

Birthstones and Their Meanings		
Birth Month	**Gemstone**	**Symbolizes**
January	Garnet	Truth, Constancy
February	Amethyst	Sincerity
March	Aquamarine	Courage
April	Diamond	Innocence, Light
May	Emerald	Happiness, Success in Love
June	Pearl	Beauty (and/or Longevity)
July	Ruby	Love, Chastity
August	Peridot	Joy
September	Sapphire	Wisdom, Clear Thinking
October	Opal	Hope
November	Topaz	Fidelity
December	Turquoise	Success, Prosperity

Unique Settings

Though the engagement ring is often valued most for its stone—and many men choose to spend their engagement ring budget on the biggest one it allows—more and more couples are looking at the setting as another opportunity for unique, beautiful design. An intriguing setting can be as much of a head turner as the diamond or gemstone it holds. These settings are sometimes inspired by different cultures, such as Middle-Eastern and African designs, or ancient jewelry design. There is also a growing trend in very modern settings—for a ring that will go with jeans and a T-shirt as much as a formal gown. They may also incorporate two metals, such as gold and platinum.

FACT

Want a really creative setting? Your skin. You can work with a tattoo artist to design a beautiful rendering for both your ring fingers. Or use the henna technique for a little less permanence.

Can't find the setting you want? Work with a jeweler to design a custom-made setting. With just a little vision and creativity, it's a great way to ensure your ring won't look like anyone else's. Or shop around—more and more jewelers are showing styles different from the more common classic solitaire and cathedral settings.

Engagement Ring Alternatives

Of course, no one says you need an engagement ring at all. Some women simply don't like jewelry, or find that expensive engagement rings don't fit into their lifestyles. Other couples opt to make their first purchase as a couple a more practical one.

Does It Have to Be a Ring?

One couple in Buffalo, New York, opted to skip the engagement ring entirely. The bride made it clear to the groom that she'd rather have a car—preferably an old, stylish one. So the groom presented her with a convertible Alfa Romeo, a gift the bride found much more practical but indulgent at the same time. Instead of telling the traditional "proposal" story, the groom recalls that car playing a big—and romantic—part in their first year as newlyweds, when they'd go on nighttime drives with the top down to cool off from the especially hot summer.

ALERT!

Forgoing the traditional engagement ring should be a mutual decision, not an excuse for the groom to substitute a ring for the power boat "she's" always wanted.

Another groom in New York City proposed to his bride . . . with a plastic gumball machine ring. The couple, who live a somewhat bohemian lifestyle in the heart of offbeat Greenwich Village, also found that an expensive diamond ring wasn't a priority in their lives and opted to save their dollars for . . . well, just about anything else.

In other words, you are not bound to convention, though a groom should always be absolutely sure his bride agrees. A groom who's overheard his bride, pre-engagement, say she would definitely never want to wear an engagement ring should ask her again. And one more time after that. Women have been known to change their minds.

Nothing Says Commitment Like a . . .

There are plenty of ways a groom can demonstrate his commitment other than with the ubiquitous metal band. These range from high-ticket items to the free of charge:

- A down payment on a home
- A dream vacation on which he proposes
- A new car
- Another piece of jewelry, such as a necklace, bracelet, or watch
- A tattoo with her name on it
- A tattoo on her ring finger
- Plastic surgery (okay, a little weird, but it's been known to happen)
- A specially written poem or song
- A handmade piece of art or a special photograph
- A family heirloom
- A kitten or puppy from the pound
- A signed, first edition copy of her favorite book
- The thing she's always wanted (only you know what that is)

The Proposal

You'll forget parties you've gone to and vacations you've taken. But one thing you'll never forget is the day he proposed. Truly this is one of the sweetest memories—and most asked about, as you announce your engagement—that you'll have in your lifetime. If you're not already engaged, strategically leave this book open where your beloved will stumble upon it. He will not only get some creative ideas. He will also quickly understand the importance of the memorable proposal.

ALERT!

As you begin announcing your engagement to friends and family, you will have to tell the story of your proposal over and over. Unless you want to say "in the parking lot of KFC" for the rest of your life, make it a good one.

The Time

Only you can decide the perfect timing to get engaged. Because men initiate 99 percent of all wedding proposals, it is often up to the woman to wait patiently, or at best have a conversation and a target date. Obviously, you want to get engaged the minute you decide he/she is the one you definitely want to spend the rest of your life with. However, there is the reality of timing, budget, and career issues entering the picture. The best advice? Don't let it come to an ultimatum. No man wants to feel backed into a corner, and no woman wants to feel that the only reason he's marrying her is because he was threatened (or vice versa).

ALERT!

The minute the first of your friends starts tying the knot, expect the wedding deluge to begin. It takes just one fearless pioneer to lead the rest to the promised land.

Creative Proposals

Ask around. You will hear some amazing proposal stories. There aren't many people who get engaged these days without something symbolic, romantic, or flamboyant going on in the background. The best proposals are highly personal, incorporating something from your history together, or your own personal interests. Stumped for ideas? Use one of the following, or elaborate on one with your own personal touch.

In the Spotlight

Like to ham it up? The following are just a few of the many creative ways to make a public display of affection.

- Buy billboard space on her route to work stating her name and "Will You Marry Me?"
- Buy a full-page ad in her favorite newspaper or magazine.
- Take her to a sports event and prearrange to use the scoreboard to make your proposal.
- Ask a local comedian to incorporate your proposal into his comedy club act (but tell him to lay off on the wife jokes).
- Stand in the audience of the *Today Show* in NYC, and try to get Al Roker's attention to get your proposal on camera.
- Good on the computer? Create a digital movie of photos and video of you together, copy it onto a film reel, and ask your local movie house to show it as a trailer to the movie you've gone to see.

For Love of the Game

If the two of you are sports-minded, there are a lot of ways to incorporate your favorite activity into a memorable wedding proposal. Rock and mountain climbers could propose at the summit. Nothing could be more gratifying than training together for a marathon, with a ring waiting for her at the end of the actual event (or a shorter event would work too—a couple who's met at work might get engaged at their city's annual corporate challenge). A tennis player might find a ring at the bottom of a tennis ball canister, and a golfer might find a sign at the eighteenth hole, asking for her hand in marriage. Whatever your sport together, be creative.

A wonderful and creative proposal doesn't have to be elaborate or expensive. The most important part of the proposal is that it be meaningful and memorable.

Isn't It Romantic?

Getting engaged is inherently romantic, but there are plenty of ideas to make it even more romantic and memorable. They range from the expensive to the low budget, with everything in between.

- Rent a helicopter and take a tour of beautiful terrain in your region, popping the question at the end.
- Rent a limousine, go to the best restaurant in town, order the most expensive champagne, and get down on one knee.
- Hire a skywriter to write out a proposal for everyone—including her—to see.
- Write her a special poem or song, and play it for her (if you're a musician).
- Go on a sunset cruise and propose as the sun dips into the horizon.

FACT

If circumstances allow, carry a mini tape recorder in your pocket and record your proposal. Store the tape in a safe place and bring it out after a long period of time—say, on your fifth or tenth anniversary—to remember how you two got started.

It's All about Location

Another great way to propose—and to have a little honeymoon before the honeymoon—is to take her on a trip somewhere exotic and propose there. If you're in a warm climate, go snorkeling together and have her discover the ring among the other rocks (but be careful not to lose it). If you're touring museums or galleries, see if the museum proprietor would allow you to include your ring as its own temporary "exhibit."

If you live somewhere cold and snowy, use it to your advantage. In fresh snow, spell out your proposal in large letters. Have her discover it by looking out a second-story window or over the roof of her building.

Or, more simply, take her back to the place you two first met, or first fell in love. If that's grammar school, take her there. If it's at a bar, see if the owner can set up something special and private for the two of you.

A Family Affair

It's always special to include others in your exciting time. Consider involving friends or family in your proposal. One groom in Baltimore proposed to his girlfriend while on a beach vacation with her parents.

Another groom in New York City called his close friends and family ahead of time to be present when he popped the question—on the starting line of a big annual holiday running race. Friends and family appreciate being part of this special, meaningful time.

Even if you don't have family present when you actually pop the question, it's not a bad idea to talk to her parents before you do. While you don't actually have to "ask permission," it's respectful to share your intentions in advance—and a great way to start off with your in-laws.

Announcing Your Engagement

A traditional engagement announcement consists of a formal note—with relatively formal language that is dictated by years of propriety—sent to family and friends by the parents of the bride or groom. This may or may not be accompanied by a formal announcement in the couple's local newspaper, with or without a photograph.

With the decrease of formal weddings, the increase of couples throwing their own weddings, and a loosening of traditional etiquette, there are many things you can do to announce your engagement creatively. Many couples prefer to not have any sort of formal announcement, relying on personal relay of information or word of mouth among family and friends. The point is, it's up to you. You can create as much or as little attention for yourselves as you choose.

ALERT!

Because of limited space, many newspapers today have a strict policy of announcing either an engagement or a wedding—but not both. See your local paper's social events section to determine its individual policy.

Of course, before you announce it to the more general public, make a personal phone call or visit to those closest to you, including parents, siblings, grandparents, and closest friends. They will all want to hear the news straight from the source, so they can congratulate you properly.

If you do decide to spread the word in a creative way, have fun with it. Today's computer-aided design programs make it easy for even novices to put together a printed piece to mail out. For an informal announcement, you might choose to send an e-mail to your friends and family. Or throw a party and announce your engagement there—kind of like a surprise engagement party. (See more on engagement parties in Chapter 4.)

Announcing Your Elopement

Announcing one's elopement can be a bit trickier than announcing one's engagement. Inevitably there will be as many people annoyed with you as there are those pleased with the news. Elopements can be a real disappointment to those who expected to share in your wedding day bliss—particularly your parents. No doubt you considered this before you eloped, and the pros outweighed the cons. Regardless, you can be just as creative in announcing you're already married by sending out a note with your new information, including any name change. Or in lieu of all the money you may have spent on a wedding, throw a party for your close friends and family as casual and anti-wedding as you like (presumably you wanted to avoid all the trappings of a wedding if you eloped). If you don't wish to receive gifts, don't announce that you've been married until your guests arrive. If they know beforehand, indicate "no gifts" on the invitation.

Chapter 3

Determining Your Wedding Style

You've decided to go ahead with a creative wedding. But how do you get started? There are a few things you'll want to consider early on in the planning that will help guide you as you get down to the nitty-gritty details. This chapter will help you determine what style is right for you.

Choosing a Style

If you're having a themed wedding, like a Victorian or a Renaissance wedding, you don't really need to determine your style—the style is dictated by the theme. But if you're having an event like a holiday wedding, or an ethnic wedding, or a traditional wedding with creative twists, it's helpful to determine what type of wedding you want right off the bat. These styles can range from formal to semiformal to informal. For each of the following wedding styles, creative elements can be easily incorporated, but the formality of the event should remain consistent. For instance, you wouldn't want to send formal, engraved invitations to a beach-themed wedding. Just as you wouldn't wear a short wedding dress to an elegant, formal evening event.

Formal Weddings

Formal weddings are typically quite proper, following a somewhat rigid set of guidelines when it comes to attire, invitations, menu, music, and location. Certainly there is much room for creativity within those guidelines. For instance, a Roaring '20s wedding could be entirely formal, with an elegant, historic location, antique cars, and attire, including tails for the men and full-length gowns for women—1920s style.

FACT

Be creative within your chosen wedding style—but be consistent. Try not to mix overly formal elements into a more casual wedding, and vice versa. It will confuse your guests and dilute your theme.

A formal wedding is set apart by high style and glamour. For a very formal evening wedding, the attire is white tie, which means tails and white bow ties, and wing-collared shirts for men. The bride typically wears a dress with a long train—as well as a long veil—for a very formal wedding. For a slightly less formal wedding or a formal daytime wedding, the bride's dress might have a shorter or detachable train and a shorter veil, while the groom may opt for a more traditional black tuxedo or formal suit. Female guests at formal weddings can wear long or short evening dresses, while men at formal evening affairs should don tuxedos or tails for white tie events, and tuxedos for black tie events.

Formal weddings are also typically accompanied by upscale, engraved invitations; an elegant location such as a historic estate, ballroom, or museum; live music from, for example, an orchestra; a sit-down, multi-course meal with wine and champagne service; and elegant traditional flower arrangements. Formal weddings usually involve 200 or more guests.

Semiformal Weddings

Semiformal weddings have many of the same trappings of formal weddings—but may be slightly more relaxed. The bride may wear a long or shorter dress, as well as a shorter veil. Bouquets may be simpler and less extravagant. For a semiformal evening wedding, the groom may still wear a tuxedo or opt to wear a dinner jacket—for daytime, a suit may be more appropriate. Female guests may wear evening dresses or evening suits, while male guests may choose between a tuxedo or suit.

The formality guidelines are meant to serve as general background—a place from which to start. And while you want to remain generally consistent with your planning, getting creative sometimes means breaking the rules. Which means if you really want a wedding that's informal in most ways—*and* a five-course meal—feel free to do both.

Semiformal weddings often still include the more formal wedding elements, including a seated meal, a good-sized wedding party, and live music. But they can also incorporate some less formal touches like a disc jockey, a cocktail reception, or a nice but not-quite-so-formal location, such as a banquet hall or inn.

Informal Weddings

Traditionally, informal weddings have been the style of choice for second weddings, daytime weddings, and theme weddings, including picnic or outdoor weddings. They are much less rigid than either formal or semiformal celebrations, with the bride wearing a suit or short dress and the groom in a suit or a classic blazer and trousers. Male and female guests alike should still wear their Sunday best, but it needn't be as dressy as a formal affair.

Informal weddings allow for much more leeway in other wedding decisions, such as invitation style, flowers, music, and location. Meals can be less formal—buffet or food station style, or even potluck.

Balancing Tradition with Creativity

There are elements of traditional weddings that you inevitably love. Perhaps it's a certain song sung in church or synagogue. Maybe it's the father-daughter dance. Then there are the traditions that you could take or leave, perhaps the bouquet toss or the cake cutting. Keep in mind that incorporating these traditions—and how they're incorporated—is entirely up to you. Just because every wedding you've attended has had a first dance doesn't mean yours has to. And just because you've been a bridesmaid twelve times doesn't mean you have to subject your friends and family to the same horror—uh, honor. The best method to determine the inclusion of certain traditions is to ask yourself "Why?" Why should we include this tradition? Does it mean anything to us? Do we want to alter it in some way to be more relevant? Can we eliminate it if we're not comfortable with it? Rather than accepting every typical part of the wedding at face value, question each element and ask if it fits your vision and style as a couple.

The very first part of any creative process is to ask yourself "Why?" Look at the reasons that something's always been done a certain way rather than assuming "that's just how it's done." Then determine if it should be changed, and/or how it can change to suit your own personal style.

Putting a new twist on an old wedding tradition can begin with the very structure of a typical wedding. For instance, why does the ceremony always come before the reception? Perhaps you'd like to receive your guests, then have a ceremony, and then a reception. Or even throw the party first, followed by a ceremony. Asking yourself "Why?" is the very first step of the creative process, which can open the door for all sorts of new possibilities you never before imagined.

FACT

One way to get creative is to wipe the slate clean, forgetting every wedding you've ever been to, every TV wedding you've ever seen, every wedding magazine you've ever glanced at. This means you won't have to "fill in the blanks" of what's traditionally dictated—instead, you'll be dictating the elements yourself.

The Ceremony

Planning a creative ceremony can provide a few more barriers to entry than, say, planning the reception. This is particularly true if you wish to have a religious ceremony. Many religions—the Catholic religion, for instance—are somewhat rigid in what is permitted and not permitted in a church ceremony. However, there is still room to pick and choose from a list of traditional readings, songs, and rituals to personalize your ceremony to fit your thoughts and beliefs. And in fact, unless you have a very clear idea of what you'd like to include in your ceremony, a bit of structure provided by your officiant can be a blessing (no pun intended), as this can be a complicated and daunting task, and a very important and symbolic one as well.

FACT

Talk to your officiant about reinterpreting ceremony traditions. For instance, you may want both your parents to walk you down the aisle (as in a Jewish ceremony). Or if you hate having all eyes on you, you may not want to walk down an aisle at all. Just because something's always been done a certain way doesn't mean you have to accept it at face value.

If you do not practice any religion, or choose to forgo a religious ceremony, you'll most likely be freer to create a ceremony of your own design. You may want to preserve some of the basic traditional elements and structure and then add your own flourishes, such as your own readings and your own vows . . . or you may want to dictate your ceremony completely from scratch. Be sure to consult with your officiant—whether it is a religious figure, a judge, a ship's captain, or a justice of the peace—to gauge his or her comfort level with the ceremony you are designing. There are many creative ceremony ideas in Chapter 13, from choosing the officiant to the site to the music.

The Reception

Clearly, the reception offers many avenues for creativity, as it is typically not bound by religious tradition the same way the ceremony may be. There are many traditions you may or may not choose to include in your wedding. For some brides and grooms, these traditions provide structure and movement to the party and are part of a grand history and continuum. For others, they may be too restrictive. The following are some of the most popular traditions you'll experience at wedding receptions. Consider each of these carefully and decide what they mean to you, and how they might fit into your overall wedding vision:

- Posing for formal portraits
- Receiving line (sometimes held immediately after the ceremony, sometimes immediately preceding the reception)
- Cocktail hour and hors d'oeuvres before dinner
- Music during cocktail hour
- Announcing the bridal party and bride and groom to the entire room
- A head table consisting of the bride, groom, and bridal party
- Speech by the father of the bride
- Speech by the best man
- Champagne toast
- Clinking of glasses until bride and groom kiss (This may be difficult to control.)
- Sit-down or buffet lunch or dinner

- Dancing after dinner, or between courses
- Bride and groom's first dance
- Father/daughter dance and mother/son dance
- Bridal party dance
- Line dances or the "Chicken Dance"
- Cutting of the cake by the bride and groom
- Smooshing of the cake into each other's faces
- Serving wedding cake at all
- Throwing of the bouquet
- Tossing of the garter
- Decorating car with "just married" signs
- Leaving the reception for your honeymoon (This is practiced more in TV weddings than in real life. Usually it is not very practical.)

Traditions . . . with a Twist

Each of these reception traditions offers an opportunity to improvise and get creative. For example, perhaps the mother of the bride is more comfortable giving a speech or the maid of honor would like to say a few words. Or instead of having music during a cocktail hour, you'd like a magic act or a strolling magician. Putting a new twist on an old tradition—or leaving a tradition out completely—is perfectly acceptable.

Some brides and grooms are uncomfortable with certain traditions, such as dancing in front of hundreds of people, or throwing the bouquet to all the "single" women. These events provide a chance to modify an old tradition to fit more modern sensibilities. Perhaps you don't want to single out the single women, who may feel uncomfortable cavorting in front of a group for the chance to be "next." Or maybe you don't want to subject your bridesmaids to dancing with the groom's friends. Open these traditions to your own interpretation . . . and create new traditions of your own.

How Far Will You Go?

How far outside the norm you go lies entirely with your comfort level. Again, keep in mind that incorporating some of the old traditions can lend some structure to your party. Your guests may feel more comfortable with some of the old traditions mixed with your creative vision. For example, if your reception will be five hours long, and food stations, music, and bar service begin as they walk in the door, there may be some confusion about when to eat, when to dance, etc. Some guests will not hit the dance floor until the bride and groom have their first dance, so if you plan to skip this tradition, invite guests onto the dance floor immediately. Or if you're not having any dancing at all, provide some sort of structure or activity—like a dessert buffet and coffee station—to top off the meal and give people a reason to get up and mingle.

Setting the Date

You may consider setting the date before you formally announce your engagement, if only because this is the next-biggest question you'll be asked once you make your info public (second only to "So how did he propose?").

FACT

The Japanese traditionally use an ancient astrological calendar called the *koyomi* to pick a couple's ideal wedding day.

With 365 days and many years ahead of you, you have lots of options when setting this date. Think things through carefully at the outset, so you can set one date and stick to it. Once you start planning the wedding, this will be extremely important when dealing with vendors. Many wedding vendors reserve the right to charge a penalty or keep your down payment if you change the date or cancel. Make sure you consider the following before you set the date.

Your Theme

If you choose one of the many themes included in this book, the theme may dictate the day . . . or the season. With a New Year's Eve wedding, for instance, you simply need choose the year. With a beach wedding, you'll have to have it in summer (unless you live in a warm-weather climate). If you choose a theme or wedding style that's more general, however, you may need to consider other factors when pinning down that date.

Your Budget

Your budget may be the single largest factor dictating your wedding date. No matter who is contributing financially to the wedding—you and your fiancé, your parents, or all of the above—a little time might be helpful in order to save enough to throw the wedding you want. A slightly longer engagement also gives you the time you might need to search for a house or apartment, without rushing—and to save for that need, as well. Coming home from your honeymoon to face thousands of dollars of debt is not the ideal way to start a life of wedded bliss. If possible, take the time to save before—you'll be extremely grateful afterward.

Vendor costs may also influence your choice of wedding date. Because spring and summer weddings are the most popular, caterers, photographers, florists, DJs, and bands often get away with boosting their prices for prime season. In addition, many vendors—including reception sites—will charge more on a Saturday than a Friday, because Saturdays are usually a couple's first choice. If your budget is tight, these factors can make a big difference to the bottom line.

Season

You may have always dreamed of a hot, sultry night for your wedding. Or for a snow-covered winter wonderland. Obviously, you know your preference, so choose the date accordingly.

Lifestyle

Depending on your career or lifestyle choices, certain times of the year may be better than others. If you're a teacher, summer is ideal. If you're a construction worker, summer is your busy time. Take these factors into consideration, as it will save a lot of stress down the line. One couple in Boston planned their wedding to fall the week after the groom's bar exam. Needless to say, he was under a great deal of added stress in the months leading up to the wedding—stress that could have easily have been avoided by setting a better date.

Other Factors

There are countless other factors that may come into play when setting your wedding date. If the bride is pregnant, for instance, the couple may choose to get married immediately—or wait until after the baby is born. If the couple is in a long-distance relationship, it may be preferable to get married sooner than later. Take your own special circumstances into consideration and don't underestimate the impact of your choice—it could save you money, time, and sanity down the line. Ⓔ

Chapter 4

Uncommon Pre-Parties

A wedding is not just a day . . . it's more like a season. From the day you announce your engagement until you finally arrive home from your honeymoon, your lives will inevitably be a frenzy of planning, parties, and celebration. The parties leading up to the wedding day can be great fun and offer lots of opportunities for creativity.

Parties Before the Big Day

Part of the fun of a wedding is all the parties and social gatherings that lead up to it. Some couples have been known to experience up to ten parties preceding the actual wedding, including multiple engagement parties, multiple showers, bachelor and bachelorette parties, luncheons, and the rehearsal dinner. Though ten is a bit extreme, it is certainly not unheard of. And with these many potential parties, there's a whole new world of creativity and fun awaiting.

QUESTION?

What if I don't want a lot of pre-wedding hoopla?
For some brides, even the wedding day spotlight might be almost too much to bear—not to mention a series of parties preceding it. If you don't want an engagement party, shower, or bachelorette party, you're certainly not required to have them. Be sure to let your friends and family know your intentions well in advance— before they've started planning.

You may throw some of these parties yourselves—such as an engagement party—and you may find many of these parties being thrown for you—such as the shower. Obviously, if you are not throwing the parties yourselves, you may have less control over the detailed planning of them, but you can still let your intentions be known.

If you're having a distinctively themed wedding, such as a Renaissance wedding or a Victorian wedding, consider theming your pre-parties as well to get your guests in the mood. Or add some related special touches to a straightforward event to foreshadow what's to come.

Whether you plan any of these parties yourselves or just plan to drop a few hints, here are some creative ideas that span from the engagement to the day before the wedding.

The Engagement Party

The engagement party is a time-honored tradition held to formally introduce the groom and his family to the bride and her family. Historically, etiquette dictates that the bride's family has first dibs on throwing an engagement party, which may be followed by a party thrown by the groom's family.

Nowadays, this custom has loosened up a bit, and engagement parties may be thrown by friends, coworkers, or even the bride and groom themselves. To avoid any misunderstandings, however, it's a good idea to consult the bride and her family before planning this event.

To Have or Not to Have?

That is the question. It's certainly not mandatory to have an engagement party. But with such a happy occasion to celebrate, why not? If you have family or friends who have offered to host an engagement party, it's not only an honor—it's also a wonderful opportunity for the families and friends of the betrothed to meet one another. The same goes if the bride and groom wish to host a party themselves.

The engagement party typically takes place soon after the engagement is announced, so there is some time between it and the other pre-parties such as showers and bachelor parties. The invitation list should only typically include those who will also be invited to the wedding, to avoid later misunderstandings. And while your final wedding guest list may not be complete at the time of the engagement party, err on the side of caution. Invite only close friends and family you are sure will be included in the final cut.

FACT

If you're planning on registering for gifts, there's nothing wrong with doing so before the engagement party. However, you should *never* include gift registry information in the invitation for the engagement party—or any other wedding pre-party. No matter how creative and untraditional your wedding, this is never a good practice.

Gifts at the engagement party are optional. Some guests wouldn't dream of coming empty-handed, while others just come to socialize and spend time with the bride and groom. If you are throwing the party yourselves and feel uncomfortable with the idea of gifts, simply indicate on the invitation "No gifts please." The same applies to parties thrown by friends or family—simply let your intentions be known.

Theme It

Just as you have creative license for the wedding, the engagement party is another opportunity to exercise your personal style. It's an occasion for fun and celebration and for people to get to know each other. If you already have a theme chosen for the wedding, you may want to incorporate elements from it into your engagement party. For instance, if you plan to have a Victorian wedding, your engagement party may be an afternoon tea rather than a raucous all-night party.

Many couples would love to throw an engagement party but are afraid it will appear to be a ploy for gifts. If you want to enjoy the company of your loved ones but don't want them to feel obligated to bring something, specify "No gifts please" on the invitation.

This will set the mood for your guests and provide a teaser for what's to come.

Of course, there are also an endless number of themes you can adopt for the engagement party that are not related to a theme wedding. Use the following ideas—or modify and pare down any of the wedding theme ideas in Chapters 6–9—to host an unforgettable engagement party.

Evening Engagement Parties

It's always easier to create an air of festivity and anticipation at an evening party. Your guests, too, will tend to loosen up and relax more at an evening party than they will, say, at a brunch party.

The 1950s kitsch cocktail party: Break out the martini shaker and recruit your friend the bartender to make cosmopolitans, manhattans, and sloe gin fizzes all night long. A 1950s-themed cocktail party will definitely be enjoyed by the bride and groom's contemporaries—and may bring back a few memories for their parents, too. Dress is definitely upscale—swingy dresses, twin sets, and Mary Janes for the women, suits or sport coats for the men. Music should consist of standards from

Frank Sinatra to classic swing. Tasty hors d'ouevres—hand passed, if possible—are a must for soaking up all those strong cocktails. Include tiny cocktail weenies, finger sandwiches, and lots of drink garnishes like olives, pickles, lemons, limes, and cherries. Have this party at home or rent out a great room—bonus points for a dance floor once things get hopping.

An evening of board games: If you'd like to throw a casual but fun and social gathering, this party's for you. It's a particularly good way to break the ice at a party that consists mainly of the bride's and groom's contemporaries—friends and coworkers—who may not be acquainted. Divide the group into teams of two or more to play against each other in heated board game battles like Pictionary, Scattergories, or Scrabble. You can create teams who've never before met each other—for instance, the bride's best friend with the groom's cousin—or allow couples to play together as a team against couples they have yet to meet. This can be a great way to break the ice and encourage your friends to get to know each other better in a more organized, less awkward way than cocktail party small talk. Serve lots of munchies and drinks to really get the party rolling, and have prizes for the winners.

Famous character party: It's a classic idea that adapts nicely to an engagement party and can be incorporated into gatherings ranging from casual to more formal. As each guest arrives, they are assigned a famous character whose name is taped to their back. The host may choose characters from pop culture, politics, history, sports, local lore, or any other category—tailor it to your guests' probable interests. The guest's job is to ask other guests "yes" or "no" questions to attempt to learn the identity. By using fun or risqué characters, you'll raise the humor quotient, providing another good ice breaker among guests who may not yet know each other.

Daytime Engagement Parties

Daytime parties can be more casual than evening parties but just as much fun.

Beach party: If you have access to a beach house or a public beach facility and the season's right, host a beach party that people of all ages can enjoy. Include volleyball, horseshoes, and plenty of lounge chairs for fun activities. Have a clam bake or barbeque with coolers of beer and soft drinks for lunch/dinner.

Weekend brunch: For a host, brunch can be one of the easiest meals to prepare at home. Quiches, salads, and sweets, for example, can be made in advance and served buffet style; cocktails including Bloody Marys and mimosas are always crowd pleasers. A holiday brunch can be a particularly pleasant way to introduce friends and family to one another—say, an Easter, Mother's Day, or Father's Day brunch. Perfect timing for a late-summer or fall wedding.

The Bridal Shower

The bridal shower is almost a foregone conclusion in the countdown to today's weddings. The shower is an occasion for women to get together to "shower" the bride with gifts to help start up a new home for the bride and groom. While traditional etiquette dictates that the maid of honor throws the shower with some help from the bridesmaids, a relative of the bride or groom often throws showers these days. Purists may still frown on this practice, as they believe it is tacky to request gifts for one's child or immediate family member, but these days most people understand the nature of the shower and what it entails. So don't sweat it if Mom or Sis is throwing you the shower.

There are lots of fun things to incorporate into a shower, from games to activities to . . . men. Men? Yes, coed showers are becoming increasingly popular, and you'll find a few theme ideas here for showers that include men and women alike.

Creative Registries

Before any and all showers are held, you'll probably want to register for gifts to make the selection process easier for guests who may be at a loss for what you want or need. Lucky for you, modern registries are no longer limited to formal china and silver. While some brides have had their china patterns picked out for years, other brides may find they need household or other items that are more practical or useful on a daily basis. And as most marrying couples of the twenty-first century have lived independently for a few years, they may already have many of the traditional things they need—like dishes, linens, and decorative items. The good news is that for brides and grooms of all preferences, there are now options.

Even if you initially feel uncomfortable about registering, remember that it's as much of a convenience to your friends and family as it is to you. Your loved ones will view it as a valuable shopping tool—not a demand or expectation of expensive gifts. Just remember to register for items in all price ranges, so guests who wish to use it have a choice.

More and more stores are offering wedding registry services, and some of these stores may surprise you. For instance, national stores like Home Depot offer the opportunity to register for gifts ranging from home improvement tools and materials to full kitchen cabinetry to outdoor landscaping tools and materials. Stores like Target allow you to register for the traditional or the unique, such as home safety items, furniture, and even cleaning supplies. In addition, there are Internet sites that allow you to register for an incredibly wide range of gifts. At *www.theknot.com*, you can register for everything from kitchenware to fax machines to sports gear to a brand new BMW Roadster—all in one place that's ultraconvenient for you and your guests.

Theme Ideas

Showers are no longer limited to polite ladies' luncheons with traditional gifts and games. Today, showers are getting more creative, with hosts planning parties that are more unique and less predictable.

Don't forget to get creative with invitations. For a spa shower, send a little packet of potpourri, a small candle, or mini toiletry items like lotions and soaps. For a sports shower, include bottled water with the invitation as the bottle "wrapper," or design your invitation like a marathoner's number.

The round-the-clock shower: This is a creative shower idea that promotes creativity in your guests, too. Guests are sent invitations specifying a certain time of day. The gift they bring should correspond to that time. For instance, an appropriate gift for 7 A.M. might be a frying pan, an egg timer, or his-and-hers electric toothbrushes. A gift for 10 P.M. might be a popcorn maker . . . or sexy lingerie. This theme can provide a fun exchange between the bride and the gift giver, who often has an interesting explanation of why a certain gift was chosen for a certain time.

Spa shower: This is a great shower to enjoy with your closest girlfriends and family members. Arrange for a block of time at a spa ahead of time, when various massage therapists, facialists, and beauticians will be available. Schedule appointments for one or two treatments for each guest, based on her requested preferences. If the host has a large budget, she may pay for these treatments herself—or subsidize them to make treatments more affordable for guests. Guests who don't wish to have treatments can join the group afterwards, to gather for a gift-giving session with a tasty spa lunch. This also works great for a bachelorette party.

Holiday shower: This is an appropriate theme for the couple who already has everything. Instead of bringing the traditional blender and crock pot for gifts, guests will be requested to bring a holiday-themed gift for the couple to enjoy for a lifetime. Gifts might include a Waterford crystal Christmas tree ornament, a beautiful platter for Thanksgiving turkey—even a U.S. flag for the Fourth of July. Food and drink can be themed to a certain holiday or a mixture of them. Again, this theme allows for guests to exercise a little creativity as well.

Sports shower: Another good idea for the couple who has everything. If the bride is an avid skier, for instance, the shower may be held at a friend's or family member's ski house—or a ski resort lodge—preceded by a day of skiing. Non-skiers can arrive later, or come early and enjoy hot toddies by the fire. Guests' gifts could be sport-related, inspired by a registry or the gift giver's imagination.

Wine shower: From the wine connoisseur to the consummate entertainer, this shower is a great way to build up a wine collection for the newlyweds. In place of traditional gifts, guests are asked to bring a bottle or two of wine as gifts for the couple. In the meantime, the host provides a selection of her own wines for a shower/wine tasting event, with a variety of white and red wines, cheeses, and other wine-friendly hors d'oeuvres for guests to munch on. This would also work well within a coed shower format.

Games and Activities

To some, the thought of shower games and activities elicits the enthusiasm of a big yawn. But today's games and activities can be specifically tailored to your crowd or modernized so everyone can appreciate them.

FACT

Activities that request guests to bring something personal such as a special scrapbook page or inspirational story will be memorable and meaningful not only to the bride but also to guests. It's a great reminder of the sanctity of the upcoming marriage, and of those who've helped the bride get where she is.

Create-a-scrapbook: Before the shower—with the invitations—the host requests a scrapbook page from each guest. To make it easy for guests and ensure all pages are consistent in shape and size, the host should send a blank scrapbook/photo album page to each recipient. Guests can then get as creative as they like, personalizing their own page for the bride. The pages might include old photographs, cutouts from magazines, or written stories or poems. They can be sentimental, funny, or a combination of the two. When put together in a book, the pages become a wonderful homemade keepsake the bride will treasure.

Wise words: This is probably more appropriate for showers of twenty or fewer people. In advance, guests are asked to bring "a word from the wise" to present to the bride—and the group. This might consist of advice for a long marriage, an inspirational story, a newspaper or magazine article about some aspect of marriage, a poem written by the gift giver, a story from the bride's past, or even a joke. Guests will be asked to read their piece aloud to the bride at one point during the shower. It's an activity that can be spiritual, hilarious, and touching for the bride and guests alike.

Recipe shower: This is a gift that keeps on giving. The host requests each guest's favorite recipe in advance and puts together a booklet for the bride of each of the guests' original, hand-written recipes—the more "secret" the better. The host can also create photocopied booklets to give to each of the guests as a favor, revealing all their friends' and families' favorite recipes—just be sure to let your guests know in advance.

Purse bingo: This is "Let's Make a Deal" for the twenty-first century. The host or another appointed guest does a Monty Hall, calling out various items to the crowd. These items should become increasingly unusual—and personal—as the list progresses. The first guest to produce that item from the depths of her purse is the winner. Examples of items include a comb, dental floss, a pair of underwear, a condom, etc.

Not Just for Women Anymore

Certainly all the shower fun and games are no longer just limited to women. Coed showers are growing increasingly popular across the country and are a great opportunity for all the wedding players to get to know each other, rather than just the ladies. And while coed showers more often resemble a cocktail party rather than a ladies' luncheon, there are countless variations based on the bride's and groom's preferences.

Venues can range from a dinner party in a family member's home to an outdoor barbecue to a rented bar or restaurant party. Gifts may be more geared to both the bride and groom, with items they both can enjoy, from high-tech items to gourmet cookery to sports equipment to American Express gift checks. Or try a variation of the wine shower—with guests asked to bring a good bottle of liquor or wine in lieu of a gift, which will help stock a bar for the bride and groom that will accommodate months or even years of entertaining.

FACT

Even if the bride will have a traditional, ladies-only shower, a second coed shower can be a great way to get the bride's and groom's contemporaries together and mingling. Also invited should be the bride's and groom's immediate families and attendants, and their significant others.

The Bachelorette Party

The bachelorette party is a relatively recent phenomenon created when modern women decided they needed a night of debauchery and revelry as naughty as their fiancé's bachelor party. Of course, many women opt for an event that's more nice than naughty, particularly if the bar scene is not her thing. There are plenty of activities for women of all tastes and styles when it comes to bachelorette party fun.

The Naughty

The most obvious and classic bachelorette party consists of a group of girls out on the town much like their male counterparts—preferably with a limo and driver to cart them around safely. The evening may consist of drinking, barhopping, and occasionally even a male stripper. If this sounds like just another weekend to you, add some bachelorette-designed games and novelties. There is a growing market of novelty earrings, fake noses, sipping straws, and much more, inspired by the male anatomy. Some scheming bridesmaids give the bride a beaded candy necklace or bracelet to wear, which random men are encouraged to devour one at a time. Or they give the bride-to-be a to-do list, with goals she must accomplish as the night progresses. These might consist of potentially embarrassing or risqué behaviors such as dirty dancing with a man of the group's choosing, collecting a pair of boxers, doing a certain number of shots, or collecting men's business cards. Even better—get a group of your girlfriends to spend the weekend in Las Vegas or New Orleans to turn things up a notch—and avoid seeing anyone you might have to face in the future.

ALERT!

The bachelorette party is definitely an occasion to have a great time, but don't let it get out of hand. Just as you expect your fiancé to respect you at his party, he deserves the same in return. Before the party begins, assign one of your more responsible friends to throw up a red flag if things start getting out of control.

The Nice

Of course, the naughty bachelorette party is not for everyone. There are plenty of creative ways to get the girls together for a day or weekend of fun everyone can enjoy.

Retro sleepover: What could be more fun than a slumber party for grown-up girls? Re-create your childhood party by having lots of magazines, movies, and munchies. Make cookies. Gossip about boys. Read *Teen Beat*. Stay up all night long. And now that you're not twelve anymore, feel free to add cocktails to the mix for even more fun and frivolity. To add just a little bit of naughtiness, rent some adult movies and giggle all night long.

Comedy club: For a night on the town that doesn't involve just drinking and carousing, get all the girls together for a comedy club. Do a bit of research to find out when a particularly good act is coming to town. Make a whole night of it by enjoying a nice dinner out before or after the show. Order the most sinful dessert on the menu.

Stag wannabe: Why should boys have all the fun? Get all the girls together for an evening of gambling and prizes, just like the boys do. Open the party up to all the women you know, young and old. Enlist the help of in-the-know girlfriends or family to act as "dealers" for blackjack and other card games. Set up poker tables for groups of four or more. Have a raffle or a fifty-fifty split. Drink single-malt scotch and smoke cigars. Regale each other with old stories about the bride. Bond.

Weekend getaway: Choose a destination and enjoy a girls' weekend away. You might choose a nearby ski resort or spa, or try somewhere a bit farther away, such as a tropical or even a European destination (depending on your budgets, of course.) Or plan a girls-only camping trip where you can all rough it and revel in a more natural environment. A weekend getaway can be a particularly workable idea for a bride with friends in various geographical areas who would have to travel for the bachelorette party anyway.

FACT

Planning the bachelorette party for the same night or weekend as the bachelor party can help squeamish brides and grooms avoid wondering and worrying what the other is up to all night. Some brides and grooms choose to begin their parties as traditional single-sex fêtes, with plans to merge the groups later to celebrate at a local bar or at someone's home.

Bridesmaids' Luncheon

So you've survived the bachelorette party and plan on enjoying one last event with your closest friends before the big day. The bridesmaids' luncheon is a tradition that honors your bridesmaids for all they've done during the wedding planning—and well before that. This is a nice opportunity to get together in a more intimate setting before your wedding guests arrive and things start getting a bit more chaotic. It is typically held on the day or two leading up to the big event. You may want to give your bridesmaids their special gifts at this time as well.

Breaking Tradition

There is no rule that states you must have a bridesmaids' luncheon, and many brides feel they don't want to schedule too much on the hectic days before the wedding. In this case, cushion your event with a bit more time between the luncheon and the wedding. Or make the decision to skip this event, but be sure to show your bridesmaids your gratitude during the rehearsal dinner or at the wedding itself. Perhaps you'd rather replace a formal luncheon with a morning-of-beauty session on the day of the wedding, where all of your bridesmaids meet to get their hair done. Or you may want to use some of our ideas to create another type of event entirely.

Creative Ideas

There's also no rule that a gathering to honor your bridesmaids has to be a luncheon. Once again, you can express your creativity by designing an event with your own personal style.

Day of beauty: Instead of pigging out the day before, invite your bridesmaids to a local spa or salon for a morning or afternoon of pampering. The bride can kill two birds with one stone, allowing her to schedule beauty treatments she planned to have anyway, like manicures and pedicures, while also enjoying good company. And you probably won't hear many bridesmaids complain about the prospect of an afternoon of pampering. If you're at a spa, arrange for a light lunch to be served to your guests at their leisure, or share a meal together once your treatments are complete.

Dinner party: You may find a dinner fits your pre-wedding schedule better than a luncheon. Feel free to host a dinner—possibly the night before the rehearsal dinner, or if it's more convenient, hold it the weekend before. If you'd like to include everyone, you may consider hosting a joint bridesmaids/groomsmen event, which would include the bride and groom, bridesmaids, groomsmen, and their significant others. This would provide another opportunity for your friends and family to mingle—making the upcoming wedding even more fun for everyone.

Friendly competition: To spend valuable time before the wedding together—and also blow off a little steam—consider including a sporting event with your "bridesmaids' luncheon." Host a softball game or volleyball game with a barbecue lunch. Create a mini golf tournament. Even if all of the group doesn't golf, they can still enjoy the great outdoors with those who do. Or get together for some doubles tennis matches. Whatever your sport, there's nothing like exercise to relieve a little stress for everyone involved in the wedding.

Rehearsal Dinner

The rehearsal dinner usually follows a formal rehearsal of the wedding day ceremony. It is typically held the night before the wedding but may be two nights before or the weekend before as well. If your wedding involves many out-of-town attendants and family members, it's usually more practical to hold it the evening before the wedding.

FACT

The rehearsal dinner is the traditional time for the bride and groom to thank their parents, their attendants, and their officiant for all their love and support. It's also perfectly appropriate—and welcome—for any and all guests to say a few words as well. To get extra creative, ask each guest in advance to write out or prepare a short anecdote or funny story about the bride and groom. Then ask them to read it aloud at the dinner, or add it to a specially created scrapbook.

The groom's family typically hosts the rehearsal dinner, but again, times are changing. If the bride and groom are hosting the wedding themselves, often times they will also host the rehearsal dinner. Or if the wedding is in the bride's hometown—but not the groom's—the families may share hosting privileges. Even other family or friends have been known to host the rehearsal dinner. No matter what, it's valuable—and usually more intimate—time to spend with your close family and friends before the big day.

The Invitation List

The rehearsal dinner traditionally includes the bride and groom, their parents, grandparents, and siblings, along with bridesmaids and groomsmen who've attended the rehearsal. Significant others of all these individuals are also invited. From there, you may choose to invite additional friends or relatives to the rehearsal dinner. It is also customary to invite out-of-town guests, who have made the effort to travel to your wedding day celebration, and with whom you can spend a bit more time before the main event. But if you'd like to keep the rehearsal dinner very small and intimate—or if the budget doesn't permit a large group—it's not mandatory. In addition, it is not appropriate to invite anyone to the rehearsal dinner who is not invited to the wedding.

Creative Rehearsal Dinners

The beauty of the rehearsal dinner is that it is loosely interpreted. Depending on the size of your group, your budget, and who is throwing it, you can create any type of event you like with the rehearsal dinner. If the groom's parents are hosting this event, be gracious and accept their suggestions. It is hoped that they'll also solicit your opinions, in order to plan an event that you'll feel comfortable with. Don't be afraid to express your opinions, but don't expect all of your suggestions to be adopted, either. And be mindful that this may be your fiancé's parents only time to feel comfortable making suggestions.

If you are throwing your own party, here are some ideas that range from the extravagant to the economical.

The formal dinner: A formal dinner is particularly nice if you have a relatively small group—twenty or less, for instance. Reserve a private room at an excellent restaurant, or call ahead and explain you'd like a good table or two for an important event. Allow guests to order off the menu, and keep the wine stewards pouring. If you have a small group, or budget is not an issue, this can be an elegant and memorable evening that will impress your guests and provide culinary delight.

The pizza party: This is perfect for groups who want a very casual, very relaxed evening to precede the wedding. Host the party at someone's house, or head out to a local pizza parlor to gorge on pizza, chicken wings, and beer. Casual affairs like this can be the perfect precursor to a more formal event the next day and will encourage people to loosen up and relax before the excitement of the big event.

Potluck pleaser: This is a great idea if you're high on family and friends—but low on budget. Ask your in-town guests to bring their favorite dish, and host it at your house or a family member's home where you can fit a crowd comfortably. This is a particularly good party to throw when you have an extensive number of relatives and friends you simply cannot leave out of the festivities the night before, and a great way for friends and family to spend time together without going into debt for the effort. If you want to contribute more to the party than just the space, supply the beverages, including bar drinks.

If you throw a potluck party, be sure to organize in advance what people should bring. You definitely don't want to end up with five tuna casseroles and no desserts.

Theme It to Your Wedding

There are as many creative ideas for the rehearsal dinner as there are for your wedding. The following are some specific ideas to correspond to the creative wedding ideas in Chapters 6–9.

Art appreciation: If you're planning an arts-themed wedding—or even if not—an art gallery is a wonderful place to hold a rehearsal dinner. Many galleries have restaurants on the premises or will rent out a portion of the building for catering. Allow your guests to walk around and enjoy the art—then provide them with an artfully created meal. If you rent the space after hours, a gallery can provide a wonderfully private and exclusive setting.

FACT

Even if you're not planning a theme wedding, you can still get creative with your rehearsal dinner. In fact, you may feel more comfortable putting your creative energy into this smaller get-together for close family and friends to enjoy.

Christmas theme: If you're planning a holiday-themed wedding with all the trimmings, why not begin the night before? For an intimate home gathering, plan to trim the Christmas tree with all your friends and family. Or for any size crowd, host dinner, eggnog, and a night of caroling. Provide everyone with sheet music so that they have access to the lyrics, and walk around the neighborhood serenading the neighbors with Christmas carols.

Country-Western theme: So you're having a country-Western–themed wedding. Prepare your guests the night before at the rehearsal dinner with an old-fashioned barbecue and plenty of music. For a real novelty, hire a dance instructor to teach novices the latest line dances so that they're prepared for all the dancing the next night. Or go to a local country-Western bar—mechanical bull a plus—for some vittles and beer following the rehearsal.

Sports theme: If you are incorporating a sport into your wedding day plans—such as running or biking—you'd better load up on some serious carbs the night before. Host a pasta party at your home or a favorite Italian restaurant. But hold back on the wine—it might affect your performance the next day.

ESSENTIAL

Feel free to mix and match any of the creative ideas from this chapter for all of your pre-parties. For instance, you may want to host a wine-tasting party or beach bash after the rehearsal, rather than as an engagement party. Be flexible to be creative!

Chapter 5

The Wedding Day Players

As much as your wedding is about you and your groom, your special day also very much involves your family and friends. But choosing who plays a special role versus who doesn't is not always easy. This chapter explains the traditional roles and responsibilities of the wedding day players and provides creative ideas about involving them in exciting new ways.

The Wedding Party

It is an honor to be chosen as a wedding attendant. The bride may choose both an honor attendant—the maid or matron of honor—and her bridesmaids from family, including sisters, cousins, aunts, or nieces; close friends from childhood, high school, college, or even work; or the groom's family. Of course, your choices need not be strictly female. If your best friend is male, you can certainly include him as an honor attendant. The priority should be to choose friends and family you are closest to, feel comfortable with, and whom you know are reliable and responsible. The same advice applies to the groom and his choice of groomsmen and/or ushers.

What's the Point?

Some brides and grooms today find little practical purpose in having a large wedding party. Rather, they find themselves honoring the tradition simply to surround themselves at pre-wedding and wedding day parties with special, honored friends and family. If you opt not to have a large wedding party, there are certainly other ways to include and honor close family and friends during your wedding.

FACT

There is an inevitable financial burden that wedding attendants must bear—wedding clothes, attending pre-wedding parties (especially if attendants live out of town), and potentially chipping in for shower or bachelorette party expenses. Be sensitive to budget constraints when choosing the outfit your bridesmaids will wear and, if necessary, pitch in to help a struggling bridesmaid.

If you do choose to include a wedding party, you can also set the stage for how much or how little they need to be involved. For instance, if there are lots of pre-wedding errands and you're overwhelmed, you may lean on your maid of honor and bridesmaids for help. Of course, you may also find yourself fully prepared and comfortable performing all these duties yourself, choosing not to burden your friends and family with any extra responsibility.

In this case, their involvement might be limited to helping choose the dress and attending pre-wedding parties. It is up to you to set the stage for how much or how little your wedding party gets involved.

Who to Choose

What comes first, the wedding party size or your choice of bridesmaids? While this decision is up to you, you'll probably find that your personal relationships dictate the number of bridesmaids you'll include. But if you're having a small, intimate wedding, it's probably inappropriate—or, at least, illogical—to have a huge wedding party. In this case, you may want to decide on a number and then decide who makes the cut.

Six of One, Half Dozen of the Other?

Some brides believe that the number of bridesmaids must exactly match the number or groomsmen or ushers. This is simply untrue. You can easily be creative with a disproportionate number in your wedding party. For instance, if you're having a wedding party dance, allow bridesmaids and groomsmen to dance with their dates or arrange for other available participants instead of pairing up bridesmaids to groomsmen. If bridesmaids outnumber groomsmen, have a single groomsman escort two bridesmaids down the aisle (a proposition your groomsmen will hardly mind). And for pictures, ask the photographer to artfully arrange an asymmetrical group. In the end, most couples find that including everyone they want is far more important than a perfectly balanced photograph or strict boy-girl seating at the head table.

Maid (or Matron) of Honor and Best Man

The maid (or Matron) of honor and best man can be anyone from a close brother or sister, cousin, or longtime friend, or even a parent, aunt, or uncle. Remember that this person will become your right-hand woman or man, giving you practical and emotional support during the months of wedding planning, and at the wedding itself.

Can't choose between two sisters or two close friends for maid of honor? Ask them both. There's no reason why two maids or matrons of honor can't share the honor and responsibility. It'll make the decision easier for you, and the maid of honor duties easier on them.

Traditional Roles and Responsibilities

There is long tradition dictating the maid of honor's and best man's roles in the wedding planning and on the wedding day. They are included here as a starting point from which to work as you plan your own creative wedding.

The maid or matron of honor:

- Helps with pre-wedding activities, such as performing wedding-related errands and addressing invitations
- Acts as head bridesmaid: creates a schedule to ensure all bridesmaids have had gowns fitted; organizes and/or schedule wedding day hair and makeup appointments; offers travel information/guidance to out-of-town bridesmaids or guests; spreads the word about the bridal registry
- Attends all pre-wedding parties; may host a shower (with or without help of bridesmaids)
- May plan and/or host bachelorette party
- Precedes the bride down the aisle
- Holds groom's ring until ceremony ring exchange
- Arranges bride's train during ceremony and helps bustle it later
- Holds bride's bouquet during part of ceremony
- May stand in receiving line
- May sign wedding certificate as a witness
- May dance with best man at the reception, or help with hosting duties
- Provides moral support during the days and hours leading up to the wedding

QUESTION?

What's the difference between a maid and a matron of honor?
It's simple. A "matron" is a woman who is married; a "maid" is unmarried.

The best man:

• Usually plans and hosts bachelor party
• May help arrange accommodations for out-of-town ushers
• May help groom in ensuring all groomsmen have been fitted for tuxes or suits
• Carries bride's wedding ring
• May stand in receiving line
• May sign wedding certificate as a witness
• Offers first toast to the newlyweds
• Returns men's rental clothes—particularly the groom's, who is probably away on his honeymoon—after the wedding

Of course, the bride and groom may take care of many of the honor attendants' traditional duties themselves, such as arranging accommodations or beauty appointments, or planning pre-parties. The bride and groom should communicate to honor attendants where they might need help—and where they're comfortable doing the planning themselves.

Creating Your Own Traditions

Of course, planning a creative wedding may also involve getting creative with honor attendants' traditional roles. And while this doesn't mean you can appoint them your personal slaves, it does mean you can incorporate some unique responsibilities and/or honors along with their traditional duties. The following are some ideas:

Ceremony participation: If the maid of honor or best man are particularly close to the bride and groom, you may want to include them in the ceremony. They, too, might say a few words about their involvement in your special union and their pledge of support for the future. Be sure to ask them first if they are comfortable with being included this way in the ceremony, then run any scripts by them before the big day.

Maid of honor toast: Though not traditionally expected of her, more and more weddings are welcoming a few words from the maid of honor in addition to those from the best man. Her speech may precede or follow that of the best man—toasts are usually made immediately prior to the meal.

FACT

Whether you're the best man, maid of honor, or parent of the bride or groom, the key to a successful wedding day or rehearsal speech is preparation. Write the speech well in advance and practice it repeatedly in front of a mirror or another friend so that you feel comfortable when faced with the prospect of hundreds of attentive listeners. If you need to, bring some notes or cue cards for backup.

Freebie: If you're having a large wedding party, you probably don't have the budget to pay for all your wedding party's attire. But if your maid of honor and best man have been especially helpful during the planning process, or if they've footed the bill for a shower, bachelor party, or bachelorette party, you may want to show your gratitude by footing the bill for their dress or tuxedo rental and accessories.

Memory collection: Create a new tradition in your family. Ask the maid of honor, along with the best man, if she'd be comfortable putting together a slide show or scrapbook featuring you, the groom, and your respective families, with old photographs, newspaper articles, homemade crafts from childhood, grammar school papers—any memorabilia that guests will enjoy at the wedding, and that the bride and groom can then have as a keep-sake. They can collect these precious items from family, the wedding party, and other friends to get a cross section of the couples' lives. Be sure to give the honor attendants credit at the reception for putting it together, and with all the time and effort put into it, you should probably also consider it your wedding gift. (Of course, if the maid of honor is already running herself ragged helping you with wedding errands and planning a shower, don't expect her to take on any more responsibility.)

House or pet sitters: If you have pets, or feel uncomfortable leaving your house vacant for a long period of time during your honeymoon, ask your maid of honor or best man if they'd like to house-sit for you. Obviously, this should include their spouses and/or children. They might welcome the chance to stay at your house if they're single and still live with their parents, or if they're city folk and you've got a country pad. Be sure not to impose on them, however, if you know it's inconvenient. And try to reimburse them in some way for their services.

Gender Benders

If the maid of honor role is filled by a man, or the best man role by a woman, you should plan to be a bit more flexible when it comes to traditional roles and responsibilities. Obviously, a woman isn't going to plan a traditional all-male bachelor party, and a man probably isn't going to want to organize dress fittings and beauty appointments—or a traditional, all-female shower. In this case, you may want to ensure that all or most of your wedding pre-parties are coed, and you might consider a joint bachelor-bachelorette party. Do whatever is logical to your situation, and use your creativity to make it work.

Instead of appointing your 6'4", 220-pound guy pal the "maid of honor," you can officially call him your "honor attendant," a more gender-friendly title that can also be applied to the role of female "best man." Or you can get creative with titles like "Man of Honor" or "Best Woman."

Bridesmaids and Groomsmen

Bridesmaids and groomsmen can provide a fun-loving supportive inner circle prior to and on your wedding day. Most women and men still consider it a big honor to be included as a special part of this important occasion and look forward to the role (in spite of the much-maligned bridesmaid dress).

Traditional Roles and Responsibilities

The following outlines the traditional roles and responsibilities of bridesmaids and groomsmen.

The bridesmaids:

- Offer to run errands and address invitations
- Attend all pre-wedding parties and may cohost a shower or bachelorette party
- May help shop for and choose the bridesmaid dress
- Pay for own dress and accessories
- Walk down the aisle ahead of the bride
- May stand in the receiving line
- May dance with groomsmen or help with small hosting duties at the reception

The groomsmen:

- Attend all pre-wedding parties and may help host the bachelor party
- Should be properly fitted and pay for own wedding attire
- Seat guests at wedding ceremony in proper fashion
- Unroll and properly place the aisle runner (if there is one)
- Escort guests with umbrellas to their cars on a rainy day
- Help in various capacities, such as aiding disabled guests, last-minute wedding errands, troubleshooting any wedding day challenges
- May dance with bridesmaids at the reception

Creating New Traditions

If the bride and groom have heavy-duty type-A personalities, have hired a wedding consultant, or have parents who've taken over the reigns of wedding planning, the bridesmaids and groomsmen may have little responsibility other than showing up and looking good at pre-parties and on your wedding day. For some busy wedding attendants, this may be just fine. But others may welcome more involvement. Here are some ideas to get them more into the thick of things.

Give them some recognition: Many times guests would like to know more about the wedding party, including how they relate to the bride and groom. The bride and groom may choose to do formal introductions during a speech at the wedding itself, saying a few words about each bridesmaid and groomsmen, how they know them, adding any fun anecdotes. Or they may want to include detailed descriptions in the wedding program for people to read as they're waiting for the ceremony to begin. Either way, it integrates the wedding party that much more into your ceremony and reception.

Put your bridesmaids in charge of wedding favors (or placecard holders, etc.): If you're making any items by hand, ask for their participation—have a little party or get-together to make it fun. If you'd like help in the idea department, ask an Internet-savvy bridesmaid to research some options for you, or tap into the experience of your favorite shopaholic for some great suggestions.

FACT

If you like the idea of your bridesmaids wearing the same dress, but aren't wild for the traditional satin and taffeta selection, shop at a department store or boutique store for more contemporary choices. Look for dresses in matte jersey, cotton, or linen in whatever length you prefer and don't rule out nice skirt/top combinations.

Tap into their talents: If you've got a groomsman who's a graphic designer, ask for his help in designing your invitation. Or if a bridesmaid has a beautiful singing voice, ask her to do double duty as a ceremony soloist—or as a special act with the band at the reception. Again, give them credit in the program or thank them aloud at the reception so that everyone else can recognize their talents, too.

Trust their judgment: The "bridesmaids as color-coordinated clones" tradition is probably one your attendants would easily forgo. By eliminating the traditional dictate for identical, often-unflattering bridesmaid dresses, your bridesmaids will be eternally grateful. If you'd like to maintain some consistency, specify a color that doesn't come in a million shades, like black, white, or navy. Your bridesmaids, who *have* been dressing themselves most of their lives, can choose a dress that's comfortable and flattering, and that may even be worn more than once.

Choosing Wisely

Choosing your bridesmaids is more emotional than it is scientific. But if you've got ten great friends and only room for five women in your wedding party, you've got a dilemma. There are some important considerations to factor in when choosing your bridesmaids to avoid problems or surprises down the road. The first of these is cost. Even though your bridesmaids cover the cost of their outfits, lodging, and other expenses, the bride's costs still rise as the number of bridesmaids increase. Remember—ten bridesmaids also means ten bouquets, ten bridesmaids' gifts, ten women plus spouses to be included in the rehearsal dinner, etc. These costs can quickly add up to more than you originally allotted in your budget.

QUESTION?

What if one of my bridesmaids is pregnant?
There are plenty of options today for a pregnant bridesmaid. She can anticipate her size at the time of your wedding and order a bridesmaid dress a few sizes larger; use a swatch of fabric to have her own, more comfortable dress tailor-made; or even opt to serve an honored role at your wedding that doesn't include a bridesmaid dress. Talk to her openly about her wishes.

Besides cost, there are a few other things you may want to consider. That nomadic friend whose responsibility-free lifestyle you admire and envy? Her attitude will probably extend to your wedding, as well. If she's always taken weeks or months to return phone calls, don't expect her behavior to change now. Choose to either put up with her laid-back attitude to your wedding, or have her fill some other role that doesn't involve showing up for dress fittings.

Also, you are not obligated to include a person in your wedding just because she included you in hers—the bride who's served in twelve weddings could end up with more than she's bargained for. And if you're unsure about a friend's or family member's ability to participate due to financial obligations, family stresses, or geographical inconvenience, don't add to her woes by insisting she be a bridesmaid. It will help you avoid inconveniences and misunderstandings on both sides later on.

In-laws

In some regions and for some families, it is expected that you will ask the groom's sisters—and even the groom's brothers' wives—to be part of your wedding party. Unfortunately, you may not subscribe to this tradition yourself. Weigh this issue carefully based upon the attitudes and feelings of your groom's family. If it will cause irreparable damage not to include them, you should reconsider. After all, it's best to start your lifetime union on the right foot. If you truly cannot stand the thought of including a certain individual, or you're being unnecessarily pressured and you don't want to have a wedding party at all, then don't . . . but expect consequences like hurt feelings or resentments.

Of course, in other families the groom's sisters may not expect to be asked at all, especially in cases where you've not grown close due to geography, age differences, or other reasons. Or if you're in a situation where the groom has, say, seven sisters and you're very close to two of them, don't be afraid to include some but not all of them.

Parental Guidance Suggested

Like it or not, your parents play a big role in your wedding planning and on your wedding day. For some brides, this means fighting off interference at every turn; for others, parents may be content to bask in the shadows. No matter what the prevailing attitude, certain experiences are universal—at some point, your parents will have to meet each other. If parents are contributing financially, they'll also want to contribute opinions. And no matter what, your parents will be involved in some capacity on your wedding day. Having an unusual or creative wedding may add to the potential stress levels between you and your parents.

Meet the Parents—The First Encounter

If you're marrying your high school sweetheart, chances are your parents have already met. For the majority of brides and grooms, however, this is far from the norm, which means they'll have to be formally introduced. While traditional formal etiquette indicates that it is up to the groom's family to make the first move, today's relaxed attitudes allow others to arrange for the initial parental get-together, including the bride's parents or even the bride and groom as a couple.

Obviously, this can be stressful, especially if you're worried your parents won't get along due to differences in politics, religion, or other attitudes. Remember—they don't have to become best friends. If they do, terrific. But if they don't, that's totally normal. Most adults can find a way to get along in a social setting a few times a year without significant problems, no matter what their differences.

When your parents meet, they may also want to discuss some of the logistics of your wedding day, including the potential for sharing costs or planning responsibility. There's also no better time to get your plans out on the table, particularly if you're planning to throw an elaborate theme wedding.

There are certainly some creative ways to make this first meeting more comfortable and less awkward for everyone. You could schedule the meeting around a shared activity, such as a music or stage performance, participation at a tennis or golf game, or as a get-together to watch a big sports event on TV. Like a first date, it provides a structure to the day or evening, as well as something besides the two of you as a focal point.

Family-to-Family Interaction

This initial meeting often sets the stage for the manner in which your families will interact as you plan the wedding. If your mother is helping you with much of the planning, she may find herself frequently in touch with your future mother-in-law about guest lists, table placements, shower planning, and the like. Or you may find yourself or your groom to be the better conduit for this information. Use your judgment.

Parental Involvement on the Big Day

Your parents' involvement is woven into the very fabric of a *traditional* wedding. The groom's parents host the rehearsal dinner. The bride's parents host the wedding, and their names appear on the wedding invitation. The bride's father walks her down the aisle (for a Jewish ceremony, both mother and father have this honor). The groom's father makes a speech at the rehearsal dinner, and the bride's father does so at the wedding reception.

Exercise your creativity with your ceremony processional. Be escorted down the aisle by your father and stepfather, both parents, parents along with stepparents, a grandparent, or older brother or sister. Or even walk down the aisle alone. Do whatever is meaningful and comfortable for you and your family.

Like all other aspects of your wedding, these roles are subject to interpretation. If you and your groom are hosting the wedding yourselves, for instance, there's no reason your wedding invitation shouldn't reflect that. If you'd like both parents to walk you down the aisle, go with your heart, not tradition. And if your parents don't care for giving speeches or dancing in front of a crowd of people, don't push the issue. Allow them to participate in your wedding in activities both you and they will feel comfortable with.

Walk-On Roles

You may have decided to limit your wedding party to a best man and a maid of honor. Or you may have so many friends and family to include that your wedding party is already at the breaking point. Either way, there are meaningful and creative ways to involve other friends and family in your wedding. For some participants, this is a best-case scenario—they can be involved in your wedding without having all the responsibility.

Readers

Even if you're not having a religious ceremony, it's easy to assign readings to special friends and family. And, in fact, it's a very important role, as one of the few speaking parts your wedding has to offer. With a religious ceremony, opportunities for readings are generally mapped out within the ceremony's structure. A Catholic wedding, for instance, has two readings and a Prayer to the Faithful included in the ceremony. For a nonreligious ceremony, you can include as many readings as you like. They may consist of poems, relevant excerpts from literature, or words written by the bride and groom. If your chosen reader has writing talent, you can involve and honor the person even further by asking him or her to write a personal passage or story to read. Potential readers may include sisters-in-law or brothers-in-law who aren't included in the wedding party, a special aunt or uncle, or good friends.

Ushers

Though groomsmen often fill the role of ushers, you may find yourself needing even more help seating guests or want groomsmen to fill another role prior to the wedding ceremony—like surrounding the groom with moral support. Whether you're having a very large wedding or simply want to include additional friends and family, the usher role provides a good opportunity. Ushers need not be male—both females and males will do just fine. Their duty is to ask guests arriving at the ceremony site how they relate to the bride and/or groom, and then seat them accordingly. Extra special ushers can be given the responsibility to seat grandparents, parents, or stepparents immediately preceding the ceremony.

Program Distributor

Along with the ushers, you can employ a friend or family member as a program distributor to ensure every guest receives a wedding program. He or she should stand near the door or entranceway and hand a program to the guests or couples as they arrive.

Guest Book Attendant

At one wedding, the bride was given a very special guest book as a shower gift to use on her wedding day. It was a one-of-a-kind, meticulously handmade book. Unfortunately, the caterer placed it in a low-traffic area, and the book was signed by only two wedding guests.

This is why having a guest book attendant makes sense. Ask one of your more social or charming friends or family members to attend the guest book and encourage guests to sign it. The guest book attendant can be put to work as guests arrive or as they depart or may bring the guest book to tables of guests after dessert to sign at their leisure.

Personal Attendant

In some regions of the country, enlisting a personal attendant is a long tradition. In other regions, it's a mystery. But a personal attendant to the bride can perform any number of functions such as organizing and toting everything the bride will need for the wedding day, ensuring her luggage gets to her hotel, helping the bride maneuver her dress in the ladies room, or acting as impromptu makeup artist/hairstylist during the rehearsal dinner and wedding.

Creative Consultant

This may end up being the must-fill role for your creative wedding. Because throwing a creative wedding can involve so much detail or an untraditional structure, a creative consultant or attendant can help you in myriad ways. A particularly open-minded or imaginative friend or family member is a perfect choice—someone who can help you brainstorm ideas, research vendors, and carry out creative ideas during the planning period.

During the wedding itself, your creative consultant can act as your surrogate by apprising the caterer, band, or DJ as to what should be happening next, and making sure the wedding flows properly from cocktails to dinner to dancing—or whatever your creative wedding structure may be.

FACT

Appointing the role of creative consultant can be particularly important if you're having an elaborately themed wedding that caterers, florists, photographers, and other vendors may be unfamiliar with. Your creative consultant can help ensure these creative touches are properly carried out before and during your wedding day, without constant distraction to the bride and groom.

Other Participants

The personalities and talents of your particular loved ones will also dictate the special role they can fill at your wedding. A graphic artist might be asked to design a wedding program or invitation, a writer might be asked to pen a special poem, an avid baker asked to create the wedding cake, or a talented photographer to snap a few photos alongside your hired gun. Again, these participants should be given credit in your program, or thanked outright during a speech or announcements.

The Officiant

If you have a close family friend or relative who's a priest, reverend, or rabbi, choosing your officiant may not be an issue. But if you're having a nonreligious ceremony or interfaith service, your choice may be more complex.

When planning a creative wedding, a civil ceremony may be more amenable to nontraditional plans. For instance, many religions are quite strict about the readings and music performed, how the procession and recession are conducted, and the exchange of vows. A civil ceremony officiant may be more open to including unconventional ceremony ideas, such as nontraditional music, outfits, readings, and/or vows. Qualified civil ceremony officiants include a justice of the peace, judge, county or court clerk, mayor, or notary public. Qualification varies from state to state, so be sure to research your options before booking and paying someone who may not be legally able to perform a wedding.

For interfaith ceremonies, your search for an officiant may be a bit more complicated. You have a number of options, including choosing one of the two religions as a foundation for both the site and officiant; finding co-officiants—one from each religion—who agree to perform the service together; or choosing a third party, such as an officiant of the Unitarian Universalist Church, to perform an interfaith ceremony. Keep in mind that many conservative clergy will not perform interfaith ceremonies or may require conversion or a commitment to raise children in his/her religion before officiating at the marriage.

Chapter 6

Location, Location, Location

Forget the white lace, that three-tier vanilla cake, and those old Jordan almonds—it's time to get creative. This chapter's weddings make the most of their locations—whether it's the beach, a dude ranch, or the friendly skies—to create unique experiences your guests will never forget.

Beach Blanket Bingo

For a breath of fresh air, there's nothing like having a wedding—and reception—on the beach. And whether you're in Miami or Maine, the beach offers unique potential to celebrate a gorgeous, unforgettable wedding for you and your guests.

Your Wedding Style

No matter what inspires you to throw a beach wedding, there are many levels on which to do so. You and your honey may envision a formal wedding with all the trappings—white linen, china, crystal, and candlelight—relocated to a beach setting. Or you may have always envisioned a casual, shorts-and-T-shirts clam bake as the perfect wedding celebration. Either way, the beach provides a perfect backdrop for parties that range from the very casual to the very formal.

FACT

For a retro-beach wedding, pick up some old Annette Funicello movies for inspiration. Play music from the late 1950s and 1960s, don kitschy outfits with polka dots, and watch everyone have a neat-o time.

For a formal beach wedding, the creativity is completely inspired by the setting. Even if you incorporate many of the traditional wedding elements, such as classic attire, food, and dancing, the wedding site will still provide instant novelty—as well as inspiration for many unique, creative touches including creative menus, décor, favors, and table settings.

For a casual beach wedding, you'll be able to utilize all the beach has to offer for your special celebration. Included among your festivities might be beach volleyball, water skiing, jet skiing, wind surfing, or wave running, plus traditional wedding trappings like good food, refreshing drinks, music, and dancing—all, of course, with a seaside twist. The following ideas can be applied to both formal and casual beach weddings.

Invitations

To unveil your fabulous beach theme, tap into your creativity with a unique invitation. By choosing a pre-made design with seaside elements such as seashells, water, fish, or palm trees, or enlisting the aid of a graphic designer to help you design something from scratch, you can inform guests in style about your upcoming seaside nuptials. For an added touch, include some tiny shells or sand in the envelope (though keep in mind that messy sand might annoy recipients.)

For a really creative twist, create three-dimensional mailers. One idea would be to re-create the old "message in a bottle," with your wedding invitation stuffed into a sea-worn bottle. You can use either traditional invitation wording or word it more creatively. Or for another three-dimensional idea, purchase large conch shells and insert the invitations within. Either of these items could be placed into a small box and mailed, or hand delivered for even more drama (and less postage) when possible.

FACT

Here's an idea to begin the wording for a "message in a bottle" invitation: S.O.S.! We are in dire need of your help . . . to celebrate the seaside wedding ceremony of Mary Smith and John Doe! (Insert Date, Time, and Venue here.) Reception to immediately follow. RSVP—traditional means preferred.

Stormy Weather

For brides who can control everything but Mother Nature, there are some precautions you should take in the event that your beach wedding has less than perfect weather: Be sure to set up a large party tent on the beach, or on a bluff or grassy area directly adjacent to the beach. Be sure it's big enough to house all your guests if necessary, and that it has roll-down sides to protect from the elements like wind or rain. Or, if you can, designate an alternate indoor site nearby (someone's home or a seaside shelter) to which you can transfer the festivities in the event of severely inclement weather.

Seaside Sustenance

Your menu will be defined in great part by the style of wedding you plan to have. If it's a casual beach bash, you'll probably want outdoor-friendly vittles that you (or a caterer, preferably) can grill and/or barbecue. This can range from simple fare like burgers and hot dogs to a kicked-up feast with steak or salmon filets, delicious grilled veggies, shrimp on the barbie, clams, crab legs, and other special treats. For drinks, set up a bar, hire a good bartender, and serve plenty of blender drinks like margaritas and daiquiris, as well as fresh squeezed lemonade and iced tea. If you can, serve drinks in coconut cups or tiki mugs for extra effect. And for even more guest convenience, strategically place ice-filled tin tubs or coolers throughout the party with cold beers, wine coolers, bottled water, and soft drinks. Decorate the coolers with seashells or bamboo to stay in theme.

For a more formal wedding, enjoy a classic sit-down dinner under the tent at sundown. Serve seafood like lobster, crab legs, or swordfish (though you may want to give allergy-prone guests another option). Again, offer plenty of tropical drinks like colorful rum runners and blender drinks, along with fresh squeezed juices or even smoothies.

During your cocktail hour, employ a calypso or steel drum band and set up an extensive raw bar with clams, shrimp, crab legs, and other delicacies.

For the wedding cake, adopt a nautical theme with an unusual shape, such as a lighthouse, sailboat, life buoy, or seashell. Or decorate a classic tiered cake with elements from the sea such as shells, starfish, or sea glass.

Natural Beauty

A gorgeous beach setting requires little decoration. However, there are a few areas where some beach-based touches will do nicely. Centerpieces can be beautiful—and creative—while easily staying in theme. For a wedding that will run into the evening, use gas-lit hurricane lamps as centerpieces to warmly light the night sky. You can surround them with flowers, sea glass, or seashells. For a nautical theme, use a simple flower surrounded by a small-sized life buoy as the centerpiece. Or use fishbowls with goldfish as centerpieces. Allow guests to take them home as favors afterward. Even a simple votive candleholder—with the candle anchored by sand—can make a beautiful centerpiece. Cluster a number of them at the center of the table, and you'll have a beautiful glow come nightfall.

Be sure your beach is clean of debris, seaweed, or dead fish on your wedding day. Different times of year present different problems, so ask questions and plan ahead—and be sure to send someone to troubleshoot problems the morning of the wedding.

Treasures from the Deep

Favors also offer an opportunity to be creative. Supply each guest with a pair of sunglasses, in case they forgot their own. Or give each guest a lei as they enter the party. For a more casual wedding and a whimsical approach, supply squirt guns, water bottles, beach balls, or flip flops.

If you're having a beach wedding that includes children, provide them with their own special wedding favors. For each child, create a package consisting of a sand bucket and shovel, a sand sifter, or other sand toys, plus "quiet time" table activities like puzzles or coloring books and crayons. They'll keep children occupied during the day and as evening falls.

For any style beach wedding, be sure there is plenty of sunscreen on hand for guests who burn easily. And for weddings that will go well into the evening hours, plan ahead by strategically placing bug zappers (the quieter the better), bug spray, citronella candles, and even blankets or pashminas to protect guests from the elements. Or surround a beach bonfire with plenty of chairs for guests to relocate to as the night grows darker and cooler. For a late-night snack, have graham crackers, chocolate, and marshmallows on hand to make old-fashioned s'mores.

String Ties and Square Dances

Even if you're from up the northeastern way, you can still throw a Western-themed wedding that will shake the cowboy boots off your Western counterparts. There are plenty of easy—and often inexpensive—ways to theme this wedding from the menu to the music, with everything in between.

Home on the Range

Before you begin planning your Western-themed wedding, you'll need to choose the site. Depending on where you live, the perfect site might be difficult to find. If you live in the middle of a large city, you may have to travel to a less densely populated area for a suitable outdoor setting such as a barn, a farm, or a ranch. Or if you're feeling particularly creative, transform an indoor city venue into a hoedown with props and decorations. Another option would be to see if your area has a country-Western theme bar. Do some research in your locale to find out whether they'll rent out the facility or provide catering. With everything under one roof, it may end up being the easiest way for you to make your dream theme into a reality.

ALERT!

As always, if you're planning to use an outdoor venue, be sure to have a foul-weather contingency plan, such as nice party tents or a nearby indoor setting to which to relocate.

Down-Home Music

Of course, the music and dancing will be the pinnacle of your Western wedding. If you are lucky enough to find a country-Western bar that will host private parties, their DJ can probably spin all the music you could ever hope for. But if you're creating your theme from the ground up, you'll need to scout out a band or DJ who specializes in the type of music you want, whether it's modern pop/country, classic country, bluegrass, or just plain blues. Research your local area online, or call your local country-Western radio station. They're bound to have ideas on your area's great local bands and DJs.

As a complement to your fine music selection, you'd also better have a good-sized dance floor. Whether it's line dancing to the latest hits or square dancing with a caller, the music is bound to inspire many of your guests to hit the dance floor. If you're afraid some of them won't know the steps, hire a dance instructor/leader to encourage dancing and to help them out; even better, hire the instructor to come to your rehearsal dinner the night before, to get the ball rolling early.

Duds

Much of the fun of a Western wedding comes with the attire you'll wear. There are so many styles for both men and women to choose from, with countless retailers ready and willing to provide them. Brides may choose a traditional white wedding dress with some Western stylings, such as a high lace bodice or Western-lace sleeves, or more Western-inspired attire such as a calf-length, handkerchief-bottom dress, or similar skirt with a cropped blouse or vest. A lace top or corset with a long skirt would also be in theme.

FACT

While beautiful Western attire is widely available for purchase, you may also want to try your local rental and costume shops for additional, and often cost-effective, options.

Whatever style you choose, cowboy boots are a must. Special wedding day cowboy boots come in short styles—and even in white—for the bride's special day.

Western attire has perhaps more options for men than any other style of dress. Men can opt to wear anything from a Western tux jacket with tails, leather pants, brocade or leather vests, banded collar shirts, frontier-style shirts, and neckwear ranging from string ties to colonel ties to continental ties to neck scarves—all, of course, with the requisite cowboy boots and cowboy hat.

For a more casual Western wedding, both women and men may opt to wear jeans as their wedding attire. The bride could wear white jeans and the groom could wear black. To gussy it up a bit, the bride could still wear a veil.

From Basics to BBQ

A Western wedding wouldn't be complete without an extensive, delicious barbecue. No matter how you choose to serve it, think barbecue chicken, ribs, and steaks; delicious side dishes like macaroni and cheese, green beans, corn on the cob, and creamed spinach; and desserts including pies—try sweet potato, strawberry, apple, and blueberry. Find a baker who will create a theme wedding cake as well. Create a three-tiered mini corral, or have it shaped in the form of hay bales.

FACT

Mealtime at your Western wedding can be any style you like, from casual, load-up-at-the-grill style to a more formal, sit-down style.

All the Trimmings

It's easy to Westernize indoor spaces—or outdoor spaces, for that matter—with table settings and other props. Set tables with gingham-checked tablecloths and blue- or black-speckled enameled dishes. For centerpieces, fill old mason jars or attractive old bottles with wildflowers or other flowers. Or use hurricane lamps with large pillar candles within as centerpieces with a Western flair. In addition, you could use cowboy hats as centerpieces, with one lucky guest from each table designated to take it home.

To create that Western feel around the perimeter of your celebration, set up split-rail fences and bales of hay throughout. Also include old-style washtubs full of ice and beer, so guests can easily quench their thirst.

Favors might consist of tiny burlap bags with goodies inside, such as candy, a deck of cards, a small candle, or bottle of lotion. Or each guest could be given a charm for a charm bracelet.

For bridesmaids' gifts, Western jewelry featuring silver or turquoise could make for a nice surprise, or a charm bracelet with a Western theme, such as a little hat, horse, and heart. Give the groomsmen a good-quality beer mug, a handsome belt buckle, or even a cowboy hat to wear the day of the wedding and beyond.

Puppy Love Wedding

Many people today couldn't possibly imagine celebrating one of the most important days of their lives without their beloved pooch. And while pet-less people may not understand their passion, dog lovers who share your canine affections will absolutely slobber over the idea of a puppy love wedding.

A Dog-Lover's Dream

The puppy love wedding is about spreading the love, not hoarding it. That means that in addition to including your own dog(s) within your special day, your guest list will also include the four-legged companions of friends and family. Luckily, dogs don't bring dates, which will cut down on per-plate costs. But, of course, special dietary concerns will go beyond the typically proffered vegetarian fare, extending to the Alpo and Purina set.

ALERT!

While dog porta-potties would be wonderful, you can't teach an old dog new tricks. So be sure to have plenty of scoops and garbage bags for the inevitable messes.

There's only one place to have your puppy love wedding—outdoors. However, the setting may vary from a state park to a farm to a (very understanding) friend's yard (make it a big one). And while you *are* throwing a wedding, there are many practical concerns you should consider *before* buying that $2,000 satin dress, which will inevitably end up with many muddy paw prints.

Unleashed

Your dog-lovers' wedding will bear no resemblance to a traditional formal affair. Of course, if you've decided to include a second species at your wedding, you're probably pretty laid back to begin with, so this may not be a big concern. But your planning—from the site to the menus to the centerpieces—will ultimately reflect your unique choice of party guests.

Love Me, Love My Dog

Unveil your theme to guests with your invitation. If you'd like to send a traditional, flat invitation, find a pre-made design that incorporates a dog element (this may be difficult to find), or hire a graphic designer or stationery shop to custom make one for you. For a fun three-dimensional invitation, consider affixing your invitation to a dog bone or dog biscuit (which could even double as a wedding favor, as humans will pass it on to their dogs).

Let all your guests know that this is a casual, comfortable wedding at which dogs will be honored guests. Don't be offended if you get declines from those who are allergic or unfriendly to dogs—it will inevitably go with the territory. If it's a real concern, and you don't want to exclude human guests from your wedding, consider including just your dog in a limited way—like walking you down the aisle—instead of having a full-blown, big-dog affair.

Getting Out of the Dog House

There are some other practical considerations to keep in mind while you plan this shindig—namely, how the dogs will get along with each *other*. There are a couple ways to combat this. The first is to put the onus on the dog owner. Most dog owners are well aware of how their pet behaves with other dogs around. If they've got a serious alpha dog who tolerates few other men or beasts, they should refrain from bringing their canine friend. Be clear about this in the invitation, so you'll avoid problems at the wedding.

The second way to combat this dog-eat-dog problem is to have a sufficiently large outdoor area with plenty of areas to stake leashes. That way, if one or two dogs get out of hand, they can be separated from the bunch.

When it comes to your puppy love wedding, space is key. Be sure to have a vast, outdoor area—preferably fenced in—where dogs can run and play freely, and where people can play with them.

Clearly, if you're having a wedding with many dogs, it's going to be an interesting and unpredictable affair. If you can anticipate problems in advance, it'll make it much easier on the day of the wedding. You may also consider employing a dog trainer for the day to help keep things under control so that you won't get distracted from the celebration.

Hot under the Collar

Now onto the fun stuff. Exactly how will this wedding differ from any other? The first thing you'll want to consider is wardrobe. Dictate casual, day-at-the-beach dress—shorts or jeans and T-shirts. For the ceremony, the bride and groom may want to wear something a little dressier, then change for the reception.

The dogs, on the other hand, are an entirely different story. Owners should feel free to bring Spot and Rover dressed in their finest—whether that's a bandana around a Lab's neck or a tutu for the toy poodle.

Then there's the ceremony. If you plan to include your canine friends in the ceremony, you will of course need to have the ceremony outside. To overshadow the cacophony of barking that is likely to occur, you may want to use microphones so that the officiant, bride, and groom can be heard by your guests. Be sure to place guest seating with plenty of room between them to accommodate a space for their four-legged friends.

For the reception, a casual menu is recommended—as is continuing with an outdoor setting. It'll be much easier to stomach the poorly trained pooch who pilfers a hot dog, rather than a filet mignon, off your guests' plates. Of course, during mealtime, the species should be separated, with canines enjoying a special menu in their own special area, with their own designated dog dishes that they can take home at the end of the day. The menu probably should not be people food, but it should be something tastier than plain old dry dog food. Go to your specialty pet food store for ideas and have the caterers serve them in style.

The meal wouldn't be complete without dessert. Instead of a groom's cake, you can include a dogs' cake, with tier after tier of doggie treats that owners can feed their dogs. For the people, a traditional wedding cake—with a dog cake topper—will do just fine.

On Leashes and Poop Scoopers

The line on leashes and poop scoops? Don't forget 'em. In fact, either would make great guest favors. See if you can get custom leashes made with your names or the date on them, like the old custom-printed matches and napkins. Or give each guest a special doggie toy or ball that they can use on the day of the wedding and thereafter.

Set up a time at your wedding for an official show-and-tell. Allow owners to show off all their favorite dog tricks and quirks for everyone to see. Give a blue ribbon to the most creative or astonishing trick.

Music

If you're having a band, be sure live musicians are properly fenced in. If you're having a DJ—the same goes, so that his equipment is protected. Hire a band or DJ who'll play as many dog-inspired tunes as possible—from Elvis's "Hound Dog" to the tunes of Snoop Doggy Dog to "How Much Is that Doggie in the Window" to Donny Osmond's "Puppy Love."

Up, Up, and Away

Imagine you and your honey silently drifting over rooftops, lakes, and forests as you exchange the vows of marriage. For impact that goes sky-high, a hot air balloon ride offers a beautiful and memorable way to tie the knot.

Wild Ride

Finding a hot air balloon near you shouldn't be difficult. To locate one, consult your yellow pages, or search online for a local service provider. If you come to a dead end, visit ✍ *www.ushotairballoon.com*, or call ✆ 1-800-76-FLY-US. The U.S. Hot Air Balloon Team will locate the nearest hot air balloon provider near you and can even arrange to schedule service.

There are a number of ways to go about incorporating a hot air balloon ride into your wedding. The first is to actually have your ceremony on board, with your officiant, the hot air balloon pilot, and witnesses present. You may also invite additional close family or friends, depending on your balloon's capacity . . . some hot air balloons can fit as many as ten or more passengers, and some limit passengers to two or three.

Obviously, if you decide to have your ceremony airborne, it will be a much more intimate affair. If you love the idea of a hot air balloon but would like all your friends and family present during the ceremony, consider holding the ceremony on the grounds where the hot air balloon launches. When you are pronounced husband and wife, take off in your balloon to the clapping and cheers of your loved ones below. Then join the party at another reception site to celebrate.

If you're going to have the wedding on solid ground, only to soar into the air as your vows are made final, toss your bouquet to onlookers from the air for added drama.

Another option would be to arrive at or depart from the reception in a hot air balloon. Speak to your hot air balloon provider to find out where they are able to land and depart from. If you plan to have your party in an open, outdoor area such as a golf course or farmland, you may be able to arrive in true style, touching down to greet your guests in a balloon. Or you may decide you'd like to have a dramatic departure following your wedding and reception, with a hot air balloon to carry you away. Once again, talk to your balloon provider—and your reception site—to determine if there are rules and regulations that could make this transportation impossible. Do so *before* you put any deposits down or book a provider.

Before booking your hot air balloon or your ceremony/reception site, be sure to coordinate the details with each vendor. You wouldn't want to put down a $1,000 deposit on a banquet hall only to find out that big adjacent lot that seems ideal for a balloon landing is actually a swamp.

The Details

The size of the balloon "basket" will likely determine who will be invited aboard. Typically, hot air balloon rides cost about $200 per person, but often you can get even better per-person group rates. In addition, many hot air balloon providers offer special wedding packages that include the officiant's fee, champagne, and other amenities. These vary from provider to provider, so talk to some local outfitters about what they have to offer.

Some ballooning companies also offer fleets of balloons to rent out, which would allow you to accommodate many more guests in the air—up to thirty or more for some companies. Imagine ten colorful hot air balloons in a synchronized launch—and the gorgeous photos you'll have afterward!

If you're planning to coordinate a big reception to follow—or precede—your hot air balloon ride, don't forget to factor in the weather. If there are high winds, rain, or snow, most balloons will not fly. And unless you're eloping, you can't reschedule the wedding due to weather. Be sure to have a contingency plan if Mother Nature isn't agreeable.

FACT

Due to weather and other factors, many hot air balloons launch at either dawn or sunset, so be sure to consider timing when planning other events around your hot air balloon ride.

If you plan to have a full-scale reception, continue your hot air balloon theme with decorations and other special touches. Find a baker who will design your cake in the shape of a balloon, cover your reception site's ceiling with countless helium balloons, and design centerpieces like hot air balloons. Also use the theme in your invitation and program design.

Chapter 7

E

Going Back in Time

The idea of traveling back in time to a period that seems simpler and more innocent is very appealing. This chapter examines theme weddings from centuries ago up to the recent past. They're all reminiscent of times that were fun and stylish—two very important elements for a richly executed, romantic theme wedding.

The Renaissance Wedding

Renaissance weddings have grown in popularity in recent years, probably due to the fact that the era, with its dress and customs, is inherently romantic. Actual Renaissance weddings hearken back to the period of the years from 1450 to 1600, though many of today's Renaissance themes incorporate elements and traditions from the Middle Ages period of 1050 to 1450 as well. This entire span covers the period of the Crusades, Robin Hood, and Christopher Columbus's voyage to the New World. If you are a stickler for historical accuracy, you may want to narrow your time frame when developing a concept for your wedding to, say, a one-hundred-year span; otherwise, call it a "medieval wedding" and bring in lore from a range of centuries.

If you decide to plan a Renaissance wedding, you can follow a number of paths. The first is to plan it entirely on your own, scouting out locations, costumes, flexible caterers, and the like. The second route is to contact the proprietors of your closest Renaissance fair. These fairs are held in outposts nationwide, and a quick search on the Internet will probably yield one near you. Often these proprietors already have wedding packages established or will allow you to hold your wedding on their grounds for a fee.

ALERT!

While you might consider it ideal for all your guests to dress in Renaissance-style costumes, indicate on your invitation that it's strictly optional. Finding a costume in an appropriate size and style may end up being prohibitive or even impossible for some of your guests, and you certainly don't want them to feel uncomfortable attending your wedding because of it.

Thee and Thou—A Special Ceremony

The site you choose for your Renaissance wedding will set the stage for the entire celebration. If you are lucky enough to reside near one of America's few castles or castle-like structures, check out whether they will host parties or can be rented out. Or choose a Gothic church, an English cottage, a old-style mansion or manor house, or a Tudor-style building (many country clubs are designed in this style). Or choose to have the ceremony and reception outdoors—think of a forest-like setting à la Robin Hood. Set up a tent to ward off evil spirits . . . a.k.a. bad weather.

For your ceremony, you may want to include some of the customs of handfasting, which was a popular practice of the era. Handfasting is a medieval tradition whose meaning scholars today debate. Some believe handfasting was a form of temporary marriage—a trial period, if you will, that lasted a year and a day—while others insist it was simply an engagement ceremony. Today, the theatrics of handfasting can be incorporated into your ceremony to symbolize anything you like—including, of course, the twenty-first-century standard of wedded bliss. (The term "handfasting" in modern use also applies to pagan weddings, which are not necessarily legally binding. If you plan on conducting a legally binding civil or religious ceremony, you can incorporate the theatrical elements of handfasting within the legal confines of a wedding ceremony, with a qualified officiant.)

FACT

Prior to the wedding you may want to enlist someone to act as "town crier," officially announcing the commencement of the ceremony. Add a trumpet blast for additional drama.

Handfasting ceremonies typically followed a course of events that went something like this: thanking the gods and goddesses for good fortune; sharing of food or wine by the bride and groom; jumping a broom; tying a cord or sash around the wrists of the bride and groom as they clasp each other's opposite hands in the sign of infinity; and exchanging vows.

Costumes

Costumes for the period are very unique, romantic, and beautiful and will definitely set the tone for your entire wedding. For a medieval look, women—including the bride—should wear long, slim gowns, possibly with an empire waist. For a later-date look (1450 to 1600), women should wear tight-bodiced dresses with full skirts. Both eras feature rich jewel tones like emerald, sapphire, and ruby.

Appropriate attire for men includes tights and tunics or breeches and billowy shirts with vests. Costumes can be custom made or rented, based on your personal preference. Furnish a trusted tailor or dressmaker with an image of your creation, or start perusing local costume shops and the Internet for rentable attire.

FACT

You'll get tons of information and inspiration by attending a Renaissance fair prior to your wedding. While there, ask organizers for tips on where they've gotten their costumes and props, and for information on customs of the day. Plus, you'll be able to purchase souvenirs for use as centerpieces, as wedding favors, or as part of your ceremony.

Clothing, of course, is just the first part of the look. Instead of a veil, the bride could wear a garland or wreath of flowers atop her head, with her hair minimally styled—if it's long, wear it freestyle and flowing (hair should not be in an elaborate up-do). Bouquets, both for the bride and bridesmaids, could be collections of wildflowers, roses, or other flowers that are loosely and casually arranged. Or you might even use dried flowers, reported to be a custom of the day. Wrap them with long, flowing ribbons for an added touch.

No Utensils, Please

Food will add a very creative and historically relevant aspect to the Renaissance wedding as well. Meat seems to have been the culinary focus back then including roasted and boiled meat, mutton, poultry, veal, goose, tongue, and sausages. And though vegetables and salads weren't a big staple, you can certainly modify any of the traditional medieval or Renaissance foods to appease guests. Work with your caterer to give your menu a creative twist that will please modern palates but offer some sort of historical aspect. Then include a menu card at each table setting with the menu written in Old English.

Liquor certainly abounded during the Middle Ages, and there is plenty of lore to draw from. Popular at the time were ales, mead (a thick wine made from fermented honey whose twenty-first-century interpretation is available in some specialty liquor stores), and plenty of wine.

If you're able to find it, serve food on metal dishware like pewter, silver, or brass, or use pottery or wooden pieces for a rustic look. It's unlikely you'll be able to find genuine pewter or brass dishware in large quantities, so feel free to improvise by using aluminum or metal-look plates and goblets. And while you may be accustomed to the "no utensils" rule popularized by many medieval-themed restaurants, you may consider giving squeamish guests the option of silverware to ensure they are not inconvenienced.

FACT

You may want to consider an "uncivilized" pig roast to add to your medieval festivities, particularly if your reception is being held outdoors.

Entertainment

The medieval and Renaissance periods are rich with entertainment offerings. First, you'll want to consider music. Common instruments to the period are bagpipes, flute, guitar, organ, harp, and mandolin. Employ a strolling musician or a band of musicians to play the haunting, clear melodies of the day. In addition to music, you may also consider other forms of entertainment for your guests, including a period-dressed magician or mime, jugglers, fire eaters, or displays of jousting or even falconry.

Special Touches

There are all sorts of additional ways to create Renaissance touches throughout your wedding. For your invitation, choose a heavy parchment paper with a medieval font or calligraphy. Or pull out all the stops and develop a wood-carved or leather-bound invitation. Ask your local invitation retailer if they have something appropriate, or enlist the help of an artisan or graphic designer to create something unique for your wedding. For the wedding program, design it like an old-time, scroll-wrapped (use a ribbon or a leather cord to wrap) announcement (the kind that were unrolled and posted on street corners). For favors, consider giving guests an artisan's (or artisan-inspired) piece of blown glass (small vase with flower), leatherwork (rustic key chain), woodwork (mini sculpture or pill box), stained glass, pottery, or metalwork. Again, your local Renaissance fair would be a great place to pick up some items—or to get ideas that you can research and purchase on your own.

The Victorian Wedding

A few centuries later came a period that easily matches the romance and beauty of Renaissance times—the Victorian era. The time period refers to the span of Queen Victoria's rule in England, from 1837 to 1901. And while such a broad time period inevitably covers many changing trends in dress, design, and tastes, there are certain fashions and behaviors suggested here as a general representation of the whole era.

Corsets and Crinolines

Without a doubt, the fashion of the period will immediately define your Victorian-themed wedding. Women's dresses during the time period went through various fads but remained similar in style on the major points—bodices were fitted (usually higher cut for the wedding day), waists were tiny, and skirts were very full, with a steel crinoline or hoop and layers of petticoats. Of course, the corset aided in making those bodices and waists as small as can be. The preferred material for wedding dresses was silk, but dresses were also made of tulle, organdy, or lace, among other fabrics. A veil was worn, particularly if the ceremony was held in a church, as were long white gloves, silk stockings, and flat slippers.

FACT

It was considered bad luck in Victorian times to marry in May—the most popular months were April in the South and June in the North.

In the earlier part of the Victorian era, bridesmaids mirrored the bride with white dresses and miniature veils. However, as the era wore on, the trend of wearing a contrasting color was popularized. Dresses were of a similar style as the bride—fitted bodice, full skirt.

The groom and groomsmen also wore similar outfits—seen most predominantly through the era were dark frock coats in black or blue, with gray trousers, gloves, and black top hats. For evening, men might wear more formal attire such as tailcoats.

Visit some local costume shops to see what's in stock from this era, or search online for retailers offering reproductions. Or give a picture—or number of pictures—to a trusted tailor or dressmaker to create a Victorian-era dress that will fit you to a tee.

FACT

The most popular blossoms for bridal bouquets during the Victorian era were orange blossoms, which were thought to represent purity. Often these were worn by the bride during the ceremony and later removed from headpieces or bouquets for the reception.

Romance and Lace

The Victorian era is remembered most for its ornate and complicated stylings in architecture, furniture, fashion, and decorating. If you choose to throw a Victorian wedding, chances are you are charmed by these romantic looks and styles and wish to incorporate many of these features into your wedding. The first thing you'll want to consider is the site. In the Victorian era, many weddings and/or receptions were held at home, so you may want to consider asking a close friend or family member with a classic Victorian home to open it for your wedding day celebration. If this isn't possible or practical, scout out a Victorian inn, a garden estate, or a museum setting with a historical feel.

Once you've decided on your theme and site, you can decide on your invitations. Modern invitations seem to have taken much of their cue from Victorian-era invitations, both in design and wording, so your task shouldn't be too difficult. Engraved, formal invitations on a quality stock paper, printed in script—much like today's—was the norm. Fonts were a bit more ornate, however, so this is one area in which you can make a statement. Talk to your stationery provider or invitation designer to view era-appropriate scripts. You may also consider hand making invitations, with hand-glued lace, paper, and other Victorian motifs. Think of an ornate, old-fashioned valentine for inspiration. For your RSVP cards, have them designed to look like an old-fashioned calling card for additional thematic effect.

The Ceremony and Reception

Church weddings were popular during this era, though many brides and grooms were also married at home. Common to each of these ceremony sites, however, was the time of day—until late in the Victorian period, it was required by law to have a morning ceremony—typically between 10 and 12 o'clock. These ceremonies were then followed by a breakfast reception, often held at the bride's parents' home.

Later in the era it was allowable to have an afternoon or evening wedding. When planning your Victorian-themed wedding, you can decide which time of day makes most sense to you—if you'd like to emulate the trappings of earlier era weddings with breakfast, tea, and little to no entertainment, the morning or daytime wedding is for you. If you'd like to incorporate dinner and dancing, hold your wedding during the evening hours. For dancing, hire a band that can play classical music by artists like Handel, Wagner, and Mozart. The popular dances of the day were reels, waltzes, and quadrilles.

For transportation, only a horse and carriage will do. A wedding custom of the time was to employ a carriage with four white horses pulling it. This would be a very beautiful and dramatic touch today.

FACT

The tradition of the groom carrying the bride over the threshold of their home upon return from the wedding—or honeymoon—originated during Victorian times. It was thought to be bad luck if the bride should stumble in the doorway . . . this practice would prevent that from happening.

No matter where you decide to hold the reception, decorate elaborately. Use lots of flowers for centerpieces and at the ceremony site, in addition to candles and other decorations incorporating lace, hearts, cupids, and angels. The Victorian wedding cake was most popularly a dark rich fruitcake with elaborate white frosting, but feel free to have a wedding cake in a more popular flavor. You can "Victorian-ize" it through decorative items like lace, rose petals, and hearts. For any style cake, have your baker bake in tiny favors or charms to be found by the wedding party and guests. This was a Victorian-era tradition to signify good luck. Be sure to alert all your guests to be on the lookout, however!

Fitzgerald Fantasy

There are few more romantic times in history than the era with which F. Scott Fitzgerald is most associated—the roaring '20s. Full of economic prosperity, new freedoms for women, and postwar victory, it was a decade of decadence in which the driving factor for many was good times.

Wonderful Wardrobes

Punctuating the style of the decade most is easily the era's wardrobes. For women, this meant straight, curveless dresses with skirts that fell around mid-calf for both daytime and evening wear. More formal dress had similar lines, with a straight bodice, low waist, and ankle-length hem, often cut on the bias. For evening wear, heavy beading was also quite popular in similar cuts.

Brides of the 1920s wore similar cut dresses, in materials like crepe and chiffon. Unlike today's veils, which are often worn off the top and back of the bride's head, veils of the 1920s usually began with an element covering the bride's forehead and much of her head and hair.

For your 1920s-theme wedding, you may choose to wear the bridal fashion of the day or decide to wear a flapper-style dress in white or ivory— one with beading would add a bit more formality. Enlist a responsible and knowledgeable dressmaker to create your outfit from scratch, or scour costume shops and online retailers to find exactly what you're looking for. Finding matching bridesmaids' dresses may present a challenge, so handmade dresses might be the solution here as well. Or you can choose the style of dress—long bias-cut dresses, for instance, or flapper dresses—and allow your bridesmaids to find a color and style of their own choosing.

FACT

Be sure to let your guests know that 1920s' attire is suggested (but not mandatory). Include in your invitation the names of local costume shops or online retailers that provide outfits from this era, to make it easier for guests to find what they're looking for.

Women's accessories of the day included long pearls, cloche hats (close fitting hats that fit over the ears), rolled stockings, feather boas, and fringe. Add a long cigarette holder for additional drama. For a wintertime wedding, the bride might don a fur (or faux fur) stole or unstructured fur wrap to cover her loosely structured dress.

As for hairstyles, choose from the famous flapper bob or the close-cut, slicked down wave, equally popular during this time period. If you have long hair, you may want to consider cutting it to fit the fashion of the day—if that's not an option, try a wig.

For men, finding the right formal attire will be a bit simpler. In fact, you'll probably be able to rent or buy a tuxedo or suit that's currently in stores, as today's formal styles are similar to those of the 1920s. Classic tuxedos in white tie or black tie would be appropriate for a 1920s-themed wedding, as would tails. Another option includes daytime cutaway coats and ascots—very sharp, very classic. Add top hats and walking sticks to the mix to accessorize in style. For more casual summertime dress, or a seaside setting, choose linen or seersucker suits. For reference and further inspiration for the sumptuous styles of the day, rent a video of *The Great Gatsby*. Prepare to fall in love again with the era.

Cocktails and Dreams

Of course, the 1920s were also marked by the era of prohibition. Ironically, drinking and smoking were a big part of the decade's cultural consciousness—forbidden fruit frequently bitten by the free-wheeling jazz babies of the day. If you'd like to have an alcohol-free wedding, the 1920s theme is the ideal backdrop and explanation. Of course, expect some guests to smuggle in flasks of illegal hooch and bathtub gin to tide them over.

If you do choose to serve alcohol, you may want to include a few "props" near the bar like big jugs filled with "moonshine," or incorporate a speakeasy look. Or serve old-fashioned drinks like gin and tonics and whiskeys and water in elegant crystal glasses with fancy stir sticks for effect.

The Flapper Age

Music will play a big role in your Fitzgerald fantasy. After all, this is the time when the modern-day dance crazes began, with flappers popularizing the Charleston, the shimmy, and the black bottom. And there's a reason F. Scott dubbed this era "The Jazz Age," with the increasing popularity of jazz musicians like Bessie Smith, Al Jolson, and Duke Ellington. Of course, old-fashioned waltzes danced to sentimental ballads were still extremely popular, as were the pop songs of artists like Irving Berlin and George Gershwin.

FACT

Dance marathons gained huge popularity in the 1920s. Hold a mini "dance marathon" at your wedding, with the last man and woman standing after a few songs receiving a prize—or some recognition.

For music, find a talented band that'll play enduring classics like "Fascinating Rhythm," "It Had to Be You," "Someone to Watch Over Me," "Tip Toe Through the Tulips," "Yes Sir, That's My Baby," and lots of other songs you didn't even know hailed from the era. Talk to the bandleader about his specific capabilities . . . often bands can easily learn a new song or two for your wedding, if you've got a special request. A large, orchestra-type band with five to ten members would be an appropriate find. Ask if they'll wear formal attire to match your theme.

Special Touches

The perfect setting for your Fitzgerald fantasy can be just about anywhere, with some decorating effort. However, to make it easier on yourself—and more authentic—scout out some art deco buildings that can be rented for public use. If you're in Miami, you're in luck—South Beach is arguably the art deco capital of North America, with many buildings of this style restored to their former glory. Check out your local area for similar options. Try old hotel ballrooms, or museum or gallery settings for a historical feel. Even if they're not strictly art deco, certain settings can still capture the historical decadence of the era.

FACT

Art deco, as defined by Infoplease.com, is a style of decorative art developed originally in the 1920s, with a revival in the 1960s, marked chiefly by geometric motifs, curvilinear forms, sharply defined outlines, often bold colors, and the use of synthetic materials, such as plastics.

If an art deco setting isn't possible or you'd like something different, create an outdoor wedding in a Gatsby-esque waterfront setting. Find a willing friend or family member with waterfront property, or rent a classic seaside cottage, lakefront home, or restaurant with easy, wide-open spaces. Set up Adirondack chairs for cocktail hour lounging, and serve a multicourse meal under a candlelit outdoor tent.

For a classy looking and era-appropriate invitation, incorporate an art deco design. Design your wedding program with a similar theme.

As an added visual, set up a giant movie screen at your reception site and run silent movies featuring Rudolph Valentino and Clara Bow—isn't it romantic?

For transportation, rent 1920s-era Model Ts to take you to the wedding, or to the wedding and reception sites. For gifts, give groomsmen silver or pewter flasks as thank-you gifts and bridesmaids little flapper purses to carry their "newly liberated" lipstick and cigarettes. As favors, give mini bottles of Chanel No. 5 to the women—first introduced in 1921, marking the beginning of the reign of Coco Chanel as fashion goddess.

Disco Wedding

The single most important factor for the disco wedding—the one that eclipses all else—is, of course, the music. For this stylized 1970s bash it all starts with music, and the rest follows.

Before you begin planning your 1970s wedding, do a little easy research. Pull out your parents' old photo albums and check out what they were wearing and doing in the 1970s. Fish through the attic and try to find some groovin' old clothes and albums. Look at your baby pictures and note the hair styles—and, more notably, the facial hair styles. This is your inspiration. Use it wisely.

Goin' Down to Funky Town

Disco. Arguably, there's still no better music to get down to. Note the popularity even today on college campuses of the music of 1970s favorites like Gloria Gaynor—and the remakes she's inspired. Your first step when planning this theme wedding is to secure the band or DJ who will make it happen. In many towns and cities, there are 1970s tribute bands who'll play nothing but—give them a listen and see if you like them.

Instead of a traditional first slow dance for the bride and groom, choreograph a disco dance à la *Saturday Night Fever* and wow your friends and family.

Or to save money and honor the original artists of disco at the same time, hire a DJ who's got plenty of selections from the era. Bonus points go to a DJ who actually worked the club scene in the 1970s and can recreate those disco days. When asking about a band's or DJ's selections, keep in mind these must-have 1970s artists:

Abba	Peaches and Herb
Blondie	Sister Sledge
The Bee Gees	Donna Summer
Gloria Gaynor	A Taste of Honey
KC and the Sunshine Band	The Village People

Strobe Lights and Disco Balls

Of course, almost as important as the music is the aesthetics, which range from attire to decorations. Finding these precious items will be half the fun.

Before you accessorize, however, you'll need to choose a site. Again, the objective is to enjoy the music, so be sure to choose a location with a great dance floor. There may be a retro 1970s-style club or bar in your city—see if you can rent it out for your wedding, or if they have any leads on another good site. You may also be able to draw that 1970s feel from another local nightclub that's not necessarily 1970s themed, many of which still incorporate the wonderfully cheesy strobe lights, lighted dance floor, and fog machines of days past. Or rent out a banquet room or hall and add the necessary accoutrements—including, first and foremost, the all-important disco ball. It's (remotely) possible that the caterer at your chosen site will have one; if not, scour consignment stores, flea markets, and the Internet to find one.

Threads

Also important to creating the perfect 1970s inspired wedding is the attire. For the men, it goes without saying—the ruffled-shirt and pastel-colored tuxedo is an absolute must. For women, it can be a little trickier. Again, looking through consignment shops—especially in a large city—may yield exactly what you're looking for. If not, get a picture of what you'd like—a satin or synthetic Studio 54–type disco dress—and have a qualified seamstress re-create it. Bonus—it'll still cost less than a traditional wedding dress.

Follow suit with the attire for your bridesmaids and groomsmen. Bridesmaids can wear disco party dresses or hot pants and blouses. For men, many tuxedo rental shops still rent out retro tuxes so the whole wedding party can match. Otherwise, make do with consignment shop finds or discoveries from your parents' closets. One never knows where they'll find that oh-so-in-demand lime green leisure suit.

You will find incredible ideas from your family's old photos, particularly for great outfits. Find pictures of Mom in her favorite groovy styles—long, colorful polyester evening dresses—and use them to work with a seamstress on your perfect wedding style.

As for guests, inform them on your disco-themed invitation that they are welcome to come wearing the best from the decade. Your contemporaries will have a great time looking for that perfect outfit, while your Aunt Judy will have an opportunity to wear that rust and orange party dress she's always hoped will come back in style.

Groovy Touches

There are countless other creative touches you can bring to your disco wedding. For transportation, rent or borrow 1970s-era sports cars like Corvettes, Porsches, and Mustangs. Instead of elaborate flower centerpieces, use lava lamps. Women should wear their hair in classic winged do's, or straight and parted down the middle. Encourage the use of heavy lip gloss and roller skates. For favors, give away mood rings, pet rocks, seahorses, or fruit-striped gum. And for a special added touch of entertainment at your wedding, hold a dance contest with a Denny Terrio–type emcee and prizes for the winners. It's solid gold! Ⓔ

Chapter 8
Love Conquers All

We're all a little bit in love with love. We celebrate romance and love whenever we can . . . we even have an annual holiday devoted to it. Romance novels comprise 50 percent of paperback book sales, and little girls fantasize about fairy-tale characters from Sleeping Beauty to the Little Mermaid. What better inspiration for a wedding than these romantic ideals?

Fairy-Tale Wedding

The most popular fairy tale to inspire weddings across the country—and beyond—is definitely *Cinderella.* Its romantic story and triumph of love and beauty over evil and ugliness is almost certainly the reason for it. It's a story that's endured though the ages and has been remade for modern sensibilities on both movie and television screens. But while *Cinderella* is the most popular and obvious choice for your fairy-tale wedding, you may also choose to include the lore of romantic fairy tales such as *Sleeping Beauty, Beauty and the Beast,* or *Rapunzel* if you wish.

Glass Slippers and More

There are certain must-haves for your fairy-tale/Cinderella wedding. The first, of course, are glass slippers. You can incorporate the glass slippers into a number of areas of your wedding, the first of which is your actual footwear. There are many styles to choose from to emulate the look of the glass or crystal slippers, including clear, transparent designs (usually in a form of plastic), or strappy designs with crystalline straps or heels. Feel free to be creative. Your shoes don't have to be exact replicas of the shoes you saw in your childhood picture books, but they should have some glass or crystal look to them—so you can show them off to onlookers and for photographs (and don't forget the ultimate photo op, with your prince placing the shoe on your foot).

You may want to use the glass slipper as inspiration for other areas of your wedding, such as a beautiful ice sculpture or a cake topper. Look for a glass slipper-themed cake topper at local retailers or online, or request one from your pastry chef/baker.

The rest of your Cinderella-inspired wedding outfit should be equally beautiful and feminine. An especially romantic silk or satin wedding gown—with a sweetheart or lower-cut neckline—with beading or jewels would be appropriate, as would an empire waist dress in similar fabrics. Wear a white fur stole and a tiara to finish the look, with hair worn long, loose and feminine, or up in a feminine chignon.

For that storybook feel, men might wear britches and white stockings, with ruffled shirts and cutaway coats with tails. However, this could be modernized for grooms who are uncomfortable with such an elaborate getup. A modern white tuxedo would also be a dramatic—and fairy tale-like—look for your groom and groomsmen.

For fun, deem your maid of honor your "Fairy Godmother," with an elaborate costume (think shimmery, white, or light-colored full gown) and a wand instead of a bouquet. Bridesmaids can wear a style of dress similar to yours, either full ball gown style dresses or empire waist dresses. (Just don't make them look like your ugly stepsisters.) White gloves on you and your bridesmaids would add an elegant and appropriate touch.

Decorations to Dessert

The Cinderella ball scene is all the inspiration you need to re-create a fairy-tale setting. For your wedding site, choose an old-fashioned hotel ballroom, an old mansion or manor house with a ballroom, a castle, or an old museum with a historical feel—and an ample area to dance. Line your tables with tulle to create a dreamy, pure look, or cover chairs with beautiful white chair covers in satin, cotton, or tulle to continue the cloudy, fairy-tale effect. Use white or pink tulips or roses for centerpieces, or any other romantic flowers in white, pink, or red. Place a magic wand at each place setting for a favor, or have a favor table displaying little chocolate mice, inspired by the fairy tale. Favors may also include decorative glass or crystal picture frames—use them to display placecards as guests walk in. There are also many favors made specifically for Cinderella weddings—check with your local wedding stationary store or with online retailers for additional options.

There are countless retailers who offer Cinderella-inspired "props" for your wedding, which range from napkins to programs to cake cutters to placecards. You can purchase the items you need from them, or use them for inspiration to create your own Cinderella-look decorations and accessories.

Before the wedding, send out invitations in pure white, heavy stock paper, with elaborate, flowery font. Include an icon on the invitation design, like a glass slipper or "pumpkin" carriage to introduce your theme. Buy them pre-made, or have one created for you. Use your old Cinderella picture books for ideas for imagery.

FACT

To find a designer to create an original invitation for you, ask friends and family for references to graphic designers they may know. If you hit a dead end, look in your local yellow pages for small graphic design outfits or freelance designers.

To arrive at your ceremony or reception site in true fairy-tale style, hire a white coach pulled by four white horses. Utilize the horse-drawn coach to recreate Cinderella's famous midnight dash . . . only this time Cinderella will be leaving *with* her prince. Have a clock chime 12 at your reception, then make a dramatic departure amid all your guests in the horse-drawn carriage.

For music at your reception, play fairy-tale soundtracks from movies like *Cinderella, Beauty and the Beast,* and *The Little Mermaid,* as well as others. During the cocktail hour or dinner, employ a strolling violinist to play classical tunes. Or hire a band that will play many old-fashioned waltzes and ballroom dance songs to re-create the feel of Cinderella's ball.

Instead of the bouquet toss, incorporate a new tradition. Hold a shoe-fitting ceremony with one lucky groomsmen looking for the woman who's his perfect fit . . . the first girl or woman guest who fits into his glass slipper will be included in a special dance or receive a special gift. If you're having children at your wedding, use a girl-sized shoe . . . and see how excited she gets when she finds out she's the evening's *other* Cinderella.

ESSENTIAL

Design your Cinderella fantasy cake in the form of a castle with a moat, bridges, fountains, and other fairy-tale touches, like figurines of Cinderella and the prince.

Romance Novel Wedding

There aren't many women who can say they've never read a romance novel. And there are many, many women who couldn't imagine living without that paperback gem waiting in their purse or bag, to escape to at lunchtime, on the subway, and right before bed.

While there are countless time periods explored in romance novels, there's none so popular—or addictive—as the Regency period. In fact, among historical romances, there's a subcategory with an extremely loyal fan base who can't get enough Regency romances. The Regency period refers to early 1800s England, during the reign of George IV, when royalty lived life to its fullest—also the time of Jane Austen and the Marquis de Sade.

Fact as Romantic as Fiction

The beauty of the romance-novel-themed wedding is that you can create a reality that's as romantic as fiction . . . become a princess for a day. From the fashion to the customs, you'll create a beautiful picture of history and romance for your special day.

Women's fashions were more relaxed during this time period than in previous times, though no less beautiful. Empire waist dresses (waists that fall from right below the breast line) with few restrictive undergarments were all the rage, worn with feminine slippers, gloves, and hats.

FACT

For a great visual of the costumes of the Regency period, rent *Sense and Sensibility, Emma,* or *Dangerous Liaisons* for inspiration. These three movies came out in the 1990s and should be readily available on VHS or DVD for rental or purchase.

Popular among men of the day were striped fabric coats—often cut in a more dramatic cutaway style that was short in front and quite long in back— with tight-fitted pants that look similar to tights. Men also wore fitted knee-length pants covering white stockings, and more feminine looking shoes with jeweled buckles. Shirts were often equally fanciful, with high colors and many ruffles down the front. Men in this era still wore powdered wigs.

Place and Time

The site for your Regency wedding may end up being similar to those suggested for a fairy-tale wedding—a castle; an old, beautiful hotel ballroom; a mansion or manor house with a ballroom; or an old museum with a historical feel. You may also wish to hold an outdoor, garden-style wedding at a beautifully landscaped country manor with rose gardens, room to stroll, and plenty of areas to sit and relax. Women guests and bridesmaids can shade themselves from the hot sun with parasols to match their beautiful 1800s-inspired dresses.

As for the reception, you may choose to have a more subtle tea and crumpets offering, particularly at a garden wedding. Or if it's an evening wedding, serve a multicourse meal that's quite formal and elegant . . . or choose to have a cocktail party reception only, with plenty of crudités, champagne, and cocktails.

Classical music would be ideal for your Regency romance wedding. Consider employing solo or duet musicians like a pianist, a harp or harpsichord player, or violists to perform throughout various times of the day or evening. A string quartet would be lovely for both cocktail hour music and dance music.

FACT

If you'd like to create vows that wow, what better inspiration than a romance novel? Choose a well-written wedding scene from your favorite romance novel, and use it directly or as inspiration to create some very proper and romantic vows of your own, in the language of the day.

For gifts for your bridesmaids and groomsmen, consider giving classic items that will stand the test of time, such as a crystal picture frame, a beautiful beer stein, or even a small Beleek or Waterford vase or glass (both inspired by England's Irish neighbor). For favors for all your guests, consider giving each of them a Regency romance of their own, or a Regency-inspired bookmark with a quote from your favorite author, or from Jane Austen. You could even make the bookmark yourself, with a color printer, a hole punch, ribbon, and a nice heavy stock paper. For your programs, create a mini romance novel of your own—elaborately relay the story of how you and your fiancé met, how he proposed, and any other romantic details leading up to your wedding. Make modern-day settings and situations sound infinitely romantic, with the type of detail and flourishes you'd find in a Regency romance.

You'll also want to consider transportation for your Regency wedding—and a horse and carriage is the only way to go. Try to locate a beautiful closed carriage for an authentic and romantic way to get there. Employ a fleet of horses to pull the carriage for additional drama. Or if you feel particularly adventurous, arrive astride your horses . . . the bride may want to ride sidesaddle with a long dress.

For a tongue-in-cheek touch to your Regency romance wedding, purchase a life-size stand-up figure of Fabio. Offer guests the chance to take a Polaroid with him for a favor. You'll be surprised at how real it'll look on film!

Valentine's Day Wedding

The perfect Valentine's Day Wedding is all heart—literally and figuratively. That's because with all the romantic touches you'll include, everything at your Valentine's Day-themed wedding will look like a giant valentine and all your guests will feel the love. The Valentine's Day wedding is a great way to seal your love—and to help your friends and family celebrate their own Valentine's Day in a very special way.

Everything's Coming Up Roses

Though it is unclear precisely when Valentine's Day traditions began—or even which, for that matter, St. Valentine inspired (there were three)—it is known that valentine cards were first mass-produced and sold in the United States in 1840. The tradition of sending valentine cards began long before, however, in Europe and in the United States—typically these valentines were handwritten notes expressing love and goodwill to the recipient.

For the "valentines" you'll be sending to your guests—a.k.a. your invitations—model the look of the traditional valentine, with cutouts, lace, pressed flowers, or perfumed stationery. There will be plenty of invitation designs with romantic themes to choose from in today's popular one-card style invitations . . . or if you have the time, talent, and inclination, make all your invitations by hand. Use quality red, pink, and white papers, attach materials like lace or ribbon, and use calligraphy for the type (hire someone or learn the craft yourself). If you'd like, make each invitation a little different. Obviously, this will be a time-consuming and demanding project, so enlist the help of family and bridesmaids if you plan to undertake it. It may be more practical to do so if you're inviting a hundred guests instead of four hundred, but no matter how many you send out, it will be a memorable keepsake for your guests to save.

If you are using traditional, printed invitations, consider including a "quote card" your guests can frame or hang on the refrigerator, with a memorable, romantic quote. Try this one from Shakespeare's *A Midsummer Night's Dream:* "Love looks not with the eyes, but with the mind; / And therefore is winged Cupid painted blind."

Obviously, your Valentine's Day wedding should be held on or very near to Valentine's Day. For both your ceremony and reception, the overarching goal will be to incorporate all the trappings of Valentine's Day. Your ceremony may end up being a traditional religious ceremony, or you may want to write a special Valentine's Day poem or your own vows for an extra romantic touch. For ceremony decorations, include lots of red and/or pink roses, and red pew/chair bows . . . you may even include a red runner to walk down.

You'll probably decide to not take your Valentine's Day theme as far as wearing a red wedding dress (though certainly no one's stopping you). But if you'd like to incorporate an element of red or pink into your outfit, there are other ways to do so as well. Perhaps it's red strappy sandals, a red velvet cape for cooler climes, or a red garter worn under your dress. The bridesmaids, however, can certainly wear the red or pink of Valentine's Day for a stunning contrast to your white or ivory dress. Groomsmen—and your groom—can match with red bowties and cummerbunds . . . or if you like the traditional black-and-white look for the men, be sure they're wearing red roses in their lapels. Bouquets for the women can follow suit, in beautiful roses of red, pink, and/or white.

ALERT!

Florists raise their prices dramatically during the Valentine's Day rush—a policy that's particularly true with roses, which are much in demand at that time. Decide you'll either accept the cost—come what may—or choose a slightly less popular flower that's in season to cut down on costs.

Straight from the Heart

Your reception will be the ideal place to display all things Valentine. Again, if you can include roses, there's nothing more appropriate, dramatic, and beautiful than rose centerpieces. However, another flower in red or pink would do. Or for contrast, use red table coverings—a velvet or sueded cotton would be beautiful—with white flower centerpieces.

Also dramatic would be to use candles as centerpieces or table accents. Rent out (or use your catering site's) silver candelabras as centerpieces for each table. Or design your own creative candle centerpiece with a number of candles in different sizes clustered and lit at the center of the table. Use large pillar candles in conjunction with small ones—in, of course, shades of red and pink.

For more table accents, sprinkle Hershey's Kisses or mini chocolates among the place settings. Or for a more upscale touch, place a mini box of truffles—wrapped in a red ribbon—on each guest's place setting to enjoy as a wedding favor.

Of course, in addition to chocolate, you'll also want to treat your guests to a decadent menu. Try to include sensuous foods popularly thought of as aphrodisiacs, such as oysters, escargot, mussels, asparagus, avocado, and tomatoes, spiced with herbs like thyme, rosemary, garlic, onion, and cloves. For dessert, serve anything with chocolate, such as chocolate mousse, chocolate cake, or chocolate cheesecake. Throughout the meal, serve plenty of champagne and wine, also guaranteed to put your guests in the mood for love.

Create a Valentine's Day–themed program for your ceremony by using two sheets of paper to create a folded mini booklet. Use a red cover lined with white paper inside (where the writing will appear), punch a hole near the fold's top and bottom, and tie with ribbon. Include a love poem if you have room.

Your wedding cake can also incorporate the elements of Valentine's Day. Suggestions include a heart-shaped, tiered cake; a traditional cake covered with heart-shaped candies—or those famous conversation hearts; a fondant cake strewn with rose petals; or simply a Valentine's Day–themed cake topper such as a Cupid or a crystal heart. Talk to your bakery about ideas as well.

Love Songs and Other Special Touches

For such a romantic-themed wedding, the music is easy—love songs. Certainly, your play list should include plenty of slow songs, but if you want the dance floor hopping, include plenty of fast ones too. See how many songs with *love* in the title you can include on the play list.

For more song-inspired fun, create this new tradition: Instead of guests clinking glasses to demand a kiss between the bride and groom, tell them their table must serenade the bride and groom with a love song. Tables can volunteer to participate with whatever song they choose—as long as it has the word *love* in the lyrics.

A final beautiful touch you may wish to incorporate into your wedding is a mini rose ceremony, wherein the bride and groom present each female guest with a long-stemmed red rose. The bride and groom may do this ceremoniously, by carrying a basket of roses and greeting each seated table in turn, either between courses or after dinner. This practice may also replace the need for a receiving line, as the bride and groom are ensured of talking to all their guests by visiting each table.

Intimate Wedding

The most intimate of weddings, of course, is called eloping. But for those couples who don't wish to have a grandiose, public affair—but do wish to be surrounded by close family and friends—an intimate wedding provides a romantic backdrop to truly celebrate the symbolism of the day.

Thus, an intimate wedding is defined by its size. The smaller the size, the more intimate the wedding. Typically, a headcount of about thirty or less will allow you to include your closest family members and friends without being overwhelmed. Of course, the intimate wedding isn't (or can't) be for everyone, particularly if you and your groom come from large nuclear families or couldn't bear to omit any friends from the celebration. But if you find you can pare down your list and explain to the non-invitees you're having a very small event, you'll be just fine.

The Guest List

Obviously, only you can create your guest list. But when it comes to a small, intimate wedding, the size limits dictate who you'll invite. Typically, this includes your immediate family, including parents, stepparents, brothers and sisters and their spouses or significant others, and grandparents. You can stop there, and keep it a family-only event . . . but you'll each undoubtedly have a close friend or two, a godparent, or another close friend or family member you couldn't bear to leave out. Or if you have limited family or aren't close to them, have a friends-only event surrounded by people you truly love and care about.

Small but Meaningful

Often brides and grooms—and guests—will say they enjoyed the rehearsal dinner more than the elaborate, large weddings. That's because the rehearsal dinner offers an intimate venue at which guests can really spend time with the bride and groom and their immediate families, rather than observe proceedings from afar.

The same goes for an intimate wedding. With only your closest family and friends—not your parents' friends, not your great-great-aunt from Saskatchewan whom you've never met—your event will inevitably have more intimate exchanges and quality time spent together.

Where, When, and How

The beauty of an intimate wedding is that you won't need to find a large banquet hall, you don't necessarily need a year to plan it, and you can forgo many of the traditional wedding trappings if you so desire. Obviously, you won't have a large wedding party—one witness apiece will suffice. You won't need to spend thousands of dollars on centerpieces, bouquets, wedding favors, a ten-piece orchestra, or 150 meals. What you may want to do is funnel those extra dollars into throwing a party at the best restaurant in town. Rent a private room—or if your wedding celebration is very small, get a table for ten or fifteen—and allow guests to order off the menu. Or provide a multicourse meal that's completely decadent, with endless wine service, the best champagne, and many desserts. You can still have a wedding cake, wedding favors, music, and all the other great wedding trappings, but because it's scaled down, you can either get the very best of everything—or save a bundle.

FACT

Even if you elope, you can still have an intimate party afterward to celebrate with family and friends. If you have pictures or a video of your ceremony, bring them to the party so everyone can feel as if they were a part of it.

There are many special touches you can include that work better with a small group than with a large one. You can show old home movies of your family—there are providers who can take your old film and create edited VHS tapes with your guidance. Or you may want to create a poem or special words for each guest present, to be read by you and the groom as a toast. Conversely, you may also want to ask guests to come with their favorite story about the bride and/or groom, to share with the rest of the party—it can be funny or sentimental, whichever they prefer. You may also wish to choose more significant wedding favors for each of your guests. It may be a copy of the video you create, or it could be a ticket to some upcoming event—so you can all get together again as a family. These could range from theater tickets to a suite at a basketball, football, or hockey game. Base it on your personal preferences.

Chapter 9

Ethnic Inspirations

Ethnic weddings provide a wonderful way to honor your ancestry. There are a host of traditions and customs that go back hundreds—even thousands—of years that are infused with symbolism and meaning. You may choose to plan a full-blown ethnic wedding or just add a few meaningful elements to celebrate your heritage.

African Weddings

With more than a thousand ethnic groups in Africa, there are as many ways to bring African heritage to your wedding celebration. However, there are some popular, more universal traditions that many African-American brides and grooms often choose to include in their weddings. Many of these traditions can be incorporated into traditional Christian weddings as well.

If you would like to have an authentic wedding that imitates the style of a very specific ethnic group or African region, talk to members or descendants of that group, or immigrants who hail from that particular area. Or research the culture more fully online.

The Ceremony

Whether you're having a traditional wedding or an African-centered ceremony, there are customs and traditions you can include to honor your ancestry. The most common African influence in today's African-American weddings is dress. There are many ways to incorporate African influence into the dress of the entire wedding party, and even guests. These include wardrobes ranging from full African garb to more subtle African-inspired accessories or accoutrements. The following are some alternatives:

- **Kente cloth.** Each piece has its own distinct weave or pattern, with its own meaning. Kente cloth can be used to fashion an entire outfit for the bride and groom. Or use it as trim for a "traditional" European-style white dress, or wear it as an accent piece—a bow tie, lapel accent, or cummerbund on the groom and groomsmen.
- **Brocade cloth.** Often adorned with adinkra symbols, brocade cloth is a heavy, beautiful quality cotton cloth that originates from the African countries of Senegal, Ivory Coast, and Guinea. Adinkra symbols have very specific meanings based on African proverbs, historical events, animal behaviors, plant lives, and more. Even if you don't include an adinkra symbol within your wedding day attire, you might consider

choosing a symbol to adorn other wedding day pieces, such as your program, tablecloths, centerpieces, or wedding favors.

- **Color.** Feel free to choose colors representative of traditional African garb, such as rich greens, reds, yellows, golds, and blues. Or incorporate a bit of color or fabric—such as beautiful gold embroidery or gold braid—into a white or ivory wedding dress for an African-inspired look.
- **Headpiece.** The "gele" is the traditional head wrap worn in many African cultures. Choose a fabric that matches your dress—whether a European-inspired white dress or an African-inspired kente-cloth or brocade dress—and you'll have a gorgeous outfit from head to toe. You can also attach a "traditional" veil to the headpiece to incorporate both African and North American cultures, if you so desire.
- **White.** The color white is also associated with traditional African ceremonies and occasions. This would be a highly appropriate color—and a stunning one as well—for the groom to wear, either in a tuxedo or within a more traditional African tunic/pants.
- **Cowrie shells.** Use them to adorn your wedding dress, your headpiece, the groom's jacket or lapels, or wear as jewelry around the neck or as a bracelet. Cowrie shells represent fertility.

Traditions

There are a number of traditions incorporated into Afrocentric weddings that hail from African culture, as well as from early African-American culture in the United States. The first of these is "jumping the broom." This is a symbolic step into a new beginning, or sweeping away the old and welcoming the new. Some say the tradition has its roots in Africa, but other sources indicate that jumping the broom began during slavery times in the United States, during which time it was illegal for slaves to marry. Jumping the broom was created as a ritual to signify the union of marriage.

FACT

For meaningful and symbolic favors, give your guests mini brooms decorated with kente cloth, or attached to a cowrie shell.

If you would like to incorporate this tradition into your wedding, you can do so either by creating a ceremony around this tradition or as an additional ritual within a traditional Christian ceremony. The broom should be beautiful and decorated with ribbon, bows, or flowers—you can decorate it yourself or purchase a pre-decorated broom. During the ceremony, the broom is placed on the floor, the groom holds the bride's hand, and they jump over it together. Discuss the timing of this event within your ceremony with your officiant.

FACT

To honor ancestors and bless elders, consider the ritual pouring of a libation. This tradition can be incorporated by your officiant immediately prior to the start of the ceremony to symbolically gather the elders and ancestors in celebration of the impending nuptials.

Another African-inspired tradition is the "tasting of the four temperaments." To represent the many stages of marriage—including the sour, the bitter, the hot, and the sweet—four food items are chosen for the bride and groom to taste during the ceremony. Different spices might be chosen for each step, or a lemon, vinegar, hot sauce, and sugar. The flavors symbolize that the couple needs to get through these stages together, eventually getting to the sweetness that their marriage will inevitably bring.

Jewish Weddings

Like an African-inspired celebration, there's no one way to incorporate Jewish traditions into your wedding. That's because within the Jewish religion, there are different rituals and traditions based on whether one is of the Orthodox, Conservative, or Reform persuasion.

Traditions

The first tradition to consider is the "ketubah," or marriage contract. Traditional ceremonies begin with the bride and groom signing this contract, which is symbolic of the covenant Moses presented to the Jewish people as they accepted God at Mount Sinai. Once used as a legal document to protect Jewish women economically in the event of divorce or widowhood, today it is a more symbolic—and often more egalitarian—gesture. Ketubot are usually ornate and beautiful and can be artistically designed around Jewish symbols or shared interests.

If you have a friend or family member who is an artist or designer, honor him or her by asking him or her to design your ketubah. Or hire an artist to incorporate special interests into the design, such as gardening, sailing, or other interests. Or if you have artistic ability, you can design your ketubah yourself.

Following the signing of the ketubah, you may choose to include the "bedeken" (or b'deken). The bedeken is the ritual unveiling of the bride by the groom immediately prior to the wedding ceremony. It is symbolic of the bible story in which Leah replaced Jacob's chosen bride, Rachel, without his knowledge. In the bedeken, the groom raises the veil from the bride's face, confirming it is really she who has come to marry him.

Following these events, the ceremony takes place. The bride is escorted down the aisle by both her parents, as is the groom. They marry underneath the "chuppah," a small shelter consisting of fabric covering four posts, decorated with flowers, ribbon, tulle, or whatever you desire. The chuppah ceremony consists of the seven blessings, recited in Hebrew or English.

After exchanging vows, it is customary for the groom (or the bride and groom together) to stomp on a wine glass—the shattering glass serves as a reminder of the fragility of human happiness. This marks the end of the traditional ceremony; the bride and groom may then retire alone together for the "yichud."

The yichud is a short time of seclusion immediately following the wedding. This tradition originated as a way for the bride and groom to consummate the marriage—now it is more commonly used as a little down time before the reception and further excitement to come.

Music

Though music at Jewish weddings most often includes contemporary dance music by a band or DJ, there are a number of traditional dances you may want to incorporate. The first of these is the very popular "hora," which hails from Israel. The hora is a joyous, lively dance in which the bride and groom are lifted on chairs, as they hold on to either end of a handkerchief. Horas can go on to include the bride and groom lifted in chairs separately and the lifting of the bride's and groom's parents in chairs as well.

FACT

Because it is tradition for Jewish male guests—and non-Jewish guests as well—to wear yarmulkes, consider giving these as wedding favors. Have your names and wedding date inscribed on the inside as a keepsake for family and friends.

Another traditional but lesser known dance is the "krenzl"—or "crowning" dance. This dance honors the mother of the bride when her last daughter is married. The mother is seated at the middle of the room and crowned with a wreath of flowers as her daughters dance around her.

Menu and Reception

Jewish weddings are well regarded for their sumptuous meals. It is a courtesy to your guests to choose a kosher caterer, as many of them may keep kosher—even if you and the groom do not.

FACT

The word *kosher* means "fit" or "proper" in Hebrew—as in "fit for consumption."

To incorporate more Jewish tradition into your wedding, you may also want to consider printing your wedding invitation—and program—in both English and Hebrew. Be sure to find a printer with the capability to print both languages.

Chinese Weddings

Many of the traditions from the many regions of China are simplified here, with the intention that they will be incorporated with some Western traditions as well. Without exception, the color red is central to the Chinese wedding, symbolizing joy, love, and prosperity. The color red is seen in a variety of ways in a Chinese wedding—in the bride's dress, wedding invitations, wedding banquet décor, gift boxes, and gift envelopes.

Traditions

On the wedding day—which itself may have been chosen according to favorable astrological signs—there are a number of traditions (with variations) you can incorporate into your own celebration. In traditional Chinese weddings, the groom picks up the bride at her home to travel to the wedding ceremony. But first he must get past the bridesmaids as a test of his love and affection. There are a number of ways he may do this, including by giving gifts of cash—wrapped in red tissue or a red envelope—or by performing specific tasks for the bridesmaids—the sillier, the better. These might include singing songs, doing push-ups, or whatever creative acts the bridesmaids think up. This demonstrates that the groom will do anything for his wife.

Because there is no traditional wedding vow script in the Chinese culture, ceremony and vows can be uniquely designed to fit your beliefs, religious or otherwise. You may choose to include music, poems, hymns, or self-written vows.

Another Chinese wedding tradition is the tea ceremony, in which the bride's and groom's parents and elders are honored. Depending upon how you decide to structure your wedding day, your tea ceremony may take place prior to or immediately following the ceremony. During the tea ceremony, the bride and groom may kneel before both sets of parents as a symbolic "asking of permission." In exchange, gifts are bestowed upon the bride and groom, which may include gold bracelets, necklaces, or red envelopes stuffed with money.

An old Chinese tradition dictates that just before she arrives at the altar, the bride should drop a fan to signify that she now belongs to her husband and his family, as well as her own.

During the ceremony, two altars are set up—one to honor the bride and her family, the other to honor the groom and his family. Eventually, these altars will be moved together as a symbolic joining of the two families. Included upon each altar should be a red cloth, a bouquet of flowers symbolic of the family's ancestors, fruit, a glass of wine, or a rice bowl with chopsticks. The rice bowl and chopsticks should only be used to represent a close relative who has died within the last several years.

The Wedding Banquet

Traditional Chinese wedding receptions are large, elaborate, and a chance to return relative's kindnesses for the weddings previously attended. This banquet may consist of a sit-down meal of up to twelve courses, mainly Chinese delicacies such as lobster, shark fin soup, abalone, and roast pig. The reception is often marked by games made up by the bridesmaids and groomsmen to trick the bride and groom. Like the clinking of the glasses during a traditional Western wedding, these games are intended to elicit a display of affection between the bride and groom and may include games such as "cherry bobbing," in which the couple tries to eat a suspended maraschino cherry before the other one catches it first. Another popular game is the hand search, in which the groom is blindfolded and must guess the identity of his wife's hand by touching a number of women's hands—after they've been dipped in ice-cold water.

It is customary for a traditional Chinese bride to change clothes up to four times on her wedding day. Consider wearing two wedding dresses, one for your ceremony and one during the reception. The ceremonial dress could include a traditional red, Chinese design, while the reception dress could be a more comfortable, Western-influenced white dress.

Incorporating Asian accents into your wedding décor—no matter how Western your venue—will add more Chinese influence to your wedding. Cover tables with red tablecloths, or use white or gold cloths with stunning red-flowered centerpieces. Decorate with red and/or gold Chinese paper lanterns, or with beautiful wicker screens to separate areas of a large, open room. Also, you may choose to use Chinese symbols on napkins, matchboxes, or other wedding favors.

Instead of a Western "receiving line," incorporate the more Chinese "retreating line" into your wedding reception. When the meal is done and the music is over, the bridal couple, their parents, and other close relatives will stand in line at the door to thank guests and wish them farewell. Not until all the guests have left does the bridal party go home.

Hindu Weddings

Hindu weddings are full of symbolic and spiritual customs, which traditionally last all day. For Hindu weddings that take place in today's Western Hemisphere, however, many of these customs have been modified to fit a much shorter time period of one to two hours. The beauty, symbolism, and tradition are not lost, however—even the modified Hindu wedding is full of ceremony and ritual that dates back thousands of years. This tradition is based upon the Veda (the sacred writings) and is considered a "samskara" (sacred trust), which is officiated by a priest and may or may not take place in a temple.

If you are planning an interfaith wedding—Hindu and Christian, for instance—why not have two wedding ceremonies? You can then honor both traditions fully. If possible, have the ceremonies on consecutive days, as dress and customs are so unique.

Wedding Day Attire

For a traditional Hindu wedding, the bride dresses in a traditional red silk sari and headpiece. This headpiece is often adorned with a small head ornament or a jeweled ornament that comes over the forehead. The bride is also heavily bedecked with gold jewelry around her neck, wrists, and even her ankles. This gold jewelry is often borrowed from friends and family. Family may also apply traditional Hindu makeup to the bride's face on the morning of the wedding.

The groom typically wears white, in traditional Indian style. This style may include "kurtas," or long tunics over loose pants; "punjabi," another style of Indian tunic; or "dhoti," which consists of one long piece of material wrapped around the groom to resemble pants. He may also wear a hat called a "mukut." His groomsmen, and the bridesmaids, follow the pattern of dress set by the groom and bride.

Hindu Ceremony

There are many rituals and customs that make up the Hindu ceremony. It begins when the bride is carried into the ceremony by her closest male relatives on a "palanquin," or a platform, atop which she sits. She is brought to her groom at the "mandap"—a canopy beneath which much of the ceremony takes place. They may exchange garlands of flowers prior to the beginning of the ceremony. Or the groom may tie a pendant around the bride's neck as a sign of happiness and fidelity (this is also known to take place at the conclusion of the ceremony).

One common ritual is the "kanyadan," or a ceremony in which the bride's parents wash the feet of the bride and groom with milk and water. The bride and groom then put their hands together, which are then covered by the bride's father's hand. The bride's mother then pours water over the father's hand, which trickles down over the couple's hands.

Another ritual is the "hastamilap," in which the bride's and groom's hands are wrapped together in string to signify the unbreakable bond of marriage. The couple's clothing may also be tied together for a portion of the ceremony.

Because there are so many regions and sects of Hinduism, there are also many variations on the basic Hindu wedding ceremony. These may not precisely represent your specific heritage, so talk to family members about the rituals and traditions of your particular region.

The walk around the "agni," or holy fire, is another ritual common to Hindu weddings. As the officiant chants various mantras and scripture readings, the bride and groom walk around this sacred fire a total of seven times, during which they exchange vows of duty, love, fidelity, and respect.

The groom may complete the wedding ceremony by applying red powder called "shindur" onto the bride's hair or forehead to signify the marriage has taken place. The bride, too, may apply a red paste to the groom's hair or forehead. They may exit the mandap to the welcoming of flower petals being thrown at them by family and friends.

Reception

The traditional Hindu wedding reception is not so different from a traditional European or North American reception—lots of great food and lively dancing. For your menu, serve traditional Indian dishes that all your guests can enjoy. These may include vegetarian dishes such as "kali dal," a classic festival bean dish; and nonvegetarian dishes, such as chicken curry, chicken tikka, or tandoori chicken; basmati or saffron rice; many flavors of chutney; and other Indian specialties. If you are mixing in North American traditions, include a wedding cake with a decorative Indian look. For flowers, choose an Indian florist who can give your wedding a more authentic Indian feel; if there is not one in your area, choose blossoms that are customary in India for bouquets, centerpieces, and to decorate the mandap, as well as for the ceremony garlands. Give favors reminiscent of India, such as incense with beautiful burners, henna tattoo kits, Indian-looking candles or picture frames, sweets from India wrapped in a pretty mesh or net and tied with a ribbon, or a CD of Indian music. If your wedding will include many guests of non-Indian descent, these favors will become souvenirs that are particularly appreciated.

Italian Weddings

Italian weddings have been immortalized in pop culture, in both film and on stage. Who can forget the pomp and circumstance of the wedding in *The Godfather,* or the fun in the Broadway show *Tony n' Tina's Wedding?*

Ceremony

The Italian wedding almost always follows a Roman Catholic ceremony, as the majority of Italians are also Catholic. This ceremony consists of the bride in a traditional white dress and white veil, who is walked down the aisle by her father and given away to her groom who waits at the altar. The wedding is usually accompanied by a standard Catholic mass, followed by the exchange of vows between the bride and groom. There are biblical readings, which can be chosen from a preapproved collection, as well as traditional wedding songs such as the "Ave Maria," "Jesu, Joy of Man's Desiring," and the "Prayer of St. Francis." The bride and groom are married by a priest. Traditions including the "blessing of the Virgin Mary" (in which the bride and groom place flowers at the Virgin's feet) as well as the lighting of the unity candle are symbolic and customary in the Catholic ceremony.

FACT

It is customary for Italian couples to tie a bow or ribbon across the door of the church, to symbolize the bond of marriage, or the tying together of two lives.

Traditions

There are many wedding traditions in the Italian culture, which once again vary by region.

To ward off evil spirits jealous of the groom's good fortune, the groom carries a piece of iron in his pocket on his wedding day. The bride's veil is believed to function similarly, concealing her from evil spirits (as well as symbolizing her purity and virginity, of course).

ALERT!

According to Italian folklore, it is bad luck for the bride to wear any gold until the groom places the wedding ring upon her finger. You may want to reconsider wearing that favorite gold necklace on your wedding day.

One popular tradition that still remains today is the carrying of the "buste," or traditional white satin bag by the bride. The buste carries the envelopes of money or checks given to the couple as wedding gifts. The bride's mother or grandmother—or the bride's father—often take over buste duty as the wedding reception continues on, to guard it and fill it with more gifts. Whoever is guarding the buste may also accept "donations" from male guests who wish to dance with the bride.

The Feast

Because food preparation is so tied to family life and nurturing in the Italian culture, it is only fitting that an Italian wedding features up to seven courses, served either sit-down style—more likely—or buffet style. Or the traditional sit-down meal may be followed by a late-night buffet once guests' stomachs have settled a bit. The meal is an extremely important part of the Italian wedding and should be planned with care. These courses may include the following:

- **Antipasto**—This is a traditional Italian first dish that includes salami, prosciutto, ham, olives, cheeses, and fruits such as cantaloupe, mixed in an Italian dressing.
- **Pasta course**—This may consist of penne, ziti, manicotti, or tortellini in a tomato-based or cream-based sauce.
- **Meat**—You'll want to serve veal, chicken, or steak for this course.
- **Seafood**—A large platter of seafood is served at each table, including lobster, king crab legs, clams, and more. Raw bars are a popular option for a buffet-style reception.
- **Hot dishes**—This course may include eggplant, sausage and peppers, or fettuccine Alfredo.
- **Cold salads**—These may include multiple-bean salads, leafy green salads, or Mediterranean-style salads combining ingredients like noodles, olives, veggies, and/or peppers and onions.
- **Dessert**—Typical desserts are tiramisu, gelato, and tartuffo (a coated ball of ice cream, cut and served in halves).
- **Wedding cake**—Italian wedding cakes are similar looking to Americanized wedding cakes—typically multi-layered concoctions with

elaborate white or ivory icing—buttercream or fondant. A more "Italian" touch may be the inclusion of fruit filling such as strawberry.

Of course, wine is a staple at Italian weddings, as is plenty of coffee, espresso, and cappuccino—presumably to help digestion after the gastro-ganza just referred to. Following dinner is plenty of dancing, including the traditional tarantella, for those guests who can still move.

FACT

Tradition dictates that the best man greet guests entering the reception with a tray of liquor so that they have a drink to toast the bride and groom. Because this may become overwhelming for one person, why not ask all the groomsmen—or bridesmaids—to participate?

No Italian wedding would be complete without "confetti," or candy-covered almonds (Jordan almonds) tied in tulle bags. Loose candy almonds can be tossed at the bride and groom as they exit the church (though check with your officiant, as there are often limitations on what is tossed), or used as wedding favors placed at each guest's place setting or in a decorated basket near the entrance of the reception. The almonds represent the sweet and bitter elements of married life.

Irish Weddings

You can incorporate Irish tradition into your wedding by adopting wedding customs, as they've always existed, straight from Ireland; or you can do it in other ways. From food to music, flowers to favors, there are myriad ways to include Irish heritage in today's Irish-American weddings.

The Ceremony

If yours is an Irish-Catholic wedding, your freedom to choose specifically Irish décor, readings, and songs may be limited. However, there are a few places in which you'll be able to get away with some Irish touches. The first is your program. Consider giving it an Irish theme, by including an Irish symbol—such as a Claddagh or Celtic cross—or by using a Celtic font. You may also want to use color, for example, use a pale green cover with a white page inside and tie it with a white or green ribbon.

FACT

The color green has only been associated with Ireland for a few hundred years. Prior to that, Ireland's colors were blue and gold, and many Irish brides, in fact, wore blue on their wedding days.

You may want to incorporate pieces of some traditional Irish masses into your religious ceremony. Three of these include the St. Patrick's Mass, the Mass of St. Francis of Assisi, and the Celtic Mass. Each of these masses includes music with traditional Irish melodies and sounds. You may also wish to incorporate live bagpipers into your ceremony, dressed in traditional Irish kilts. This can be a haunting and beautiful tribute to your Irish heritage. Check with your officiant about the best timing for bagpipers within your ceremony.

The Music

There are many ways to give your wedding reception an Irish flair. The most predominant of these is through music. Anyone who's ever celebrated St. Patrick's Day knows there's no dearth of traditional Irish music; there are, however, some special songs specifically suited to weddings. The most popular of these is the "Irish Wedding Song." Consider asking a friend or family member with a great voice to sing it, or ask your band if they know it. If you're hiring a DJ, bring a recording of the song if he doesn't have one; if you live in an area with a large Irish population, chances are he does. Also consult with your band or DJ about music for the remainder of the wedding. If you can, hire an Irish band. If not, intermix the recordings of modern-day Irish bands like the Chieftains, the Cranberries, and the Corrs with more traditional Irish music. There are also CDs available specifically for Irish wedding celebrations.

You can also include bagpipers during your wedding reception. Bagpipe music could be a beautiful prelude to dinner, ushering guests in from the cocktail hour, or signaling the end of the meal and the beginning of dancing.

ALERT!

While bagpipers make a wonderful addition to an Irish-themed wedding, remember their sound can overpower attempts at communication. If your wedding is taking place in a small, confined space, a shorter performance is better. If you're having an open-air wedding, it's not as much of an issue.

Food and Drink

A wedding is an occasion to celebrate. And nobody can celebrate like the Irish. There are many traditional menu options to help get this celebration rolling, as well as plenty of options for traditional Irish drinks to make it last all night long.

Typical Irish fare may include potato dishes—potato-based soups and side dishes; fine Irish cheeses, as a separate course; various styles of Irish soda bread; and entrees such as poached salmon, ham, leg of lamb, or pork. You may also want to consider the fare that we see in U.S. versions of Irish pubs, such as corned beef and cabbage, shepherd's pie, or carved roast beef and turkey. These are heartier, down-home choices and may be a less expensive way to stay in theme.

As for drink, there are plenty of options. Traditionally, sherry is the first drink served for the Irish toast to the bride and groom. Beyond that, consider choices like cider, Irish whiskey, beer (Irish brands like Guinness, of course), and traditional Irish meads, such as Bunratty Meade. Mead is a honey wine based on the oldest known drink recipe in Ireland, and it is thought to promote virility. It is the same drink that Irish newlyweds were historically expected to drink during "mi na meala," or the month of honey, following their wedding. The bride and groom were given plenty of this liquor to enjoy during the month—or "first full moon"— following their wedding, and it was believed to ensure a good beginning for the new marriage—and the promise of many children. This is where the term *honeymoon* comes from.

Other drinks you may wish to include at your reception are Irish Coffee and Irish-based liqueurs such as Bailey's Irish Cream.

The Look

There are many ways to visually incorporate the beauty of Ireland into your wedding as well. For instance, include on the invitation an Irish design such as a Claddagh symbol, a Celtic script, or an Irish family crest. Or consider having an invitation custom designed. For consistency, model your programs using the same design elements.

> At your reception, consider using tablecloths of Irish lace, or giving small hankies of Irish lace as favors. It may be difficult to find these in quantity, but if you can, it could provide a beautiful Irish touch.

You can also choose your flowers based on those that grow naturally in Ireland. For bouquets, centerpieces, and corsages, try stems including Bells of Ireland, foxglove, roses, and rhododendrons. You may also try to find live shamrocks to include in bouquets or boutonnieres—again, these may be difficult to locate, but a great touch if you do.

For favors with Irish symbolism, give guests miniature horseshoes (for good luck) or tiny bells (to ward off spirits—these can also be rung when the bride and groom exit the church). Attach a tag with a traditional Irish blessing or prayer, plus your names and date to commemorate the occasion.

Greek Orthodox Weddings

The Greek Orthodox wedding and reception are full of tradition and ceremony from beginning to end (which often occurs in the wee hours of the following morning). The elements of the very symbolic ceremony go back centuries, and the reception that follows is full of much revelry, drama, and fun.

The Engagement

A traditional Greek Orthodox wedding day includes not only the ceremony and reception but also the engagement. Historically, in Greek families, the groom-to-be would go to the bride's home on the morning of the wedding to ask the bride's father for her hand in marriage. Once permission was given, the groom's best man (or "kumbada") would then accompany the couple to the church and, with the priest, assist with moving along the different elements of the formal marriage ceremony.

FACT

The best man's role is extremely important and symbolic in the Greek Orthodox wedding, going well beyond the mere "best man speech" and help in planning the bachelor party.

Though today's Greek-American engagements last much longer than a few hours, with the "typical" engagement lasting six months to a year, this engagement "ceremony" is still part of the traditional wedding day for Greek Orthodox families.

The Ceremony

There are seven basic parts to a Greek Orthodox wedding ceremony. Many of these actions are conducted three times, to symbolize the Holy Trinity—the Father, the Son, and the Holy Spirit. These steps are as follows:

- **The blessing of the rings:** Both the bride's and groom's wedding rings are blessed by the officiant. They are then exchanged by the bride and groom three times, with the assistance of the best man. This exchange, during which at one point the groom wears the bride's ring and the bride wears the groom's, signifies the reliance the couple will have upon one another throughout their lives, and that the strength of one will sometimes make up for the weakness of the other.
- **The lighting of the candles:** The officiant will then give the bride and groom candles, which they will hold throughout the service. The lit candles symbolize the couple's willingness to receive Christ's blessings. Historically, the candles represent the lamps of the five biblical maidens, who lit the way for Christ when he came in the darkness of night.
- **The joining of hands:** As the priest reads a prayer, the bride and groom join right hands to symbolize their unity. They continue to hold each other's hand throughout the ceremony.

- **The crowning:** The priest then crowns the bride and groom with the "stefana" (a crown of gold and/or flowers). These crowns, attached with a ribbon, are exchanged three times by the bride and the groom, with the best man's help. The crowning ceremony symbolizes the glory and honor bestowed upon the couple during the sacrament of marriage, as they are crowned the king and queen of their new kingdom—or home—that they will create. From this point on in the ceremony, neither the bride nor the groom speaks.
- **The common cup:** This portion of the ceremony honors the biblical account of Jesus at the wedding of Cana at Galilee, where he performed his first miracle, turning water into wine. In the ceremony, the bride and groom partake of the wine, drinking from the cup with their hands crossed.
- **The ceremonial walk:** With the best man, the couple then walks around the table on the altar three times, while the priest sings songs and recites prayers. The table holds a bible and a cross. The walk represents the fact that the church is the center of life and a successful marriage.
- **The blessing:** After the ceremonial walk, the priest then blesses the newly married couple and removes the crowns. Only then do the bride and groom release hands. They are then officially married.

The Reception

The reception that follows at the Greek Orthodox wedding is just as full and involved as the ceremony. Dancing is the focus of the reception, and it can go on all night long as guests join in the traditional Greek line dances such as the Kalamatiano, Hasapiko, and Tsiftertelli. Another Greek tradition involves smashing dishes on the floor, which signifies good luck. An honored guest may be chosen to do the honors, or more than one guest may participate.

FACT

To ensure that her life is sweet, the bride may carry a bit of sugar in her glove.

A variety of Greek dishes are traditionally served at the reception, and dinner may be followed by breakfast the following morning, if the wedding is expected to last that long. Greek sweets are a big part of the wedding festivities, with treats like baklava, diples, and Greek cookies served along with the wedding cake. As with Italian weddings, it's traditional to give away candied almonds wrapped in netting, symbolizing fertility. There should be an odd number of almonds in each package.

Polish Weddings

The Polish wedding is full of tradition, history, and cultural customs that date back hundreds of years. Most of the following traditions come directly from Poland, and the focus is on food, fun, and some traditional and symbolic rituals.

History

The wedding has historically been one of the most important family celebrations in Poland, with much time devoted to the planning and celebration of this exciting occasion. Polish weddings in the mid-twentieth century were characterized by a great deal of planning and labor in the days leading up to the big event, with many of the women in the family joining forces to cook, bake, and clean. Much of these efforts surrounded the meal—still and always a vital part of Polish culture.

Of course, for cocktails at your wedding, only the best Polish vodka will do. Serve it with a choice of mixers alongside beer and wine.

During this time period in both the United States and Poland, Polish weddings followed a timetable consisting of a morning ceremony (usually Catholic) followed by a lunch prepared by the family for all the wedding guests. This lunch consisted of homemade chicken noodle soup, followed by a hot meal of chicken or another meat, potatoes, vegetables, and homemade cookies.

A break would follow lunch, then the reception would begin in the early evening. The reception would include another hot meal—this time it might be roast turkey, pork, duck, or veal, with a dessert of fresh pies and pastries. To incorporate Polish heritage into today's Polish wedding menu, you can include the above classics alongside more traditional Polish fare, such as barszcz (beet soup), pierogis (dough pockets filled with cheese, sauerkraut, or potatoes), golumpki (cabbage rolls filled with ground meat), and nut rolls (pastry filled with ground nuts). Find a polish caterer or another caterer who'd be willing to give some new recipes a try. Or if you and your family are very ambitious, prepare some of these Polish dishes yourselves in advance. Have a pierogi party—you can make hundreds of these tasty treats in a day with enough manpower. Freeze them, then thaw and serve on your wedding day, along with other menu items.

Rituals and Customs

Food continues to play an important role in some of the traditional customs of the Polish wedding. The sharing of bread and salt is an important tradition and historically took place as the bride and groom entered the reception. The parents of the couple would then greet them with bread, lightly sprinkled with salt. The bread symbolizes that the couple should never go hungry, and the salt represents overcoming the potentially difficult times to come. To incorporate this meaning into today's reception, why not include all your wedding guests in the bread ceremony? You may wish to include it at the commencement of dinner. At this time, your parents might say the traditional blessing as well as welcome everyone to the reception.

FACT

Traditionally, the wedding cake is not served at the Polish wedding reception but rather is cut, boxed, and given to guests to enjoy at home.

Another Polish tradition, which grew out of the historic engagement custom in Poland but is now sometimes incorporated into the wedding festivities, is the "zerkowiny." During this ritual the bride's and groom's hands are joined with an embroidered cloth and tied together above a loaf of bread. This represents the two becoming one couple, and the wish that they should always have bread beneath their hands.

Fun and Games

Of course, no Polish wedding would be complete without plenty of polkas. You may consider hiring a polka band for your reception for an all-Polish wedding . . . or mix it up for guests Polish and non-Polish alike by choosing a band that can play both polkas and American dance music. If you plan on holding the "oczepiny ceremony" (the unveiling and capping), be sure to have the proper music on hand. In this ceremony (traditionally performed at midnight), guests form a circle around the bride, and the bride's veil is removed and replaced by the "czypek," or small lace cap. The maid of honor may then wear the veil and dance with the best man and then pass it on to the next bridesmaid to dance with the next groomsmen, and so on down the line. This signifies good luck for single bridesmaids—that they, too, will find happiness in marriage. For the bride, the ritual represents shedding her maiden status for womanhood.

FACT

The oczepiny ceremony can also be held as the bride and groom enter the reception. In this instance, the veil is removed and replaced by a necklace of tiny baby dolls, while the groom is crowned with a funny hat. This is meant to signify fertility and fun in the marriage to come.

The money dance is also a Polish tradition. Historically, the wedding guests had to pay for the privilege of dancing with the bride by pinning money to her dress. (The money would often go toward wedding or honeymoon expenses.) Today this dance has more practical applications as an apron dance, whereby the maid of honor wears an apron that guests toss money into so that they can dance with the bride. At the end, the groom throws in his own wallet to show he'll pay most for the privilege of dancing with—and keeping—his new bride. (E)

Chapter 10
A Very Good Sport

No matter what your life's passion—stamp collecting, scuba diving, or skateboarding—there's a way to include it in a meaningful way in your wedding day. This chapter details a number of creative weddings based on some favored pastimes. Use it as a starting point for the infinite possibilities of making your passion part of your special day.

It's All Uphill from Here

Many individuals have found their soul mates on the ski slopes. And why not? The exhilaration of the sport combined with the relaxed atmosphere of a ski resort is the perfect backdrop for falling in love.

If your passion is skiing, or you and your fiancé met on the slopes, why not consider going back to your roots as a couple, and plan a wedding on the slopes.

In Season or Off-Season

There are a number of ways to incorporate your sport into your wedding. If you love skiing but are set on celebrating a late-spring, summer, or early-fall wedding, consider holding your wedding at your favorite resort or ski club—off-season. The setting will still be gorgeous, and you can still probably arrange to be married hillside. Check with the resort to see if they'll open the lifts and/or gondolas to trek guests up the hill or mountain. If that's not possible, hold your ceremony at the base of the mountain and let the landscape provide the best décor you could ever want.

ALERT!

If you plan to hold a mountaintop ceremony, you'll have to do your homework. Some resorts will be very accommodating, while others will probably want nothing to do with your grand plan. So if at first you don't succeed, keep trying until you find a place that will embrace your plans as enthusiastically as you do.

If, however, you are set on exchanging your vows on skis, many resorts will accommodate your wishes. Again, check with them about details, but some resorts have been known to close off a certain run (at a certain price) to accommodate the bride and groom, wedding party, and wedding guests. Those who can't ski can be taken up and down the mountain on snowmobiles (or lifts), and the guests who ski can take full advantage. Be sure to find a photographer who can ski, or employ a photographer who can snap photos on top of the mountain—and from a snowmobile as you newly marrieds descend the mountain once the ceremony ends.

The Ultimate Ski Bunny

If you do decide to marry slope-side, your attire will require some modifications to accommodate the weather, of course. If your ceremony will precede a ski run down the mountain, the bride may consider more comfortable ski wear rather than a dress, for instance, white ski pants and a white ski jacket—with a special wedding corsage. For the groom, try a dinner jacket look—white ski pants with a black jacket . . . or wear all black for a dramatic contrast to the bride.

FACT

Turn your ski wedding into a ski weekend by having a rehearsal dinner at the ski resort where your wedding will take place. Invite your guests to ski all day, to be followed by a casual, après-ski rehearsal dinner by the fire in the chalet or lodge.

The really daring bride may consider wearing a traditional white dress or skirt (be sure it's full enough to permit movement and short enough that it won't catch on your skis). Either way, feel free to don a veil—sew one to your ski hat, or wear it the traditional way.

Your wedding party can show their solidarity with matching Nordic sweaters of the same color, which they can wear over ski gear, or with matching skirts for the women and pants for the men. Bonus: Your bridesmaids will be grateful for something they'll actually wear again. Also, you and the groom may also consider wearing these sweaters over more traditional attire.

FACT

If you're wearing ski gear for the ceremony but have your heart set on a traditional wedding dress, change into one after your run down the mountain. Then make a dramatic entrance into the reception with your groom, resplendent in your formal attire.

A Smooth Run

After the ceremony, the resort can no doubt accommodate your party on the premises. Again, no matter what the season, you can incorporate a ski theme into your reception beyond just the venue. If your wedding is in the warm-weather months, inquire whether you can have an outdoor setting, with tables and a dance floor set up at the bottom of the mountain. Or for any season, consider hosting the reception in the chalet or restaurant that your guests can conveniently ski or drive a snowmobile to.

You can design everything from your invitations to your wedding favors with a ski-flavored flair. Design your invitations with little ski icons, a mountain look, or a traditional Nordic pattern as a border. Consider guest favors, such as pretty mugs with little bags of powdered hot chocolate inside, lip balm, sunscreen, or other ski-related items. For your bridesmaids and groomsmen, you may consider giving them matching ski hats and gloves or lift tickets for a future ski outing with the whole gang.

FACT

If you'd like your ski wedding to be a more intimate affair, there are resorts that offer packages for private ceremonies that include a qualified officiant, a photographer, and extras like corsages, champagne, and, of course, your lift ticket. They will perform the ceremony in a secluded mountain location, from which you can then ski away!

If you can find a creative cake designer, ask him or her to design your cake to resemble a ski mountain. Or have a traditional white cake topped with a bride and groom skiing. For an additional dessert or in place of a wedding cake, you may also consider serving snowball-shaped desserts like the Italian tartuffo or ball-shaped groom's cakes sprinkled with white coconut.

For decorations, consider an all-white look inside to mirror the beautiful white outdoors. Choose all-white centerpieces with roses, tulips, or other flowers; all white linens; white china; and/or silver candelabras with white candles.

Gills and Thrills Wedding

If you've ever gone snorkeling or scuba diving, you know there's nothing like the peaceful solitude that surrounds you underwater. There are many ways you can incorporate an underwater ceremony into your wedding day, whether you crave a small, intimate ceremony and celebration or a party that includes all your friends and family.

Underwater Fantasy

The first step in your underwater fantasy is to get certified, if you aren't already. Your next step is to decide on a destination. If you live in the Florida Keys, you'll have the choice of sticking close to home. However, if you're from the deserts of Nevada, your guests undoubtedly will be required to travel. The destination will probably, in turn, determine what style of reception you'll have. If you plan to travel to the Great Barrier Reef off the coast of Australia, don't expect many wedding guests. But if you live in a coastal town, you can incorporate a large reception into your underwater wedding plans with much greater ease. Again, here are a number of options.

Tiny Bubbles

Of course, if you're planning an underwater wedding, the ceremony is the main event. What can you expect? First, you'll need to team up with a diving company that is willing to go along with your plan. If possible, find a group that has experience with weddings; they'll be better able to help you with details. Check with the diving company about communication gear, which is essential to the underwater wedding. This gear will enable you to hear the officiant, as well as speak your vows so that everyone underwater can hear. Many times this communication gear allows listeners on your scuba boat to hear the proceedings, as well—which is particularly helpful if you're inviting friends and family to attend on the scuba boat. If communication gear is not available, you can use slates with written vows and responses to the officiant's questions, in order to communicate with one another.

The diving company can also probably help point you to a certified diver who can officiate at your proceedings. In addition, if your witnesses are not certified divers, they will need training before the big day. Be sure they are willing to commit to this endeavor before counting them in officially.

The length of your ceremony should be kept short, with just the basic legal requirements and a few other elements included—particularly if you're using written communication. If you'd like a more elaborate ceremony, consider including the basics underwater, and then adding a more complete ceremony on land—or on the boat.

Don't forget to hire an underwater photographer and/or videographer to capture the proceedings . . . your land-loving friends and relatives will be an eager audience.

The Reception

If you are including friends and family in your wedding celebration, you can plan as simple or as elaborate a reception as you wish. For a more elaborate reception, investigate hiring a yacht or party boat large enough to host a traditional reception dinner or cocktails. You can meet up and board the larger boat from your scuba boat, or you can dive directly off this boat, if it's permitted.

Some scuba operations also offer glass bottom boats as an option. This could be an exciting way to include a lot of guests in your ceremony—without requiring them to go underwater, too.

Whether you host a reception on a boat or yacht or decide to ground your operations on solid land, there are plenty of special touches you can include to continue your seafaring theme. Of course, your invitation provides a perfect opportunity to introduce your unique wedding style to invited guests, with water and a sea-theme as your inspiration. For menu options, serve seafood, or include a raw bar. Tropical drinks in fun coconut cups or tiki mugs would provide a refreshing change for cocktail hour.

If you can, hire a calypso band (or play similar music from a sound system) for pre- and post-meal dancing. Use seashells, seagrass, sea glass, and other nautical elements for decorations. For favors, give guests sunglasses, sunscreen, or snorkel gear if it's a daytime wedding, or mini flashlights or glow sticks to help navigate the outdoors at night. If you're holding your reception on the water, have plenty of Dramamine on hand in case the seas get rough.

FACT

For a more unconventional reception that still allows for guests, charter a boat large enough to hold plenty of people but small enough to allow guests to snorkel off the side. (A good-sized catamaran would work well.) Hold a casual, picnic-style reception with sandwiches, salads, beer, and wine. Wait to serve spirits until after snorkeling's completed.

Wine Lover's Wedding

You may have an elaborate wine cellar that holds hundreds of premium wines . . . or you may barely know the difference between a cabernet and a merlot. Either way, a wine-tasting theme at your wedding will set your day uniquely apart from other celebrations. With the wine-tasting theme, you can have a relatively traditional wedding with a sit-down meal and dancing, or you can make wine tasting the main event and have a simpler reception with just wine, cheese, and hors d'ouevres.

Pinpointing the Perfect Place

You can hold a wine-tasting wedding anywhere. However, if you live near some local wineries, you may want to start your search with them. Usually, wineries are situated in beautiful countrysides, and many or most have indoor facilities built to complement the surroundings. Call your local wineries to determine whether they have the resources to host a special event—chances are, they rent out the space and will probably have recommendations for caterers they've worked with in the past, if you plan to serve food. Most wineries will be eager to work with you, as your wedding provides a great opportunity to promote their wines to a captive audience. Keep this in mind when negotiating price.

Of course, not everyone lives near wine country. However, you can still easily arrange a beautiful and memorable wine-tasting event. Check with local restaurants known for their extensive wine selections, or with caterers or banquet facilities for their suggestions. Again, these proprietors will probably be enthusiastic about including a wine-tasting event, as they make most of their profits from the alcohol served at weddings. A less expensive route may be to purchase your own wines to include in the reception, particularly if you're having your wedding at home or at a private dwelling. Most caterers or banquet facilities will not allow you to bring in your own wine or alcohol, however, as it cuts into their profits.

Very Good Taste

Having a wine-tasting wedding will provide your guests with a more interactive experience, and a chance to try something that may be new to them. For this reason, conduct your wine tasting with as much detail as a winery would. That means including a number of wine selections in both red and white; serving room-temperature water (cold water numbs the taste buds) and/or bread to clean the palate between tastings; and furnishing spittoons for spitting out wine once it's tasted. Employ qualified sommeliers who can educate guests about what they're tasting, and to answer questions about the wines and also about proper tasting technique (particularly the use of spittoons).

ALERT!

For guests who just don't care for wine, be sure to provide other beverages such as beer, mixed drinks, and soft drinks to serve during cocktail hour and/or dinner.

The wine-tasting event would ideally begin during your reception's cocktail hour, if you're having a traditional reception with meal. Serve decadent hors d'oeuvres chosen specifically to offset the wine during this time period. These may include a variety of cheeses, pâtés, seafood, crudités, and other hors d'oeuvres—hand passed. If you're including an hors d'oeuvres table, add menu cards that indicate which foods offset which wines. Also, to make it more fun for guests—and to help them remember their favorites—give each guest a "tasting card" and pen or pencil with which they can record their wine-tasting experience. This can double as your wedding favor, if you place the cards in nice frames, or include a pretty pen or pencil engraved with your names and wedding date.

If you are serving dinner, allow guests to choose which wine they'd like to drink with dinner based on their preferences during cocktail hour. Or based on your menu, you may serve special wines with each course, chosen to best complement the flavor of the food. Work with your caterer to determine the best pairings. This would give guests an opportunity to try the wines "in action," so to speak.

To continue your enthusiasm for wine in other aspects of your celebration, consider staying in theme for decorations and wedding favors. Instead of flower centerpieces, include beautiful fruit-inspired centerpieces that reflect the flavors of the wines—of course, grapes will be central. Many wines also include other fruit flavors such as peach, pear, apple, pomegranate, etc. Coordinate these fruits into your décor—for centerpieces, bouquets, and other areas where you would traditionally use flowers.

When you serve dessert or wedding cake, continue your wine tasting with a dessert wine or "ice wine," a type of sweet wine that is suited to the after-dinner palate, and quickly growing in popularity.

For favors, give your guests wine-related mementos. Depending on your budget, these may include a bottle of wine for each couple (or miniature bottles of wine to cut down on cost); a unique corkscrew; a beautiful wine stopper (there are many styles available in home stores today); even fresh grapes in a small, decorated box or basket (what a lovely touch!). Display the favors together on a table, or include favors at each place setting to give the table setting an elegant touch.

For more wine-inspired décor, incorporate an Italian countryside look, with lots of rustic candles, distressed furniture, and/or murals. Or re-create the look of a vineyard—indoors—with lots of earth tones and decorative wines. Consult with your florist and caterer about creating a truly unique look.

Artistic Wedding

If you're in a creative field related to writing, art, music, food, decorating, or more, there are plenty of ways to take your professional talent and personalize it for your wedding day. Or if you have latent creative talent but work in a noncreative field, why not take your pent-up energy and let your talents shine for your wedding celebration? Whether your talent is your profession or your hobby, including it in the festivities is a very appropriate way to personalize your wedding.

From Favors to Flowers

With so many elements involved in planning a wedding—invitations, flowers, programs, ceremony, centerpieces, favors, music, decorations, cake, transportation, food, and drink—there is inevitably a way to include your and/or your groom's special talents (or a close family member's or friend's). Nothing makes a wedding more unique and memorable than wedding elements that reflect the couple's true personalities. And nothing could reflect those personalities more than an expression of personal creativity.

The Visual Arts

If you or your fiancé have talents in the visual arts, there are many ways to incorporate them into your ceremony and reception, beginning with your invitation. Whether you're a commercially employed graphic designer or a classically trained artist (or even a dabbler with some amount of artistic ability), you can use your talents to design a one-of-a-kind invitation, rather than purchasing the pre-made variety.

You may consider making each invitation individually with paint, watercolors, pencil sketch, or even an elegant collage format. Or if you're adept at computer design, custom design and commercially print your invitation to reflect your tastes or your wedding style (casual, formal, or a particular theme). Or use premium or handmade papers, vellum, ribbon, or other media to create an invitation uniquely your own. If you need help with the mechanics (gluing, tying, or stuffing envelopes), enlist the help of your bridesmaids or groomsmen.

If you have a specific talent that's not covered in this section, simply go through each element of your wedding planning—from the invitation to transportation—to seek out ways to include a personal, creative touch utilizing your own brand of creativity.

You may wish to coordinate your invitation design with your program design to maintain a consistent look or design for all your printed pieces. If you wish to incorporate placecards and/or menu cards at your reception, the design may be used here as well; even thank-you notes could be custom coordinated with your original invitation.

There are plenty of other places—on centerpieces, banners, and other wedding day decorations—to display your visual talents. For instance, include a self-portrait of the bride and groom surrounded by a matte frame, and display it at the entrance or exit so that everyone can sign it or write a special note on it. You'll then have a keepsake to hang in your home. Or design part or all of your centerpieces, depending on your talent—for example, hand paint vases or make your own pottery to hold flowers. Or include your own sculpted masterpieces on each table.

The Written Word

If you or your fiancé have writing talent, there are plenty of places to use it in your wedding celebration, beginning with the invitation. Instead of going with the traditional, standard invitation wording, why not craft your own invitation message? Include a poem or quote written by you or by a favorite writer; word the invitation with a heartfelt, personal message. It's your party, you can write what you want to.

Another opportunity to put your writing skills to work is during the ceremony, for which you can write your own vows, or even craft your own ceremony (unless it is a religious ceremony with specific guidelines). Check with your officiant to determine how much freedom you have, then pour your heart into what you'd like to express to your groom—or vice versa—on your wedding day. This exercise will also help you reflect on what marriage really means to you beyond the pomp and circumstance of the wedding day, and what your expectations, hopes, and dreams truly are.

ALERT!

If you're writing your own vows, be honest and heartfelt—but try not to be *too* intimate. There are some thoughts that should only be exchanged privately.

The ceremony program also offers a good medium in which to be creative. Besides a unique design, you can also go beyond the traditional ceremony readings, songs, and a "thank you" to family and friends. While including these practical features, you can also give your guests something to sink their teeth into as they await your walk down the aisle. Include fun (and flattering) descriptions of your wedding party and how they're acquainted with the bride and groom; include the story of how the bride and groom met; or include a favorite poem or excerpts from a love letter exchanged between the two of you (make sure the groom knows beforehand, particularly if it was written by him). Your guests will enjoy getting to know your personal story better and will feel more involved in the celebration.

Other opportunities to let loose your writing talent include speeches to be given during the rehearsal dinner or at the wedding itself; a song written for your band to perform; a poem to read to your groom with your guests as the audience (you can have it framed to give to him as your wedding gift); letters with goodie bags to greet out-of-town guests in their hotels or rooms; or some special words to attach to your wedding favors.

Other Talents

No matter what your creative passion, you can incorporate it into your wedding day. If it's needlepoint, embroidery, or sewing, you can fashion handmade favors such as little pillows or handkerchiefs for your guests. Like to cook or bake? Make your own fudge, cookies, or whatever you do best for guests to enjoy or take home as favors (and be sure to let everyone know they're made by the you). Do you play a musical instrument or sing? Incorporate your own song into the ceremony, or plan a special performance during part of the reception. You'll have much satisfaction creating something for your own celebration.

Chapter 11
Holiday Weddings

There's something extra special about a holiday wedding. Maybe it's because everyone's in vacation mode, and spirits are high around holidays. Many of your guests will have time off from work, which makes them more relaxed and open to enjoying all the festivities of the season. For your holiday wedding, tap into these high spirits to throw a party that's really unforgettable.

Christmas Wedding

For many people, there's no more special—or happier—time than the Christmas season. Full of giving hearts and good spirits, the Christmas season, despite its often less-than-pleasant weather in many areas of the country, is a popular time for weddings. In addition, the food, decorations, and wedding attire can truly reflect the richness and beauty of the season in countless ways and will provide a stunning backdrop for all your celebrations.

An Anniversary You'll Never Forget

Obviously, a Christmas wedding doesn't need to (and probably shouldn't) fall on Christmas Day or Christmas Eve. In fact, you'd be hard pressed to find a priest who would agree to officiate a wedding ceremony on these two very important holy days. However, that doesn't mean you can't throw a Christmas-themed wedding with all the trappings. Any date between Thanksgiving and December 25 will do; most venues officially begin their Christmas season right after Thanksgiving weekend, or at the very latest the beginning of December.

If you're planning your reception in July, you'll have no way of knowing how your chosen reception facility decorates for the holidays. Ask to see pictures of past holiday affairs to be sure you like the style of décor. Chances are they won't remove these items for your wedding.

One thing to keep in mind as you plan your holiday wedding is price. While you may be able to save a bundle on decorations, you may also be subject to higher holiday pricing due to greater demand for party space, caterers, and the like, who are busy with corporate Christmas parties and other holiday gatherings. The earlier in the season, the easier you'll be able to schedule time and space—and may be able to save a bit more money, too.

Holiday Wear

The outfits of the bride, groom, and wedding party provide an obvious way to express the season's best. For those of us used to the lighter, sleeveless dresses of the oh-so-popular June bride, December brings its own brand of beautiful attire that we've not necessarily seen a hundred times over. Dresses in white velvet, or with long fitted sleeves, are as appropriate as traditional silk or satin sleeveless, strapless, or short-sleeve gowns. And winter can be particularly fun for the bride's accessories—consider wearing a white, faux-fur wrap or white sweater with faux fur at the wrists and collar; a beautiful white faux-fur cap and muff; or a white coat in cashmere or another luxurious fabric.

Your bridesmaids can look equally festive in the rich colors of Christmas—deep reds or cranberry, emerald greens, silver, and gold. Simple black dresses in velvet or other fabrics would work as well, with accessories that reflect the season such as a Christmas bouquet of poinsettias, or a pretty silver or gold Christmas-themed broach. Consider giving such an item as your bridesmaids' gift.

For the men, tuxes or suits are obviously in style during any season. If the groom and groomsmen are wearing tuxes, a silver- or gold-hued cummerbund, vest, and/or bow tie would reflect the season, as would boutonnieres of traditional Christmas foliage like mistletoe, holly, or small poinsettia blossoms.

Decorations

Your holiday decorations, as well, bring a host of opportunities to let your holiday spirit go wild. If your venue does not come decorated for the holidays, there are plenty of ways to reflect the Christmas season, starting with centerpieces. Holiday centerpieces can be as simple as red flowers, such as roses (or, even better, poinsettias) with plenty of greens, or as elaborate as custom-made Christmas wreaths made of ivy, berries, and other Christmas foliage encircling candles. You could include a small "Charlie Brown"–style Christmas tree in the center of each table, decorated with ornaments guests are invited to take home as favors. If you'd like to go flower-free, a simple cluster of candles amid pine needles could be beautiful, as could a large vase or bowl filled with metallic Christmas ball ornaments.

For decorations around your reception venue, be sure there's a large Christmas tree on hand—you may wish to make this the backdrop for your ceremony if you're not marrying in a church setting. Drape ivy and/or holly around stairway banisters, and hang mistletoe from the rafters and doorways (and watch the fun ensue as groomsmen jockey for position).

Don't forget to include your Christmas theme in your invitation. Look for designs with traditional Christmas icons such as a tree, silver bells, a stocking, mistletoe, Santa, a gift, a sleigh, a reindeer, or a more subtle tie-in, such as paper with a trace of silver and gold. Or include scented pine needles in the envelope for an added touch.

Your cake can also reflect these traditional Christmas elements. You could have it designed to resemble a large, beautifully wrapped present, with a bit of color here and there for good measure. Or choose a traditional cake and garnish it with ivy and/or holly, or with tiny Christmas ornaments.

You may also wish to drape Christmas lights around certain areas of your reception, such as the front of the head table or existing foliage. With lights, less can often mean more, so try to be subtle and use tiny white or twinkle lights. Or forgo lights and create a warm atmosphere by using lots of candles throughout the reception area.

The Christmas Goose

Of course, you don't need to serve traditional Christmas goose to stay in the holiday spirit. However, you may want to consider serving holiday favorites—kicked up a notch, as they say—such as turkey, ham, Cornish hens, or specially prepared steaks. Follow your own family's holiday menu traditions. For drinks, include cold-weather favorites such as hot cider, eggnog, warm coffee drinks with liqueurs, and hot chocolate. A special coffee bar featuring flavored coffees, cappuccino, and espresso could be an impressive and welcome addition to a cold winter wedding.

That's Entertainment

There are many little "extras" that you could incorporate into your Christmas wedding, for children and adults alike. Consider inviting Santa to pay a visit. If you're including children in your reception, have Santa give a special wrapped gift to each child. Or if you'd prefer, let Santa deliver your bridesmaids' and groomsmen's gifts, as well as any gifts to your parents or to the groom. Santa may also be tapped to deliver wedding favors; he could walk from table to table handing them out.

You can carry out your Christmas theme at your rehearsal dinner, too, by surrounding it with a traditional winter activity, such as ice skating, caroling, or sledding, followed with hot chocolate. Then enjoy dinner by a roaring fire for a unique and exhilarating rehearsal celebration.

Another Christmas activity might include Christmas caroling. Set aside some time when those who'd like to participate can sing a few songs for the party. Provide each guest with song lyrics at their table so they have the option of comfortably joining in. Or hire some carolers to start the singing, inviting all who care to participate to join in.

Christmas Gifts

No Christmas-themed wedding would be complete without gifts for the guests! There are many Christmas-related goodies to offer them; consider wrapping items in small boxes with beautiful shiny paper and big bows and displaying them all together on a table when guests enter. You could also use them as placecard holders, with placecards tucked in the ribbon—this way you'll be sure each guest gets a favor.

Favor ideas include Christmas ornaments; candy canes; Christmas stocking (with stuffers, if your budget allows for it); Christmas candy or cookies; snow globes; potpourri of pine, holly, and other winter foliage; a Christmas candle; or pretty Christmas bells.

New Year's Eve Wedding

Because New Year's Eve is traditionally an evening for dressing up and stepping out, the New Year's wedding should be an elegant, formal, and festive affair. If this is your dream date for a wedding, be sure to start planning very early to ensure you'll get the space you really want, and beware of escalating prices, as this is one of the busiest—if not *the* busiest—party nights of the year.

What Will I Wear?

Of course, the traditional white, full-length gown is appropriate for almost any wedding. To stay in theme for your New Year's Eve wedding, however, you may want to dress in a more modern style of wedding dress—a fitted gown, or a gown with silver or gold beading or sparkles; or you may want to go the glamorous route with a traditional dress and tiara in a very dramatic style. Either way, you'll probably want to make this a black-tie event for your guests, with the groom and groomsmen paving the way in formal tuxedos or even tails and top hats. For your bridesmaids, you may want to choose dresses in a metallic color such as silver or gold, or allow them to choose their own floor length dresses in black. Or choose beautiful beaded party dresses/gowns that they'll feel comfortable in and look great in, too.

Timing Is Everything

Throwing a New Year's Eve wedding is not much more involved than throwing a fabulous New Year's Eve party—champagne, confetti, and noisemakers characterize the best of them. Obviously, timing for this celebration is extremely important, as all your activities will revolve in some way around the countdown to midnight. Use midnight as your starting point, then work backward—and forward—to plan for cocktails, mealtime, speeches, dancing, dessert, and anything else.

One of the most important options to consider is the timing of the ceremony. You may choose to incorporate traditional timing, with the ceremony followed by a reception, or you may wish to marry at midnight, with your wedding kiss taking place just as the new year rolls in. If you do choose to hold your ceremony at midnight, you can still have all the traditional elements of a wedding celebration, including a cocktail hour and dinner—this time they'll just take place *before* the ceremony.

Be sure you've hired your photographer to work well past midnight, to catch everyone in candid shots ringing in the New Year.

If you do decide to have the ceremony prior to the reception, you can still weave the midnight hour into a distinctive part of your wedding. For example, you may want to stage a dramatic serving of dessert or wedding cake, with waiters coming out with flaming Baked Alaska or an equally show-stopping treat just after midnight. Or you may designate midnight as the time when the wedding speeches and toasts take place, including that of the best man, the father of the bride, and anyone else who would like to speak.

For this holiday, *glitz* is the operative word. People generally go out on New Year's Eve with the understanding that this is a special night—they dress up a little more, spend a little more money, stay out a little later. Let that fuel your own wedding plans, and you'll create a party your guests will never forget.

Food and Drink

Most restaurants serve an extra-special menu on New Year's Eve. Let your wedding be no exception. Go all out on food and drinks for this affair, with plentiful passed hors d'oeuvres and stations of cocktail hour foods to choose from. Because your New Year's reception will probably begin later than normal, and dinner may not be served until 9 or 10 o'clock, ample hors d'oeuvres during cocktail hour will ensure guests won't go hungry—or become too intoxicated—for lack of proper vittles. As for alcohol, don't skimp on the quality. Serve top-shelf liquor for mixed drinks, good-quality wine, imported, bottled beers, and specialty featured drinks like flavored martinis. Of course, champagne should be served at midnight, so be sure there is plenty on hand for all your guests.

Follow your cocktail hour with an extravagant sit-down meal of multiple courses, with the best cuts of beef, fresh seafood, and fresh fruit and vegetables to treat your guests. Consider dishes such as filet mignon, lobster, crab, salmon—dishes all your guests may not enjoy on a regular basis.

Of course, your wedding will probably get going just as other weddings traditionally end—midnight. Plan for this and offer late-night snacks and plenty of coffee to ensure your party continues into the wee hours.

A Festive Look

For an elegant yet festive New Year's look to your wedding, include plenty of balloons. Try covering the ceiling in black, white, and silver balloons. For more drama, as the clock strikes midnight, have confetti rain down on guests and/or turn on a smoke machine or bubble machine. You may also wish to include a large clock or two that guests can watch as the minutes tick by.

For wedding favors and other decorative accoutrements, make champagne, noisemakers, and party hats the focus. Include a large table of noisemakers and hats for guests to grab as they enter the reception, or use them as an extra decoration for the tables. For centerpieces, why not include bunches of helium-filled balloons tied to champagne bottles at each table? That way, guests can open champagne on their own, and there will be plenty of corks popping for a midnight sound effect. For wedding favors, give your guests engraved champagne glasses or mini bottles of champagne to take home—or a cool clock or watch to commemorate the time and date of your wedding.

Halloween Wedding

For many people, there is no better holiday than Halloween. And for weddings, there is no more inspiring day for creativity, zaniness, and fun than this holiday. Whether your vision is a more casual Halloween wedding with all the familiar orange-and-black trappings or a formal masquerade ball with some subtle Halloween touches, there are plenty of ways to make Halloween a creative and unusual backdrop for your wedding celebration.

Fun for the Whole Family

For a more casual Halloween wedding, simply draw from the holiday itself for inspiration. Obviously, your color scheme will include a lot of black. Some brides choose to wear black themselves for Halloween weddings and dress their bridesmaids accordingly.

You love Halloween. Others, unfortunately, may not. If you're inviting your guests to wear costumes, be sure to let them know it is optional.

If you plan to include all the traditions of Halloween as we celebrate it, start with the invitation. Check out traditional Halloween party invitations for inspiration; you may wish to have one custom designed based on your findings. You can make it as elaborate or as simple as you like—an invitation written on black or charcoal colored paper—with silver or white writing—could be a simple, elegant format. Or go all out in the spirit of the holiday with a design that incorporates ghosts, bats, tombstones, pumpkins, witches, or other symbols of Halloween. If you'd like, invite your guests to come in costume.

Haunted House

Whether you're having a kid-friendly or more formal affair, the right venues for your ceremony and reception can make a big difference. If you're having a religious ceremony, choose an old or Gothic-style church or synagogue to set the tone. For your reception, look for sites such as historical buildings, shadowy old museums or galleries, an old hotel ballroom, an old Victorian home or bed and breakfast, or a reputed "haunted" house. These types of venues will serve as the ideal backdrop whether you plan to have a formal masquerade ball or a party that includes bobbing for apples.

If you are having a more laid-back affair, you can create your own haunted house, particularly if your guest list includes children. Talk with your caterer about creating a special area of your reception location to set up traditional Halloween activities such as a mini "haunted house," haunted hayrides, bobbing for apples, face painting, or tarot card and palm reading. Include a smoke machine or dry ice to create atmosphere. Employ actors dressed in costume to entertain children. Have a ghost story hour for kids and adults alike. Make sure the wedding goes late into the evening so that there's plenty of time to enjoy all the activities.

ALERT!

If there will be young children at your wedding, be sure that costumes aren't too scary for them. You don't want a bunch of crying, frightened children at your reception.

Trick or Treat

If you're going all out in Halloween theme, there are plenty of easy ways to decorate your reception venue. Start by decorating with fake cotton cobwebs, "R.I.P." tombstones, makeshift ghosts and goblins, coffins, smoke machines, hanging bats, black lights, and whatever else inspires you for the holiday. Give guests favors such as bags of candy, wax lips, Dracula teeth, noses with glasses attached, or other gag gifts. Strew candy over tables for decoration, and create Halloween-themed centerpieces with witch hats, jack-o'-lanterns with candles inside, cauldrons filled with candy, or Halloween masks. Hold a contest and give awards for the best costume, most creative costume, scariest costume, and funniest costume.

Masquerade Ball

For a more formal, traditional wedding with a mysterious, moody ambience, Halloween also serves as a perfect date. If all the youthful amusements of Halloween are not your thing, you can still create a romantic, dark, and luxurious reception with a Halloween/New Orleans feel.

If you're wearing a traditional white dress, choose conservative bridesmaids' dresses in a subdued burnt orange or rust hue, or in black. Your flowers can reflect the color of the holiday—and of the fall season in general—if you choose roses in an orange/rust hue for both your bouquets and centerpieces. They can be formal and lovely with a tight bouquet style for roses or a loose, laid-back collection of daisies or sunflowers in the appropriate color.

ESSENTIAL

> Carve your names or initials into decorative pumpkins for an elegant touch.

At your reception, you can create an ambience that's romantic and moody with centerpieces of silver or black candelabras, or tall wrought iron candleholders with pillar candles. Lighting your whole reception room by candlelight (alone or in conjunction with very dim overhead lights) would create a wonderful atmosphere. Pumpkins make great accents for your guest tables, cake table, or placecard table. In fact, you may want to attach placecards to miniature pumpkins or gourds—they'll look beautiful set up on a table as guests enter.

If you'd like guests to come dressed in more traditional formal attire rather than in costume, you can still incorporate a masquerade ball look to stay in theme. Ask guests to bring or wear a traditional masquerade ball mask of feathers and sequins—the kind that sometimes come with stick holders—for a more festive atmosphere.

For music, employ a Cajun-inspired band or a New Orleans–style jazz band. Give away voodoo dolls as favors. Serve foods that are related to the theme, such as pumpkin or squash soup, and/or desserts that incorporate the season's best apples. And of course there's always pumpkin pie . . .

Fourth of July Wedding

Many people couldn't envision any other season but summer for a wedding. So . . . what better time to celebrate than the day that is guaranteed to have fireworks flying?

Stars and Stripes

Obviously, you can have any style of wedding on Independence Day, ranging from the very formal to the very casual. There is, however, something about the Fourth of July that invites us to adopt a more casual attitude; so we will consider an Independence Day wedding a more laid-back affair. You can still incorporate special touches that will set it apart from any other Fourth of July celebration, however. Instead of beer and hot dogs, why not serve excellent steaks, gourmet salads, and fun cocktails, for instance? You can still serve a formal sit-down meal, even if your wedding is outside, by setting up tables beneath an attractive party tent. Or adopt a more laid-back format with a buffet-style reception—or include an upscale barbecue whereby guests can choose between grilled steaks, chicken, or seafood, prepared fresh before their eyes. Another nice summer touch is to include grilled corn on the cob, grilled clams, mussels, or shrimp, or even a raw bar from which guests can partake before lunch or dinner.

For a traditional, casual menu, serve Fourth of July favorites like potato salad, macaroni salad, fruit salad, burgers, sausage, and hot dogs, with lots of condiments. Don't forget desserts like apple pie à la mode and, of course, anything with chocolate.

The venue will play a big part in your Fourth of July wedding. Choose a reception locale that's outdoors, such as a beautiful park setting, a beach location, a private yard that's large enough for all your guests, or a restaurant, banquet hall, or unique site with an indoor/outdoor setting. If you're having your wedding ceremony and reception entirely outdoors, be sure to set up sturdy party tents that can protect everyone from the elements if the weather doesn't go your way.

For a more casual event, bring props for traditional Fourth of July activities, such as horseshoes, bocce balls, croquet, Frisbee, badminton, and volleyball. (If you're having a beach wedding, see Chapter 6 for additional ideas specific to seaside celebrations.) You may also wish to invite guests to take part in water sports such as sailing, jet-skiing, wind-surfing, waterskiing, or surfing.

Decorations

If you prefer a more upscale, outdoor affair, you can set up beautiful party tents that come fully enclosed to protect against the weather or can be opened if your day turns out to be perfect. You can make your setting as elegant as you like—consider an all-white look for summer, with white linens, white china, good silver, and centerpieces with beautiful summer blossoms in elegant holders such as pewter or silver vases. These party tents will allow you to hang lighting and other decorations—you could wind white blossoms and ivy around tent supports for an elegant touch or hang white Chinese lanterns to best reflect the outdoors.

Of course, for a more casual affair, such as a picnic-style reception, you'll want to include touches of red, white, and blue throughout your décor. Display the American flag in unique ways, such as through mini flags lining your walkway or incorporated into a centerpiece of flowers. Serve dessert or wedding cake with sparklers. Choose tableware with a red, white, and blue theme, or table linens with red and blue accents, such as white tablecloths with blue and red cloth napkins. Include plenty of refreshments in convenient locations to complement the bar service, such as big tubs filled with ice and beer, flavored malt beverages, and soft drinks.

For a fun invitation that includes your theme—without losing sight of your wedding day—include a graphic of fireworks. Invite your guests to witness the fireworks.

Your cake can include the thematic elements of the Fourth, as well. Have your cake baker design your cake in the shape of the flag, or to look like fireworks exploding in midair. Or include red and blue flower blossoms on a traditional cake for a more subtle tie-in.

For wedding favors, give guests bug spray, sunscreen, sunglasses, beach towels, a great summer paperback, a specially designed bookmark, or even a combination of these outdoor staples. Of course, the day wouldn't be complete without a fireworks show. If you are setting off fireworks yourself, be extremely careful, assigning someone responsible for this duty (or, even better, hire an experienced person to handle it). Play some music in the background for greater effect—play your wedding song again, or other romantic love songs.

If it is illegal in your state to set off fireworks yourself, choose a venue where you'll be able to witness an organized fireworks show—or include transportation that will take your wedding party and guests to and fro a fireworks show nearby.

Chapter 12

Make a Weekend of It

Even without an organized theme, there are many ways to infuse creativity into your wedding, mainly by structuring things a little bit differently. So whether you'd like a wedding that lasts all weekend, a destination wedding, or an elopement, this chapter shows you the basics of doing it creatively.

Defining the Budget

Your budget may drive the decision-making process on the wedding styles included in this chapter—for better or for worse. In fact, though it seems elaborate, you may end up saving money by throwing a destination wedding; and many of the activities you'll include in a weekend wedding don't have to break the bank. Eloping is your best bet for saving many of the traditional wedding costs, of course, but you may find you'd like to factor in some funds for a post-elopement party, which will escalate your budget. The point? Don't assume any of these styles will be more or less expensive—like a traditional wedding, the bottom line cost is all in the details.

Organization Is Key

For any of the weddings in this chapter, organization and time are the keys to successful planning. If you are planning a wedding away from your hometown—and particularly in a foreign country—there are many issues you'll need to address above and beyond the typical details of dress, flowers, and menu. Long-distance planning adds the extra element of travel, which can be unpredictable and complicated, as well as the question of legality if you are marrying out of the country. In addition, planning a wedding from afar simply becomes more complicated because you are not able to meet with planners and vendors face to face. However, with the Internet, fax, and even three-way calling, many of these communication barriers have broken down in recent years.

Weekend Weddings

A weekend wedding is a celebration that does not begin and end with the ceremony and reception. A weekend wedding, instead, includes additional parties and activities for all the wedding guests throughout an entire weekend. These activities may include a rehearsal dinner; salon or spa primping; sporting activities such as golf, horseback riding, skiing, or tennis; and a post-day wedding gathering. If you've attended any wedding out of town, chances are you've experienced the "weekend wedding," even in an abbreviated form, as you may have attended a rehearsal dinner and maybe a follow-up brunch or lunch the day after the wedding.

FACT

The weekend wedding is also ideal for type-A personalities, as this type of celebration requires intensive planning, a high degree of organizational skill, and plenty of follow-up to ensure all the details are in place.

Consider the Options

When beginning your planning of a weekend wedding, consider your goals. Is one of your priorities to allow your and your groom's family to get acquainted for the first time? Is it a chance for all your friends from high school and college to finally meet? Or is it a reunion of sorts, at which most of the guests will already know each other? Use the answers to these questions to help define what you'd like to accomplish—breaking the ice among your guests, or letting your guests spend long-awaited quality time together, or a little of both.

Next, you'll want to create your guest list, so that you have an idea of the number of people you'll be hosting. Planning weekend activities for 250 will prove a greater challenge than planning for 50. You may want to limit your extra-nuptial activities to out-of-town guests, the wedding party, and close family only, to have more manageable groups to work with. After all, a spa day for a hundred women would not be an easy (or inexpensive) feat to pull off.

ESSENTIAL

If you'd like to include all your invited guests—from both in and out of town—in all your weekend wedding festivities, plan activities that are crowd-friendly, such as picnics, casual beach parties, or gatherings that don't require a precise head count in advance.

Finally, you'll want to consider budget. Will you be footing the bill for guest accommodations? Will you be paying for planned activities such as golf, sight-seeing tours, or salon services? Or will your budget be strictly limited to the rehearsal dinner, wedding, and post-wedding brunch or lunch? Either way, you can still plan plenty of activities, but make them optional so guests can choose whether they'd like or can afford to participate.

Create an Agenda

Once you've determined a basic budget and guest list, begin planning. If your weekend wedding will take place on a regular, non-holiday weekend, you'll want to plan activities for Friday, Saturday, and Sunday. Many guests, particularly if they are invited to a rehearsal dinner on Friday, would rather arrive in town on Thursday to ensure they don't get stuck traveling. So, include all of Friday in your plans to accommodate guests who arrive early. Or if you're having your wedding on a long weekend, make it a mini vacation for your guests, with activities planned for every day of the long weekend.

FACT

Some activities will require a head count in advance, such as a golf or tennis outing. If you're planning this type of activity, include RSVP cards in your initial "save the date" card so that guests can express their interest early. You can then contact them later to confirm before organizing foursomes or reserving court or course time.

Once you've determined an itinerary for your weekend, send out a "save-the-weekend" notice to your guest list, so that they'll have enough time to make travel reservations, and reservations for accommodations. Be sure to supply guests with appropriate lodging options at different price levels, with addresses and phone numbers for each. Often, you can arrange group rates, which cut the costs down for everyone (and will often include a complimentary night's stay for you and the groom). Later you can send your formal wedding invitation with ceremony and reception details.

Fun for Everyone

The fun part is planning your activities. Obviously, every weekend wedding will differ based on the time of year, location, interests of the bride and groom and their families, and number of guests, but the following are some ideas you can adapt for your own use. If you'd like to give guests options or schedule more than one activity for a certain time period, or if togetherness for all your guests is the overriding strategy, plan for only one activity at a time. Here are some suggestions:

- **Salon or spa treatments.** Whether it's your treat or every woman for herself, no one will complain about a little pampering and primping before the wedding. Invite any interested men as well.
- **Tennis.** Rent out some courts and arrange a mini doubles tournament for lots of social interaction.
- **Sailing or boating.** Charter a fishing boat or sailboat to treat all your guests to a day on the water.
- **Horseback riding.** Reserve enough horses in advance to ensure you'll accommodate all interested parties.
- **A day at the club or beach.** If you belong to a pool club, beach club, or other country club, arrange for your guests to have permission to use the facilities, including pool, golf course, tennis courts, etc. This way, your guests will all be in one place but still be able to choose their activities.
- **Golf.** Golf is one of the most popular pastimes for weekend weddings. Play a best-ball tournament to even out the stakes among different level golfers.
- **Skiing.** Arrange transportation to and from the resort, and set aside time when everyone can meet up for lunch or hot chocolate by the fire.
- **Sledding or ice-skating.** In winter, rent sleds or toboggans and let your guests relive their childhoods. Or rent out a skating rink for an hour or two and invite all your guests to come work up an appetite before the rehearsal dinner.

Upon their arrival, be sure every guest is given a detailed itinerary of the weekend, including activities, specific times, phone numbers, and, if possible, who is participating.

- **Sightseeing.** If you're in a city or a location that invites sightseeing, arrange for an organized tour of the area. If you're in a large city, such as New York, do some research to see if there are any wedding-related tours, or take guests on a popular one, such as the Sex in the City Tour or Sopranos Tour.

- **See a show.** Give your guests the option of seeing a matinee or evening show, if your schedule allows.

- **See a concert.** If there's a great act in town on the weekend of your wedding (bonus points for cross-generational appeal), find out who'd like to go and get a group of tickets in advance. You may even get a group rate if there are enough takers.

- **Special events.** Scour your local Web pages for events taking place around town on your wedding weekend. Or if you have a favorite annual event such as an art festival, food tasting event, or historical celebration in your town or city, plan your wedding to coincide with that particular weekend. (Keep in mind, however, that it may make finding accommodations difficult—so plan ahead and reserve a block of rooms.)

- **Sporting event.** Get a group of tickets for the Sunday NFL game that falls on your wedding weekend. Or attend a Thursday or Friday night hockey, basketball, or baseball game with in-town and out-of-town friends and family.

- **Partake in a local pastime.** If you live in wine country, plan a tour of a local vineyard. If you live near the Grand Canyon, plan a day-long excursion. Take your guests to Niagara Falls if you live in New York State. Take advantage of local attractions—even though you may have seen them a hundred times, chances are that your guests have not.

- **Picnic.** The day before or the day after your wedding (it might be too much for the day of), host a casual, outdoor picnic where your guests can mingle and get to know each other in a laid-back, relaxed setting. Include a multitude of activities such as horseshoes, volleyball, or badminton. This is a particularly good way for guests to get acquainted, if most do not already know each other.

- **Brunch.** The morning after the wedding, a brunch is a great way to see your guests one more time before they travel back to their respective hometowns. Make it a casual, buffet-style get-together to which guests can come and go at various times.

No matter what the activity, arrange for transportation from a common location such as the hotel where most of your guests are staying, or supply guests with accurate, detailed directions to each destination. Arranging transportation for your guests will be easier if they are staying at the same or nearby hotels.

Destination Weddings

A destination wedding is a wedding that takes place in a destination other than the bride and groom's current hometown or parents' hometown. Generally, a destination wedding occurs in a vacation location that may include the tropics, a ski resort, a cruise ship, a faraway foreign outpost, or other favorites. Destination weddings can include as many or as few guests as the bride and groom wish—they can range from intimate affairs of ten people to elaborate wedding-and-vacation packages including hundreds of guests.

The Guest List

This brings us to the guest list. One of the first things you should do before making any plans is to formulate your guest list. And when it comes to a destination wedding, you can go any number of routes.

Being a bridesmaid or groomsman can be expensive enough just for the dress or tux rental. Add in travel and accommodation expenses and it may become prohibitive. Be clear with your potential wedding party about costs before assuming they can definitely participate.

For a small destination wedding, you may decide to include only your parents, siblings, a maid of honor and best man (with their spouses or significant others), or a small group of select friends or family. If you would like to pay for your guests' travel and accommodations, budget will play an obvious role in your final guest list. However, keep in mind that you can also subsidize expenses for your guests—in other words, pay for part but not all of their expenses, such as plane tickets or hotel costs—if you'd like to include more guests. Or you can ask your guests to pay all the costs themselves, though this can be a bit presumptuous. If you do not offer to pay the vast majority of your guests' expenses, bear in mind that you may have more than a few rejection RSVP cards in your mailbox.

ALERT!

Do not assume that all your invited guests will be able to afford the costs associated with your destination wedding. Allow them to be comfortable saying "no." Time may also be a constraint, particularly for guests with young families or career obligations.

For these reasons you may decide to keep your destination wedding small and design it as more of a family vacation with your wedding as the focal point rather than as a large wedding in a faraway place.

Getting Organized

Obviously, deciding on your destination is the most important aspect of planning a destination wedding. This is a highly personal decision, based on many factors including your interests, the time of year, and your proposed guest list and budget. Both distance and your final destination will dictate final travel costs—it'll cost a lot less to marry in Las Vegas than in Fiji for the same level of accommodations. But if you shop around for travel deals with a travel agent or on the Internet, you may be surprised at what you'll find—particularly if you're planning your wedding celebration outside of tourist season.

The following are a few popular destinations.

Inside the United States:

Hawaii

Las Vegas

Lake Tahoe

California Coast (Monterey, Big Sur)

Key West

Martha's Vineyard/Nantucket

New Orleans

Disney World

Outside the United States:

Caribbean Islands

Puerto Rico

Mexico

Italy

Ireland

France

Greece

Monte Carlo

Sri Lanka

Australia/New Zealand

South Pacific Islands (Bali, Fiji, etc.)

Besides the appeal of the setting itself, another factor to consider is your destination's legal requirements for recognizing a marriage. If your destination is within the United States, this may be a simpler process—simply check with authorities in your locale of choice to determine what is required (for example, marriage license rules).

Be sure to contact the embassy, consulate, or tourist information bureau of the country in which your wedding will take place to determine legal requirements well in advance of your wedding date.

If your wedding will be held outside the United States, however, the process can be a bit trickier—and requirements for documents and other preparations vary widely from country to country. Your best bet is to contact authorities in your destination country. Investigate exactly what is needed well in advance, before you schedule travel plans or make definite bookings. Proper documentation may include passports, birth certificates, divorce decrees, or death certificates of former spouses. There may be formalized procedures in your destination country as well, such as the posting of marriage banns—a public announcement of your intention to marry. There may also be rules for foreigners that may not apply to local residents, so be sure to do your homework. You wouldn't want to have all your travel dates and accommodations booked only to encounter a legal snag that prevents the marriage from being official.

The Wedding Planners

A second factor that may influence your destination decision is the available resources of the area. If you'd like to minimize your planning, go with a resort or hotel that has a wedding planning staff—or at least a willing concierge—on hand to assist with planning. Many times the staff can help arrange all the details of your day, from your ceremony to food to music, which can be a big help, especially if there are complicated legal requirements. This type of wedding "package" may be more convenient and efficient than planning every last detail from afar by yourself.

A travel agent can help steer you in the right direction and may have wedding contacts in the area you've chosen. Or you may consider hiring a wedding consultant who resides in your wedding location, if you are planning all your wedding details à la carte and need someone who knows the local florists, musicians, caterers, transportation options, and the like. Even a wedding consultant in your local area should be willing to plan all the details of your destination wedding and may even travel there beforehand to iron out final details, if required.

Setting the Date

Before arbitrarily setting a final, inflexible date, there are a couple things to consider. The first is, obviously, your own schedules, closely followed by the schedules of the loved ones you plan to include in your festivities. If your maid of honor will be eight months pregnant on your chosen date, you'll need to factor that in; if your parents have a vacation already scheduled, work around it. In other words, consult with those must-attend guests before setting the final date.

With proper planning, you can throw any style destination wedding you like—from an intimate affair for ten to a formal reception for one hundred. Use the tips from previous and coming chapters to host a wedding that's just your style—no matter where the final setting.

You should also factor in the weather and scheduled events of your destination before setting your date. Obviously, you probably don't want to schedule your wedding for the same weekend and location as an event such as the Superbowl (hotels and airfare will be overbooked and over-priced). In addition, you may want to consider booking your festivities during your destination's off-season, as this can be a significant cost-cutting measure (which may allow you to include more guests than you originally anticipated). Of course, if your resort is knocked out by a hurricane, the savings won't matter, so consider all your options carefully. Often there is a "shoulder" season that combines the best of both worlds—good weather and good pricing—with little risk.

Be sure to buy travel insurance—for you and your guests—in the event that weather or unforeseen events cause last-minute changes to travel plans.

The Party's Over

The beauty of the destination wedding is that the excitement can last and last. If you can swing it, a destination wedding that goes beyond just a day or two may be just the thing for you, your family, and your friends. You may decide to spend a few days to a week ironing out last-minute details at your destination of choice before the actual wedding takes place, or you may decide to hold the wedding right away so that you can relax and celebrate your honeymoon on the premises once everything's gone smoothly. If you're having a lot of guests, you may want to arrive a few days before them, to ensure the accommodations are adequate, the ceremony and reception vendors are under control, and all the details are taken care of.

Of course, you're already well equipped to enjoy your honeymoon—just walk outside. If your guests are staying on after the wedding, you may want to issue a self-imposed day or two of solitude for you and your groom, or you may decide the more, the merrier and enjoy every minute of your destination with friends and family.

Eloping

When you think of eloping, do you think of a cheesy Elvis chapel in Las Vegas with drive-thru weddings? Well think again—elopements are simply destination weddings, only without the guests. This means you can have a beautiful, memorable, and meaningful ceremony at the destination you've always dreamed of, with a limited amount of time required to make it happen.

For the easiest elopement, contact a wedding coordinator or concierge at a resort or hotel. Chances are they've helped many couples before you and may have all-inclusive package deals to simplify your wedding planning.

Just the Two of Us

Before you decide to elope, you must consider one thing—the repercussions. Yes, it's *your* wedding. Yes, it's about the two of you. But no, your close family and friends probably won't see it that way, so beware of hurt feelings and resentment about your decision. There are ways to combat potential hurt feelings, however. For instance, you may want to tell certain family members and friends in advance or even invite them along (see the section on Destination Weddings). Or you may choose to elope and then hold a reception after you return—you may feel more relaxed about throwing a party after the fact, particularly because you're already husband and wife. You can even have your ceremony photographed and/or videotaped to show your friends and family at the party, or individually—it may help take some of the sting off not being included originally.

FACT

The best part of eloping is that the minute the ceremony's over, you're already on your honeymoon. Choose a destination you can spend some time enjoying afterward, or elope where the legal requirements are simple and then jet off to a favored destination.

When it comes to planning your elopement, the factors you need to consider in planning a wedding in a far-off locale are the same ones you'd consider for a destination wedding. Legalities in particular can be very specific to your wedding locale, particularly if you are marrying outside the United States. If you want to elope quickly, there are destinations more amenable to quickie weddings—which is part of the reason why Las Vegas has become so popular for eloping couples.

Pros and Cons

While cost, planning stress, and family considerations may make the prospect of planning a traditional wedding daunting, remember—you only get married once (with any luck). If you do decide to elope, you may look back and wish you'd celebrated your wedding with friends and family. Keep this in mind before making a final decision. And if you've had a change of heart upon your return, there's no reason why you can't plan a party then.

Elopement Etiquette

If you decide to elope, you've also decided to give up the barrage of gifts you're bound to receive at a traditional wedding. It's in poor taste to register for gifts if you elope, and while well-meaning family and friends may still give you gifts, you should by no means expect them.

It's also a good idea to inform loved ones about your marriage upon your return. Send "at home" notes to family and friends announcing your marriage and informing them of any name or address changes. You may also include a personal note explaining why you've eloped so that recipients are less likely to feel left out by your decision. Of course, your reasons for eloping may be personal, so an explanation is by no means required.

Chapter 13

Creativity on a Budget

Worried that your budget won't allow you to be creative enough? Don't be. The most creative weddings are often much more cost-effective than you might think. This chapter discusses some typical wedding costs and how being creative can cut those costs—while still allowing you to throw a unique and beautiful wedding with your own personal stamp.

Major Contributors

Before you begin planning any wedding—from the most traditional and formal to the most creative theme wedding—it's imperative to know who will be paying for it. Tradition dictates that the bride's family pay for the lion's share of the wedding expenses, including the bride's attire, reception costs, decorations, favors, and the cake. However, this custom is drastically changing as marriages themselves change: Brides and grooms are marrying older and have their own jobs and savings to fund a wedding, plus today's couples often want complete control over the planning of their wedding, which can be difficult to exercise if someone else is footing the bill. What's more common today is a melding of financial resources, with the bride, groom, bride's family, and groom's family all contributing toward the final bill.

FACT

The average U.S. wedding today costs approximately $19,000 ($31,000 in the NYC tri-state area).

So, before you begin planning that elegant affair for three hundred people, be sure you're clear on who'll be paying—and who won't. This means engaging in candid conversations with each set of parents to determine what they're able to contribute. Or simply plan to pay for the wedding yourselves, and earmark any contributions that come later for honeymoon expenses or for new household needs.

Which Comes First—Wedding or Budget?

So which should come first? The grand wedding plan with all the fun details, or the budget figure that dictates those details? That's really up to you. Obviously, if you have a specific and finite amount of money to apply toward your celebration, your plans will have to adhere to your budget—thus your budget will come first. If you have no idea how much things cost, however, and are willing to beg, borrow, or steal to have exactly the wedding you want, you may want to begin with the grand plan. After all, you can always scale down the less important aspects of the planning if budget constraints become a definite reality.

Time Is on Your Side

When it comes to planning a wedding on a budget, time is by far one of the most important factors. Time can be the most effective resource you have in planning exactly the wedding you want, with the budget that it requires. For example: You've just become engaged. Neither you nor the groom has a great deal of money saved, and your parents aren't contributing to the wedding costs. Should you max out your credit cards in order to have the wedding in six months? Or should you bide your time, saving money each month, and have a longer engagement that allows you to pay your wedding costs up front?

You'd be much better advised to extend your engagement by a year or so, avoiding all those astronomical interest fees you'll get with credit cards, and beginning your marriage debt free. And any money you receive as wedding gifts can go toward a down payment on a home, or toward household items you might still need.

It is a much better idea to save money in advance for wedding costs than to pay high-interest credit card bills later. That may mean planning a slightly longer engagement to save money—but hey, what's few extra months when you'll be spending the rest of your lives together?

Estimating Costs to Determine a Budget

No matter which comes first—the budget or the wedding plan—it's a good idea to have something to use as a starting point. Table 13-1 outlines average U.S. wedding costs for today's weddings. These costs are approximate and will vary according to geographic region.

Table 13-1 Average Costs for a Typical Wedding

Item	Cost
Invitations, thank-you notes, etc.	$375–$450
Flowers	$775–$1,800
Photography/videography	$1,200–$1,500
Music	$750–$1,000
Ceremony fees	$150–$250
Limousine	$300–$425
Attendants' gifts	$300
Wedding Rings	$1,000–$1,800
Engagement Ring	$3,000
Pre-wedding parties	$600
Bridal attire	$1,000
Groom's formal attire	$100
Reception (for 150 to 200 guests)	$5,500–$7,500
Wedding cake	$300
Wedding favors	$250
Decorations	$600
Total	**$16,200–$20,875**

Obviously, you can go much higher or somewhat lower on all these costs, based on many factors including number of guests, wedding date, venue, style of wedding, menu, and choice of vendors. In addition, you can get around many of these costs with some creative savvy, and by thinking outside the box when you plan your wedding. The most important thing to remember is this: There are no rules. Just because your cousin Susie, big sister Jane, and best friend Mary served a ten-course meals does not mean you have to as well. Examine what's really important to you rather than just falling into what's "expected." If you keep an open mind and adopt a creative outlook, you can throw a wonderful wedding that doesn't have to break the bank.

There is no one way to plan your wedding. Embracing your creative side instead of doing what's traditionally dictated will allow you to have a wedding that's equal parts memorable and financially feasible.

Creative from Start to Finish

There are specific ways to cut the cost of your wedding—or to achieve the desired effects on a limited budget. One way to do this is to cut in some areas in order to spend more in others. For example, if you have a fabulous idea for a three-dimensional invitation that you know will cost much more than a traditional flat invitation, you may decide to forgo giving wedding favors or to skip making a wedding program. Or you may cut your guest list in order to serve a three-course seated meal rather than a buffet. Cutting in areas that aren't as important to you is the first commonsense way to achieve your goals on a limited budget.

The second way is to use all your resources. That means calling in favors from Rolls-owning Uncle Leo, cake designer Aunt Flo, and wedding singer Cousin Billy. Ask if you can borrow the Rolls, or if they can swing a price break in place of a wedding gift. Chances are they'll be more than happy to help you out.

Where no rich uncle exists, the following will outline the many ways to creatively circumvent the "typical" ways of throwing a wedding, with tips for being financially savvy in the face of the well-heeled wedding industry.

Invitations

If you're going custom made, see if you can hire a graphic arts student to design your dream invitation. They won't charge as much as a freelance artist or design studio and may even do it for free if it will help fatten their portfolio.

If you don't want a custom-made invitation, the Internet is a great place for bargains on invitations—often you're skipping the middleman, who tacks on additional cost. In addition, skip the engraving for significant savings; invitations will look and feel just as elegant with today's raised printing methods, such as thermography, which are much less expensive.

Also, remember to factor in the cost of postage. Adding an additional stamp or two to each invitation can add to costs, especially if you're sending a large number of invitations. Talk to your stationer about minimizing the final weight of the invitation. Also, consider designing your RSVP card as a postcard to save postage costs as well. Postcards are an efficient and convenient way of tracking responses—no tiny envelopes to open!

Flowers

There's nothing like the look and scent of fresh flowers—but, of course, they can get very expensive, very quickly. If you or a friend or family member has any artistic ability, consider fashioning your own bouquet from flowers you've grown yourself. If you don't trust your ability (or your friend's or family member's), find a florist who'll work with your budget. A couple ways to cut flower costs is to choose less expensive blossoms—forgo the roses for carnations—and choose flowers that are local and in season. Or go with wildflowers or even dried flowers for significant cost cutting.

Certain spaces are naturally decorative. If you choose an outdoor setting such as a park or garden for your ceremony and/or reception, or marry around certain holidays, chances are your space will already be full of beautiful flowers and decorations.

You may also wish to skip costly flower centerpieces in favor of something equally pretty but much less expensive, such as a grouping of pillar candles, large bowls of water with floating candles (or flower petals), fish bowls with goldfish, or anything else that's related to your particular theme. Instead of buying bowls, candleholders, or other centerpiece fixtures from a florist—who will mark up these items significantly—scout out local craft stores and other discount stores for the pieces you're looking for. Also keep in mind that your centerpieces don't have to match—antique or unique bowls, candleholders, or other times in different styles for each table can be a beautiful and creative accent. Pick an item (e.g., bowls, vases, platters to hold pillar candles, etc.) and look for these unique treasures at flea markets, garage sales, or your grandmother's attic. Guests will love to look at the variety of items you've chosen, and you'll have them to keep after the wedding's over.

Photography and Videography

There's no rule that says you have to have a professional photographer and videographer. You will certainly want to capture the day's events, however, for posterity so consider asking a friend or family member with a good camera and a little skill to help out. Complement your collection with photos taken by the guests themselves—include disposable cameras on each table for guests to photograph the proceedings and each other.

If you don't want to take chances with amateurs, hire a photographer but limit his or her hours to cut costs or wait to order the final album and prints until you have the funds to do so after the wedding. Cut video costs by purchasing an unedited package—this will minimize the videographer's time-consuming task of cutting, editing, and adding background music. You won't miss any of the action, and you can always have it edited later when more funds are available.

Sometimes you can get a cheaper deal by booking one company for a photo/video combo rather than hiring a photographer and videographer separately.

Wedding Favors

This is one of the best areas to get creative—and save money—at the same time. There are many favors you can make yourself, such as sachets, bookmarks, boxes of candy or fudge, cookies, pretty refrigerator magnets, sprigs of dried flowers, hand-painted glasses or mugs—the list goes on. Typically, you will spend much less buying the raw materials and making favors yourself than buying a similar item fully finished. This is where time is once again on your side. The more time you have before the wedding takes place, the more opportunity to research favor ideas, scour craft (or other) shops for the best prices, and put them together. Ask your bridesmaids for help and a have a fun favor-making party in the time leading up to the wedding. Bonus: Your guests will love receiving something special and handmade in place of the typical throwaway trinket. (See Chapter 18 for favor ideas you can buy or make yourself.)

Music

A DJ will typically be less expensive than a band, because you are paying for only one person's time rather than five to ten band members' time—or possibly more. If you definitely want live music, keep in mind that the smaller the band, the less expensive their fee—usually. There will obviously be exceptions for more popular, in-demand bands.

ALERT!

When deciding between a band or DJ, keep in mind the size of the space you'll have. If the reception location is on the small side, there may not be room for a ten-member band. A DJ's equipment will take up less space.

You can always negotiate the band's fee as well. If your wedding is the last Saturday in January, you'll have a lot more bargaining power than if it's the last Saturday in June. A band would almost always rather have a gig that pays a little less than the regular fee than no gig at all. If your heart is set on a certain ten-member band, see if they do gigs with fewer members at a lower price—in a confined space, you'll hardly recognize the difference in sound. Also, see if your band can play fewer hours to cut down on the cost. You can play CDs during the dinner hour, for instance, when no one will be dancing anyway.

Transportation

Ask a friend or family member (remember Uncle Leo?) to borrow that vintage car or Lincoln Navigator—then ask your brother-in-law, cousin, or friend to do the driving honors. Or hire a smaller limo or town car that will carry only you, the groom, and your parents, rather than the entire wedding party. You can also opt for a small—but social—customized bus, an often cheaper (and fun) alternative to the traditional—and sometimes uncomfortable—limo.

Research your area for limousine companies and rates. Often, smaller mom-and-pop shops will charge less than the dominant limousine fleet companies in your area, because they have less overhead and fewer advertising costs. Another popular trend is walking. Coordinate your ceremony and reception sites to be within walking distance, so that the entire wedding party, followed by guests, can hoof it to the reception.

Bride's Attire

Once again, time can be an important cost-cutting factor when it comes to shopping for bridal attire. Under pressure, you'll tend to buy the first gown you really love—cost considerations aside—in order to have enough time to order it, get two rounds of alterations, and have it in time for your bridal portrait. However, with some additional time, you'll be able to shop smarter. Like the sense of accomplishment you feel buying those adorable Calvin Klein pants on the cheap at a little-known sample sale, you'll also feel great getting a bargain on what's probably the most expensive item of clothing you'll ever purchase.

The good news is there are plenty of sample sales and clearance events to keep bridal gowns moving off the racks. In order to hit these often-elusive sample sales and clearance events, you need perfect timing—and detective work. Often they're not widely advertised, so keep your eyes and ears open for these events by talking to friends, family members, wedding vendors, and anyone else who might be in the know. These sample sales, store clearance sales, and warehouse outlets will often include at significant savings designer dresses you've drooled over in bridal magazines. Of course, what you see is what you get—you usually can't order special sizes and must purchase your dress off the rack.

Another creative way to save money on your bridal gown is to buy a bridesmaid's dress in white, particularly if you're not set on the traditional, full-length white wedding gown. There are many beautiful bridesmaids' dresses offered now by top bridal gown designers.

If you can't hit these sales or have no discount bridal outlets in your region, you may also consider renting a dress, or even purchasing a pre-owned dress (after all, it's only been worn once). Scan the classifieds for dress ads—there are always a few. Go to nicer consignment shops and talk to the shop owners. Ask them to call you if any bridal gowns come in. Or ask your mother to pull out her wedding dress. If it's not exactly your style or size, have a seamstress or tailor update it to reflect your taste . . . the best of old and new. You may also consider having a seamstress make you a dress from scratch, based on a designer-style dress you've seen in a magazine, or the combination of favorite parts of various dresses—the sleeves from one dress, the bustle from another, the neckline from a third. Often having a dress made will be less expensive than buying a similar dress from a retailer—plus you can get exactly the style and fit you want.

Of course, you can also simply decide to not have a big white dress and to wear something you feel comfortable in—in white, ivory, or any color you choose.

Rehearsal Dinner

Your rehearsal dinner does not have to be a catered affair. In fact, many of your guests will welcome a more casual event, particularly if you are having a more formal event the day of your wedding. Instead of a catered or restaurant event, hold a backyard barbecue or a pizza party—or even a potluck dinner—following your rehearsal. The idea is to have time to spend together, not to bowl everyone over with a formal meal. No backyard? Have the party at a relative's or friend's place.

You are also not required to hold a rehearsal dinner. It is more of a courtesy to those participating in the wedding or who've traveled out of town. So if you just can't swing it financially, or decide you don't have the time or inclination to hold an additional party immediately prior to your wedding, skip the rehearsal dinner. If you're doing many of your wedding elements yourself, such as cooking, bouquet preparation, or other last-minute touches, you may not have the time, anyway.

Reception

Planning a reception during certain times of the year—June, for instance—means you'll pay a premium. That's because so many brides are gunning for the same dates, and the rules of supply and demand definitely apply. Thus, the first way to save on your reception costs is to plan your wedding for a less popular time, such as fall or winter, and for a less popular day of the week, such as Friday. Often reception venues and caterers will charge lower fees for less popular times.

Obviously, the cost of your reception is also directly related to the number of guests you'll invite. You will be charged per head for both food and alcohol for each guest. So another commonsense way to cut costs is by limiting the number of guests, especially if you do not want to skimp on the menu.

If you don't mind compromising on the menu, there are certainly ways to cut costs here as well. Serve a chicken dish instead of steak or seafood; limit the hors d'oeuvres. Skip the butler-passed appetizers and include plates of cheeses and crudités; limit the bar to beer and wine only, or close the bar during the dinner hour (this is especially easy to do if there is wine service during dinner).

FACT

Despite what your caterer may suggest, you don't need more than your wedding cake for dessert. Eliminating dessert can help you save an extra $3 to $5 (or more) per guest.

Even choosing a different time of day for your wedding can affect cost. A brunch or lunch will cost much less than a dinner, and guests will most likely drink less alcohol. A consumption-based bar fee can thus end up being much lower than the cost of a consumption-based or by-the-head evening bar.

Or host a cocktail reception only and skip the full meal completely. You can serve a few hors d'oeuvres as well and still keep costs low.

In addition, when you're scouting around for cost estimates for any wedding service, don't spill the beans immediately that you're planning a wedding. Often vendors charge more for wedding services than they do for other parties—just because they can.

If you're not planning the traditional hall- or restaurant-based reception, there are plenty of ways to cut costs creatively. If you're having a home wedding, for instance, you can supply your own food rather than hire a caterer. Ask family and friends to chip in and help cook some dishes you can serve at the reception. Also, you will cut costs significantly by buying and serving your own alcohol—the bar is where most caterers typically make most of their profits. By buying cases of liquor, beer, and wine on your own, you can save thousands of dollars on the bar bill—and you may even be able to return what wasn't consumed. Work out a deal with your local beverage center for optimum savings.

Use the worksheet in Appendix C to keep track of wedding expenses as you budget for your event. E

Chapter 14

(E) **Special Circumstances**

You have a lot to think about already with the details of planning a wedding. But what if you are pregnant, divorced, or of a different religion than your fiancé? This chapter details how to handle sticky situations with grace and aplomb, and have the wedding you want despite perceived obstacles.

Interfaith Weddings

It's only natural that in our, as some would say, melting pot of a nation, more and more interfaith and intercultural marriages are taking place. Marrying someone of another faith or culture can be stressful well before you reach the wedding day. Not only might you meet with family resistance, you'll also find that many of the traditional ceremonial wedding practices you've grown accustomed to will not fit your particular circumstances. You may have the additional burden of fashioning a ceremony that suits both your faiths, cultures, and families. You can plan your wedding day itself to reflect both your (and your family's) beliefs, as well as your fiancé's, as a symbolic start to the blend and balance you plan to incorporate into your lives together.

Combining Traditions

By creating a ceremony that incorporates the beliefs, practices, and traditions of both of your religions and cultures, you can honor your heritage and families while creating a meaningful ceremony of your own design. In Chapter 9, various ethnic and religious wedding practices are discussed in detail. These chapters are a great place to start, with overviews of wedding traditions and practices of various cultures. As you design your ceremony and reception to reflect both of your heritages, consider the rituals and practices that are meaningful to you. Talk to both sets of parents about their traditions, and listen openly to what they feel is important as well. You may also wish to speak with clergy from each religion to get additional perspectives on your ceremony—as well as some advice and perspective about your future together. Then you can plan a ceremony of your design that reflects the most important elements of your religions and cultures.

Your next step will be to find an officiant who will agree to perform an interfaith ceremony. Some religions are open to this, such as Protestantism, while others are stricter about conditions for performing weddings, such as Catholicism, Islam, and Orthodox Judaism. You may consider asking an officiant to preside from each faith; stick with an officiant from one faith; or pursue a third party, such as an officiant from the Unitarian Church. The Unitarian Church is particularly open to performing weddings of different faiths and may be more open to combining the rituals of two faiths into one ceremony.

If you do decide to combine traditions of two religions into one ceremony, consider explaining certain practices or rituals in the wedding program. That way, all your guests can understand what's going on and feel they are participating in every element of the ceremony.

Another option to consider is holding two separate ceremonies—one for each religion. This will enable you to include all the rituals, traditions, and practices in their entirety. You could hold both on the same day, one after the other, or you could even make a weekend out of your wedding celebration, hosting two ceremonies and two receptions on two separate days. This way you can celebrate each faith or culture without compromising tradition.

The Reception

The wedding reception offers an additional opportunity to combine and celebrate traditions from both your backgrounds, in a format that's a bit looser and more open to interpretation than the ceremony. The most obvious—and welcome—way is with food. Work with a caterer who can create menu items from both your backgrounds; for example, if you're having an Italian/Indian wedding, be sure your caterer can provide delicacies from each culture, from cannoli to curry. If you're combining Jewish and Christian traditions, find a kosher chef to honor religious beliefs (non-Jewish guests won't know the difference).

The most effective way of combining additional traditions—such as traditional dances, toasts, or other symbolic practices—is to pick and choose what is important to you as a couple. For instance, a big part of a Jewish wedding is dancing the hora—a Jewish wedding probably wouldn't be the same without it. Similarly, traditional dances in the Italian, Greek, and Polish cultures would be missed as well. Combining the dances of two cultures can only add to the excitement and enjoyment of your guests.

An interfaith wedding and reception provide an exciting opportunity to fashion your own day based on the rituals that hold the most symbolism and importance to you as a couple. It's also a wonderful way to introduce your guests to a new culture, and to create a completely original celebration no one will soon forget.

If there are traditions or practices you're not so keen on, this is your chance to eliminate them. For example, some brides have eliminated the bouquet toss as an antiquated and uncomfortable tradition, particularly for solo or still-single female guests. The point? You don't need to include a tradition just because it's always been there. Examine each ritual and tradition carefully for its meaning and symbolism before including it in your wedding. This is a built-in process for an interfaith wedding, for which you will most likely combine the best and most important elements of each of your backgrounds.

Of course, like the ceremony, you may also have two separate receptions to honor both your backgrounds in full. Again, a great way to include all your guests for both celebrations is to have the parties on consecutive days, such as during a full weekend celebration. You may find it to be the best—and, in some respects, simplest—way to honor both families and sets of traditions.

Second Weddings

Over the past twenty years or so, second weddings have changed a great deal in nature, having progressed from small, intimate, or somewhat quiet affairs to full-blown extravaganzas that mimic first weddings. Possibly this is because 43 percent of marriages in this country each year are second marriages for one partner or both. Like an interfaith wedding, when planning a second wedding, you are bound to come up against many opinions—from the supportive to downright hostile—so be prepared for potential criticism. However, handled the right way (by taking children's feelings into consideration, for instance), your second wedding can be as beautiful as a first wedding.

Children and Stepfamilies

When children are involved in a second marriage, the wedding is not simply the joining of husband and wife—it is the joining of families.

If either of you has children, you may consider involving them at the marriage proposal stage. In other words, if the man is proposing, he might propose to both the woman and her children at the same time. This will help children feel included and secure during a time of big changes.

It's recommended that the marrying couple involve children as much as possible in the planning and wedding day activities. This means telling them about your plans to wed before you tell anyone else (if they haven't already been a part of the proposal, that is), and incorporating their involvement in a meaningful way. For instance, a mother might include her daughter in making decisions about flowers, menu, photography, or music; a father may take his son on a shopping trip for an engagement ring.

On the wedding day itself, children can be involved in many ways. They are often included in the ceremony and during the exchange of vows. For instance, instead of just husband and wife saying "I do," children can also have their vows and words of commitment to the new family. Talk to your officiant for recommendations about how to include children in your ceremony. At the reception, be sure children sit with you for the meal and are involved in special toasts, dances, the cake cutting, and other traditions. It's also a good idea to assign each child an adult "buddy," so that when they can't have your attention they'll have someone to go to, such as a favorite aunt, a grandparent, or a cousin.

QUESTION?

Is taking a honeymoon appropriate for a second wedding?
Yes, post-wedding rest and relaxation is a good idea for any wedding. If either of you has children, though, it's probably wise to take them along and make this more of a new family vacation and celebration rather than a traditional honeymoon.

If you are divorced and share custody of children, a final strategy is to be sure your ex knows your plans to marry in advance as well. This respectfully includes your ex in a decision that will ultimately affect the lives of your children, and him/her by extension.

Second-Wedding Etiquette

A second wedding can take many forms. It may be the first wedding for one partner, but the second for the other; it may be a second wedding for both partners. Obviously, if it is a first wedding for one half of the couple—particularly the bride—there may be more pressure to throw an elaborate wedding with all the traditional trappings. Fortunately, it is less and less unusual to see a "second" wedding that is as large or involved as a "first" wedding, so planning a large wedding is no longer taboo. However, you should keep in mind a few basic points of etiquette that will help you through any sticky social situations without a hitch:

- **Don't invite your ex-spouse(s)**. No matter how well you get along, this can be very confusing to you, your guests, and your children.
- **Contrary to popular belief, you can wear white.** And you can wear a traditional wedding gown. However, you should probably avoid very elaborate attire, such as a blusher veil or long train. But the days of wearing a dressy suit only for a second wedding are definitely past.
- **Formal etiquette says you can register for gifts.** However, if your first wedding has taken place in the not-so-distant past, if it ended in a quick divorce, or if you have all the household items you can handle, consider skipping the registry. In fact, you may wish to specify "no gifts" entirely or indicate a charity to donate to in lieu of gifts.
- **It is also acceptable to have an engagement party or bridal shower.**

Again, use your judgment here. A bridal shower is much more appropriate if this is a first marriage for you (and a second for your groom), though obviously circumstances for each couple differ. It is also okay to decline the offers of friends and family to throw you a shower if you do not feel comfortable with it.

Creative Ideas

There are many ways to use your creativity to host a celebration that has special meaning specific to a second marriage. For your ceremony—either religious or secular—you may want to examine the readings, vows, and other spoken elements to discern whether you feel they are appropriate or a comfortable part of your ceremony. For instance, one divorced bride eliminated the "til death do us part" line in deference to the reality of her past; another bride didn't feel it was appropriate for her father to walk her down the aisle. One couple had a religious wedding—but at an entirely different setting than the groom's first—to avoid any comparisons to wedding number one. In fact, it's best to avoid duplicating any of the details of either of your first weddings, as this is a new union with new—and different—cause for celebration.

The size and style of your second wedding is not predetermined by etiquette. Big or small, casual or formal—do what feels comfortable for you as a couple and as a family.

The size of your wedding is up to you. If it makes you more comfortable, you may choose to have a small, intimate ceremony followed by a larger reception. Or you may want to go all out with the ceremony and reception, mirroring the traditional "first wedding." Of course, to create a wholly original and fun celebration—and possibly even deflect the focus that this is a "second" wedding—you may also decide to throw a theme wedding (see Chapters 6 through 11 for specific ideas). Or you may wish to keep this wedding smaller and more intimate for both ceremony and reception. The point is, do what feels comfortable for you as a couple, and try not to worry about your critics. There's always bound to be someone who doesn't agree with you, whether it's your first wedding or your third.

Include whatever traditions are important to you, such as first dances, tossing the bouquet, toasts, cutting the cake—or eliminate them if they do not feel right to you. Part of being creative is examining the meaning behind tradition and then tailoring that tradition to fit your beliefs and lifestyle. So feel free to create your own, new traditions if they make sense to you.

If you or your fiancé have children, there are many ways to involve them and make this into a family celebration. During the ceremony, they may stand at the altar with you and even be part of the vow exchange—write your vows as a family to reflect your true feelings. Or if children feel uncomfortable speaking, they can be included as junior bridesmaids or groomsmen, or as flower girls or ring bearers. You can also involve them in other elements of your ceremony, such as the exchanging of rings, or the lighting of the unity candle, or by doing a reading.

What to Expect When We're Expecting

There's an old wives' tale that states that every wedding upsets somebody, and this may be especially true for a wedding in which the couple is expecting. But between planning a wedding and planning for the baby, you'll have little time—or inclination—left to worry about other peoples' opinions. And with a little organization and planning, you can still throw a great wedding that celebrates your love, no matter what anyone says.

It's All about Timing

If you're pregnant and plan to marry, the first issue you'll want to consider is timing. You may decide that having your wedding as quickly as possible—before you're showing—is the best route to go. The advantages of marrying sooner rather than later are that you'll be able to wear a standard-fitting wedding dress, if that is your wish, and your guests may not even know you are pregnant.

You may decide that you'd like enough time to plan the wedding you want, however, which will probably mean getting married in the later months of your pregnancy, or waiting until the baby is born to get married. The advantages of getting married before the baby is born are that your child will be born to parents that are already married, if that is important to you, and that you can plan and celebrate your wedding day before the intense demands of caring for an infant take over. Of course, you can always hold a quiet civil ceremony now and have a religious ceremony and reception later . . . do whatever makes you comfortable. Keep in mind you may not be feeling in optimum physical condition during pregnancy, which may encourage you to wait until after the baby is born as well.

The Dress

If you do decide to marry during your pregnancy (or you get pregnant while you're engaged), rest assured that the white dress and veil are no longer symbolic of virginity. You are free to choose attire ranging from a traditional white wedding dress to a conservative suit—or anything in between. If you do choose a traditional wedding dress, there are certain styles you should gravitate to for reasons both aesthetic and practical. In order to best flatter your shape, choose an A-line (not body hugging) style or an empire waist (where the "waistline" falls from directly beneath the breast line). Depending on how far along you are, a pregnancy may be barely noticeable with these styles. And they serve a practical purpose as well, giving you more room and material to work with in the event that you should become bigger than you anticipated by your wedding day (which will be a relief to your tailor or seamstress). These styles will also be much more comfortable to wear than a dress with a defined or fitted waistline.

The Wedding

There are those who would unequivocally say that a small, quiet ceremony and reception is best for the pregnant couple (or new parents); however, you should do what you feel comfortable with. If a large wedding has always been your dream, and you wish to celebrate your union with your family and friends, there's no reason to give it up, except perhaps finances. That $10,000 to $20,000 you would spend on a wedding weighed against the costs of your new baby's needs could add another perspective. However, if you aren't on a tight budget, go ahead and plan the wedding you want. Wear white if you wish. Dance all night. Honor all the traditions, or create your own. If you are marrying after the birth of your baby, or will follow a civil ceremony with a more public religious ceremony after the birth, consider involving your child in the ceremony as part of your symbolic commitment as a family.

Same-Sex Ceremonies

There are so many good reasons to have a same-sex ceremony that it's no wonder they seem to be growing in popularity. Though gay and lesbian unions are still not legally recognized (except in the state of Vermont), more and more couples are choosing to celebrate their love and commitment with friends and family, with a symbolic ceremony and reception that mirrors a traditional wedding.

No matter who's getting married—same sex or opposite sex—the reception is an opportunity to let loose and celebrate your commitment with family and friends. There's nothing particularly different about a reception for a same-sex wedding. Choose the type of party you'd like and incorporate the ideas from the rest of this book to create a reception you'll love.

Because there is little precedent for them and no legal requirements, same-sex ceremonies may be the ultimate in creative celebrations. They are wide open for interpretation and personalization. Some couples use the framework from traditional weddings; others create a ceremony from the ground up. No matter how the ceremony is ultimately planned, though, it is an opportunity to create a symbolic and meaningful ritual that everyone involved—the couple, friends, and family—can honor together.

Why a Commitment Ceremony?

Even though same-sex marriages are not currently recognized legally, there are many other reasons to have a commitment ceremony. The first is to publicly declare one's life-long love and commitment to a partner, involving friends and family as witnesses to that love. A commitment ceremony can be that next symbolic step in a relationship—formalizing it and creating a more serious, committed platform for the couple, and creating a more solid, recognized union among friends and family. This formal request for recognition can be a powerful reason for having a ceremony.

If you're not crazy about the labels "wedding" or "commitment ceremony," there is other popular terminology you can adopt. Create your own label, or consider some of these: Affirmation Ceremony, Bonding Ceremony, Holy Union, Lifetime Commitment, Union Ceremony, Lifelong Commitment Vows, or Relationship Blessing.

These ceremony elements may follow the structure of a traditional wedding, with a greeting by the officiant, readings, the declaration of vows, the exchange of rings, and the pronouncement of marriage—sealed with a kiss. When designing your ceremony, it's a good idea to examine what each of these steps means to you, and to then tailor them to your personalities, your relationship, and your values. For instance, you can handpick readings that are meaningful to you—from traditional religious or bible passages, poetry, and passages from favorite books, plays, or movies to self-written musings. Or you can invite some or all of your guests to participate with readings that they select themselves—it might be a favorite story, joke, book passage, quote (famous or otherwise), speech, religious reading—anything they like that has special meaning for your day (it will lend an element of surprise and spontaneity to your ceremony as well). This is a wonderful way to include friends and family in your ceremony in a meaningful and symbolic way.

The remaining elements of the wedding ceremony can follow suit, with your own personal slant on the proceedings. Write your own vows or adapt them from traditional vows; create your own ring ceremony—with a ring, another piece of jewelry, or another symbol that represents your commitment to one another; include your favorite songs, religious or secular; and include any other special touches, such as a marriage contract, to seal your commitment ceremony. Many gay couples will create their own symbolic contract or wedding certificate—or commission one from an artist or friend—that they and their witnesses (or all their guests) can sign at the ceremony as another symbol of their commitment to one another. This contract—like the Jewish ketubah—can then be displayed in the home.

Because your ceremony is not intended to legalize your marriage, you may chose any officiant you like to run the proceedings—a friend, family member, judge or justice of the peace, or a religious figure, such as a minister or rabbi. In some religions (Reform Jewish, some Protestant), the decision to honor same-sex marriages is up to the clergy member—there is no overriding organizational policy that supports or denies them. So, talk to specific clergy members to determine if they are willing to participate. If your place of worship will not honor your commitment ceremony, there are those that will. Consult with your local Unitarian Universalist or Universal Life Churches, who support same-sex unions.

If you do decide to have a secular proceeding instead of a religious ceremony, many of your creative ideas may be easier to implement. You won't have your church's or temple's religious constraints on chosen readings, songs, or vows—or any other elements you may bring to the ceremony.

A Rose by Any Other Name

There's no real precedent for invitation wording for same-sex unions, so again, you can use your creativity to fashion a statement that has meaning to you as a couple. Some couples have been known to write a full letter to friends and family explaining the reasons why they've decided to have a commitment ceremony; other couples simply send a more traditional invitation with their own personal message. You may find for simplicity's sake that you'd like to mirror the wording of a traditional wedding invitation, which might begin as such: "The honor of your presence is requested at the commitment ceremony of xxx and xxx" or "Together with their families and friends, xxx and xxx request the honor of your presence at their commitment ceremony."

Legal Considerations

Beyond your symbolic union and public statement to family and friends, there are additional issues to consider when making a lifelong commitment to your partner. Because gay couples are not legally recognized as a married unit, per se, they are not protected by federal law the same way heterosexual couples are. There are, however, some legal steps you can take in order to protect yourselves.

With regard to a civil union ceremony, currently the only state to perform same-sex civil unions is Vermont. Unfortunately, your legal rights as a "married" couple are only protected if you reside there. However, it can't hurt to have a legally recognized union in the event that your state—or the federal government—eventually recognizes same-sex partnerships as well.

More importantly, for issues relevant to both health and finance, you should meet with a lawyer to draw up a will and a power of attorney for both you and your partner. Unlike a heterosexual married couple, whose assets automatically go to the spouse in the event of a death, gay couples have no such protections. A will can ensure your lifelong savings or joint assets are rightly assigned.

FACT

It is perfectly acceptable to register for gifts and plan a honeymoon as part of your celebration.

Power of attorney will ensure legal rights in emergency situations, such as those involving health or incapacitation. Documented power of attorney will grant you or your partner hospital visitation rights, decision-making rights for emergency medical care, probate rights, shared property rights, and asset agreement rights.

Like any committed couple, it's important to have your practical affairs in order as you begin your lives together as lifelong partners.

Other Issues

It comes as no surprise that there will be some who will not support the idea of a same-sex wedding, so you'll need to be prepared for this. If your parents or certain family members have not been supportive in the past, you may decide to celebrate this special day with only those who are supportive; talk, if you can, with your family in advance to determine their comfort level, and then decide whether you'd like to include them or not. It's possible that your commitment ceremony will help cement your relationship in the eyes of family or friends, thus creating more acceptance or understanding in the long run.

Again, this is your day. You can fashion it, mold it, and create it to be anything you'd like, without formal precedent or tradition to hold you back. Have fun, and congratulations!

Chapter 15

Creative Ceremonies

The heart of the wedding is, of course, the ceremony itself. It's what makes a wedding a wedding, and not just a lavish party. And it offers many options for infusing creativity into your wedding to make it unique and unforgettable.

Parting with Tradition

We've all been there countless times—the traditional church, temple, or secular wedding ceremony, listening to the same readings, songs, and vows. These places and pieces are classic, traditional, and ritualistic for a reason—the importance of the event dictates a certain gravity that these pre-chosen readings, vows, and songs all demonstrate. The classics also provide a sense of tradition and continuity from generation to generation.

However, these rituals may not be right for every couple. You may decide a religious setting or officiant does not feel right, that the popular readings and songs don't quite capture your interpretation of this day, or that the classic wedding vows may not express exactly how you feel.

Distinctive Sites

There's no rule that says you have to get married in a traditional place of worship—even if you plan to have a religious wedding. And while some clergy may frown upon a "location" ceremony (and some may refuse to perform it anywhere but in a religious setting), other clergy will be more than willing to perform your ceremony where you want it.

Of course, if you are not having a religious ceremony, your ceremony location is much more flexible. If you're choosing a particularly unusual location (say, underwater), your choice of officiants who are willing to participate may still be quite limited; however, if your ceremony will take place in a park or on a hillside, chances are you'll have no trouble finding a willing officiant.

When choosing a ceremony site, first examine your shared history as a couple and mutual interests for inspiration. You may already have a dream location in mind—a place that is special and personal to you and your groom. This may be the place you first met, the place you first said "I love you," or the place he (or you) proposed. It may also be a place that your interests dictate—a golf course, a ski mountain, an art gallery. By personalizing your ceremony location, you will feel comfortable—and correct—exchanging your all-important vows and expressing your lifelong commitment to one another.

ALERT!

For most ceremony sites, you will need to get permission in advance—and may even have to pay a fee. Be sure to secure permission before planning your entire wedding around this specific location.

If there's no place that immediately comes to mind, you may simply wish to hold your ceremony in a location that is particularly spiritual, beautiful, or reflective of your values. The possibilities are endless.

Wide-Open Spaces

An outdoor wedding can be incredibly spiritual, and particularly appropriate if the two of you spend a lot of time enjoying the outdoors. Whether it's land or water that appeals to you, there are plenty of sites to choose from. You probably won't be able to simply set up shop in most public, outdoor areas, so remember you'll need to contact the parks commissioner, private owner, or other relevant authority to get permission or a permit to marry there. Here are some possibilities:

- In a beautiful, private clearing in the woods
- Beside a mountain or hill
- At a private or public garden, perfectly timed so that flowers are in full bloom
- On the beach
- On a cliffside, overlooking the water or a green valley
- In the desert
- On a boat or yacht
- On an island—ferry (or row) over all your guests in private boats
- Near a beautiful man-made lake or quarry
- Beside a waterfall
- On a footbridge, crossing a stream
- In a gazebo
- In an orange grove (orange blossoms are a symbol of purity and virginity)
- At the zoo, near your favorite outdoor exhibit
- In a nature reserve
- On a farm

- On the grounds of an estate
- In a vineyard
- In a Japanese garden
- In a city garden
- On a rooftop
- On a hiking trail
- On a golf course
- On a football field
- On a tennis court
- At a theme park
- On your college campus
- At a marina or yacht club
- On a military base
- On (or near) a volcano
- On an ice-skating rink
- In a pumpkin patch
- At a country fairgrounds
- On an observation deck
- On a movie studio lot
- In a hot air balloon
- In your backyard

Indoor Splendor

There are also many beautifully designed—and creative—choices for indoor ceremonies that often go beyond your standard banquet facility or restaurant. Choose a location that reflects your personal interests. Or simply choose one that's beautiful and inspiring. These may include the following:

- At an art gallery
- In a museum (small or large, famous or obscure)
- In a particularly beautiful or historic lobby
- In an old hotel
- In an aquarium
- In an auditorium or theater space
- In a nationally preserved historic building
- In an old or restored public mansion

- In a famous hotel or restaurant (The Rainbow Room, Tavern on the Green)
- In a friend's or family member's beautiful home or estate
- In a castle
- At a hacienda
- In a nightclub
- In a library
- In an old saloon
- In a bowling alley
- In a spa
- In a classic Victorian home
- On a train
- In a casino
- On a cruise ship
- In an airplane
- In a blimp
- In a municipal building such as a beautiful old town hall
- In your college chapel
- In a planetarium
- In an airplane hangar
- At the zoo (indoor exhibits)
- In a gym
- In a boxing ring
- On a basketball court
- In a greenhouse
- In a sports arena
- In a cave

Whether you're indoors or outdoors, a candlelit ceremony can create a serene and beautiful atmosphere. Give each guest a candle to hold during the ceremony, and consider replacing bridesmaids' bouquets with special, decorated candles. Have a friend or family member participate by lighting guests' candles. Don't forget the drip shields!

Extreme Locations

There are also some specific sites that may not be right in your back-yard—but may be worth the drive (or flight). Some of these locations will probably not allow for weddings directly on site; you will need to contact the appropriate authority for permission. You can always compromise and get creative; however, maybe your ceremony is in a location's sightline, rather than directly on or in it. Here are some suggestions:

- Niagara Falls
- The Grand Canyon
- The southernmost tip of Key West
- The northernmost point in Alaska
- The Empire State Building
- The Statue of Liberty
- Plymouth Rock
- The mall in Washington, D.C.
- The bayou
- Old Faithful (in Yellowstone Park)
- The Cliffs of Dover
- Stonehenge
- Canada's Ice Hotel
- The Ruins of Pompeii
- The Pyramids of Egypt
- The Bermuda Triangle (be careful!)
- Mt. Fuji
- Mt. Everest
- The Great Barrier Reef
- The Panama Canal
- Mayan Ruins

Practical Magic

It's easy to become overwhelmed by the idea of a particular site because of its beauty or the statement it makes. You should still, however, consider some practical issues before committing to a site. The first is size. If you're inviting four hundred guests, be sure there is enough room to set up appropriate seating, an "aisle" for the bride to walk down, and ample area for the bride, groom, and officiant—or more, as with a Jewish ceremony that includes a chuppah and the parents of the marrying couple. If your heart is absolutely set on a ceremony site that will only accommodate a small number of guests, you may decide to keep your ceremony small and intimate, then invite more guests to the reception.

The second item to consider is privacy. You may love the idea of marrying amid the historical grandeur of Grand Central Station, but there are two things you won't have—quiet and privacy. Even less extreme examples—such as a public park, a botanical garden, or a restaurant—may not offer you the privacy you desire for your wedding ceremony. Keep in mind that you will not be able to control onlookers and curiosity seekers if you choose a public forum for your ceremony.

A final item to consider is light and sound. If your location is dark or dim, be sure to arrange for appropriate lighting, whether it's candlelight or floodlights. Also, if there is a loud din that will compete with your ceremony (waterfall, planes overhead, foot traffic), consider using small microphones so that your guests can hear and better witness your ceremony.

Music That Moves You

There are many classic music selections to choose from for every musical portion of your ceremony—favorites you've probably heard at the weddings you've attended in the past. Selections like Bach's "Jesu, Joy of Man's Desiring," Mozart's "The Wedding March," Pachelbel's "Canon in D," and Beethoven's "Ode to Joy" are popular standards used during various phases of your ceremony. These musical phases include the following:

The prelude—the time when guests enter, are seated, and eagerly await your journey down the aisle

The processional—during which you walk down the aisle

Interludes—such as the time you light your unity candle, exchange rings, or break the glass

The recessional—during which you dramatically make your exit as husband and wife

The standard classics are popular for a reason—they are beautifully composed, appropriate for the different phases of your wedding, and full of grand tradition. However, you may choose to do something more personal and/or more contemporary for your own ceremony.

Making a Statement

The music you choose for your wedding makes as much of a statement as your chosen readings and vows, and there are a number of ways to creatively include music in your ceremony. The first is to play the traditional classics—reinterpreted. For instance, instead of the standard organist or string quartet playing the classic wedding songs, hire a different type of instrumentalist to reinterpret them. These may include percussionists, a jazz combo, a xylophone player, a harmonica player, a bagpiper, or even a hip hop-inspired group. In other words, adopt the style of music that suits your lifestyle, background, culture, or attitude—a string quartet is not for everyone.

You may also choose to include artists who play different songs in their own style, such as a folk singer/guitar player, an a cappella singer, a jazz quartet, a blues band, a country or bluegrass band, a rap artist, a Motown band, or a New Orleans–style band. Or include soloists on the flute, harp, harpsichord, drums, mandolin, trumpet, piano, or any instrument that reflects your personal taste and vision for your ceremony.

FACT

If either or both of you are musicians or vocalists, personalize your ceremony by performing a song or two yourselves. Write a song to your fiancé as a wedding gift, and unveil it at the ceremony. Or perform an existing favorite. Your guests will really enjoy the personal touch.

Of course, music does not have to be performed live. You may also include recorded music. While most often adopted for ceremony interludes, recorded music—particularly contemporary recorded music—can be a creative and welcome addition to any portion of your ceremony. If contemporary favorites are more your style than the classics, choose songs that have romance *and* resonance. These may include Broadway show tunes, movie soundtrack singles, or even movie soundtrack scores—that background instrumental music that can be so evocative and memorable. Or pick appropriate songs from your favorite artists. Here are some particularly romantic artists with great discographies to choose from:

James Taylor	David Grey
Marc Cohn	Barbra Streisand
Sarah McLachlan	Luther Vandross
Aimee Mann	Simon and Garfunkel
Dave Matthews	

The Wedding Program

Many brides and grooms believe that the wedding program is strictly limited to the list of ceremony readings and songs, the list of bridesmaids and groomsmen, and a thank you to your guests for attending. However, this is simply not the case. While it's great to outline everything that will happen in the ceremony, the wedding program is an underutilized way to communicate with your guests about any number of topics.

For instance, instead of simply listing the names of your wedding party, why not also include a short, pithy, or funny description of each of individual? Your guests will feel as if they better know the people in your wedding party, and it's also a great and unusual way to honor your bridesmaids and groomsmen.

You may also include the story of how you and the groom met, when you first knew you were in love, or any other personal story that will make the proceedings feel even richer with meaning. Or you may include a favorite poem, passage, or quote that you feel reflects the meaning of the day; the lyrics of a favorite song; or a note or passage you've written yourselves to commemorate the day. It's not always easy to speak to every guest at your wedding. Your wedding program is a great opportunity to communicate your personal feelings on the proceedings, or to help your guests better understand the two of you as a couple.

If you are having an interfaith wedding or are including rituals or traditions that may be unfamiliar to your guests, the ceremony program is also a great medium to communicate the meaning of various ceremony practices. Include as much detail as you like—your guests will feel more involved and included and will take away a new experience and understanding of your culture or religion.

Writing Your Own Vows

Writing your own vows is another very meaningful way to personalize your ceremony. There are many ways to include self-written vows in your ceremony—from adapting the standard vows, writing vows from scratch, and writing them together as bride and groom to surprising each other with heartfelt words on your wedding day.

You may also consider giving your program a different creative twist, such as designing it to look like a theater playbook, a sports program, a CD jacket, a TV guide—then tailor the text to fit the format.

Some religions are quite strict about what they will and won't permit during the exchange of vows. Before you invest too much time writing vows, be sure to know and understand your religion's rules on this issue. Also, your officiant may be a source of help and inspiration for self-written vows. Talk to him or her for additional ideas and advice about what works best. He or she may also help you to examine your feelings on marriage and for one another, providing additional inspiration for the content of your vows.

In general, your vows should be a declaration of why you've chosen to spend your life together, how you plan to honor your spouse, and what you believe about your future together.

First Things First

Like writing a term paper, letter, or business report, it's difficult if not impossible to begin writing until you know exactly what you want to say. As with any writing assignment, it's necessary to do the proper research first. Luckily your research for this project won't entail hours at the library or searching vainly online; however, it will demand a bit of self-reflection and honesty. The best way to do this is to ask yourself a few questions. For best results, write down the answers to these questions on a separate sheet of paper. You can then pinpoint common threads, or at least have some solid notes when you do begin to actually write:

- Where did the two of you meet?
- How did you know the other was "the one"?
- How did he (or she) propose?
- When did you first realize you were in love?
- What are some of your favorite times together?
- How do you make each other feel happy and fulfilled?
- Were there any obstacles to your relationship that you overcame together?
- How long have you been together as a couple?
- What is the meaning, to you, of marriage? Of commitment? Of trust? Of honesty?
- How do you feel about lifelong commitment?
- How does the idea of having a life partner make you feel?
- How do you feel about sharing your lives with children?
- What will life be like growing old together?
- What will life be like facing challenges together?
- Do you share a common religious bond?

- Have religious or cultural differences enhanced your relationship?
- Are there any other common bonds or interests that have brought you together?
- What do you respect about each other? Love about each other? Admire in each other? Envy in each other?
- What about each other makes you laugh?
- How does he/she make your life complete?

Once you have determined the answers to most or all of these questions, you'll probably find there's a great deal to draw from as you begin thinking more seriously about your vows.

Getting Down to Business

You may decide that writing your vows is strictly an exercise for two—whereby you write your vows together. Or you may enjoy the element of surprise, writing your vows separately to be spoken first on your wedding day. Either way, the questions in the previous section will help you determine what is important to communicate during this exchange. And though you can certainly write your vows freestyle—in the form of a short story, anecdote, poem, or whatever form appeals to you—you may wish to stick to a more structured formula to keep things simple. Vows can be as short or long as you like, but remember, it's you that'll be under the hot lights. Short and sweet is often preferable to long and winded—for both you and your guests.

An easy and common structure that follows the course of traditional vows goes as follows:

Begin with the starter:
"I, John Doe, take you, Jane Smith, as my _____."

Continue with the explanation:
"Being in love with you means_____."
　　or
"You have always made me feel like _____."

Finish with the pledge:

"In good times and bad I will always _____."

or

"I hereby promise to _____."

By following this fairly simple structure, you'll find it easy to begin crafting your message. Feel free to deviate, of course; this is simply meant to provide a starting point for your writing efforts.

You may also wish to write vows that simply require an "I do" as a response. If you feel shy about speaking at your ceremony for any length of time, this can enable you to still put your personal imprint on vows without the added pressure of speaking them aloud. Write your vows in traditional style: "Jane, do you take John as your _____? Do you promise to_____ etc., etc.?" Fill in the blanks with your interpretation of love, marriage, and commitment based on your own personal relationship.

Helpful Tips

There are some helpful tips to keep in mind as you begin writing your vows. Remember that as intimate and celebratory as this day is, your vows are also a public declaration for all to hear. Try not to embarrass your witnesses, officiant, or guests with overly intimate details that should be left between the two of you. That doesn't mean you shouldn't be sincere and personal, however—find the balance between the two and you'll be fine. If you're not sure, ask a trusted friend or family member to hear them beforehand and to offer an honest opinion.

The second thing to remember is to be natural. Don't write your vows according to what you think they should sound like—make them sound like you. That means you don't need to use overly flowery or official sounding language. While remaining somewhat formal (no impromptu vows filled with pauses, "umms," "likes," or "you know what I means"), you can also be natural and conversational in the style and tone your normally speak in. Sincerity is the key to writing vows you'll feel comfortable with and that have deep meaning.

On that note, shorter is usually better than longer. You'll be better off skipping the ten-minute monologue (or saving elements of it for your reception speech) in favor of short and meaningful vows. Otherwise, in addition to boring your guests, you'll also become aware of how long ten minutes really is when you're speaking in public.

Don't rely on memory alone to recite your vows. There are a couple of ways to combat the issue of memorizing them. Write them beforehand on index cards or a sheet of paper. Ask your best man or maid of honor to hold onto these "cheat sheets" until the appropriate moment. Or when you write your vows, structure them so that they are first spoken by your officiant, then repeated by you—as with traditional vows.

Finally, when you do speak your vows, be sure to speak slowly and clearly. If it's important to you that all your guests hear your vows, and you are marrying in an acoustically challenged venue, consider wearing mini microphones, or using the officiant's microphone when it's your turn to speak. This way all your guests can be sure to hear what's going on, and no one will miss all the hard work and thought you've put into creating these special vows.

Give your vows to each other as a wedding gift. Ask a calligrapher or artist to render them on a piece of paper or canvas, then frame it and hang in your home as a reminder of your love and commitment for one another.

Sample Vows

The following are some sample vows that follow the simple structure just outlined. They are meant to function as examples only—infuse your own personal story and details to individualize them. As you'll notice, some examples also include snippets of traditional vows, illustrating how you can weave the traditional and personal together to create statements that are powerful, meaningful, and memorable.

Example 1:

I, Jane Smith, take you, John Doe, to be my husband, my best friend, and my soul mate. Together we have already taken the world by storm through our travels, unforgettable times with family and friends, and support for each other's careers. Now I pledge to take the next step with you, where we will truly be united as one, sharing our entire futures together, and building a family of our own. John, your kindness, generosity, and thoughtfulness are what made me fall in love with you in the first place—now I look forward to enjoying all these wonderful traits as I continue loving you for the rest of our lives together.

Example 2:

Jane, commitment can be an intimidating thing. But when it's made to someone like you, nothing could feel more natural or meant to be. Through my parents, I've had a wonderful living example of what it means to be committed, and I pledge to do the same for you—through sickness, health, fun, sorrow, joy, and pain. You mean the world to me, and I promise to always honor you—body, spirit, and soul—as long as we both shall live.

Example 3:

I, John, take you, Jane, to be my lifelong partner in everything we do. We've been through so much together already, ranging from incredible joy to great sorrow, that I know we can get through whatever else life presents us along the way. Since the day I met you in high school study hall, I've dreamed about you, respected you, laughed with you, and loved you. Finally, today, my ultimate dream has come true—marrying you.

Example 4:

I, Jane, take you, John, to be my husband. Since I've met you, you've changed my life in so many beautiful ways. You've become the balm for my loneliness, the laugh track for my bad jokes, the support system for my dreams and aspirations, the cheerleader for my accomplishments, and the best friend to share all my life's experiences. From a simple walk in the neighborhood to a trip around the world, there's no better companion for me on life's journey than you. I will love you and honor you all the days of my life.

After the Ceremony

Besides the now-taboo thrown rice (it's been known to kill birds when they eat it off the ground), there are many ways to make a dramatic and memorable exit from your ceremony. Before deciding on any of these, however, check with authorities at your ceremony site to determine what's permitted. There are often strict rules about throwing certain items, based on clean-up and other issues.

Once you're aware of the rules, consider some of these options:

- Give guests jingle bells to ring as you and your groom exit. Tie them with ribbon and attach a little note with your names, the date, and any quote or poem that you find appropriate. This can be a particularly nice exit during the holiday months.
- Give guests kazoos or harmonicas to play as you exit. Personalize them with your name and the date imprinted on them.
- Release a flock of white doves as you exit, or as you are pronounced husband and wife. Doves symbolize love, peace, and faithfulness. (Typically, the doves used are actually homing pigeons, which are trained to find their way home after being released.)
- You may also try this idea with butterflies. Give each guest his/her own butterfly to release after the ceremony.
- Have guests blow bubbles as the couple exits the ceremony. Give each guest their own little bottle of bubbles—have your names and the date transcribed on them. Bonus: Airborne bubbles look very cool captured in black-and-white photos.
- You may also substitute bird seed for the traditional rice or confetti—your site may approve this over other items as it'll probably disappear from the ground minutes after you do! Ⓔ

Chapter 16

You've Got the Look

When you look good, you feel good. That's seldom truer than on your wedding day. And when you're surrounded by beautiful things, how can you not feel good? This chapter gives you lots of ideas for creative touches in your attire, your décor, and your flowers that will set your wedding apart from all the others.

Buck the Trends

Despite the seeming evidence to the contrary, you can express your individuality through attire, flowers, location, and decorations. You don't have to go with cookie-cutter dresses, banquet halls, and bouquets. The key to expressing your own style is to first think hard about what is important to you—then go from there to fashion all the details.

Though they certainly can be, these style decisions don't need to be extreme. What these decisions can do, however, is buck the $10 billion-a-year wedding industry, which often dictates what you should and shouldn't do in order to promote its own interests. By examining each element of your wedding and how it can reflect your own personality and needs, you can create a unique ceremony and reception that allows you to feel comfortable and, most importantly, have fun.

From Glad Rags to Sunday Best

The first image that comes to mind when one thinks of wedding attire is, of course, the big white dress. And while many women have dreamed of wearing this Cinderella-fantasy dress their entire lives, for others the image of themselves surrounded by white satin and tulle doesn't quite fit.

FACT

Angelina Jolie wore a "tuxeda," or a woman's styled-and-fitted tuxedo, at the 2001 Academy Awards—comfortable and sexy. You might try this look if you aren't the dress-wearing type.

The good news is that there are alternatives to the classic wedding gown. If you are adopting a theme for your wedding, these alternatives are obvious—a medieval style for a Renaissance wedding, cowboy boots and a hat for a Western wedding, retro-1970s style for a disco wedding. Even if you're not having a theme, feel free to wear something besides the big white dress. There's no reason to feel uncomfortable and awkward just because of others' expectations on your wedding day.

Express Yourself

So you've decided that the white ball gown isn't your thing. What is, then? It's almost impossible to go into detail here about what you should wear on your wedding day—every woman has her own style of dressing. However, here are some factors you can think about that will help you on your way to fashioning an outfit that's comfortable, special, and reflective of your personality:

- **What is your day-to-day style?** If you're totally into Goth, there's no way you'll feel comfortable in a white satin wedding dress. If your idea of ultrafeminine is slacks instead of jeans, the white dress may induce a gagging reflex. The point? There's no reason to suddenly look like someone no one will recognize just because it's your wedding day.

- **What are your interests?** Is it motorcycles? Wear a custom-made white leather motorcycle jacket and boots. Surfing? Try a body-hugging mermaid-style dress. By incorporating your lifestyle and interests into your wedding attire, you'll feel comfortable and appropriate as you walk down the aisle.

- *What's your budget—or your financial tolerance?* Maybe you have a limited wedding budget. Or maybe the thought of spending over a thousand dollars on a dress you'll wear for a few hours is morally reprehensible to you. If you like the idea of tradition but not what it will cost, there are many ways to get bridal attire bargains that allow you, your budget, and your conscience to happily coexist. (See Chapter 13 for specific ideas.)

- **What do you envision?** Perhaps you have a vision of yourself in a classic knee-length white linen dress and a simple strand of pearls— or maybe it's a white micro-mini with thigh-high white rubber boots. Either way, remember that your wedding photos are like your yearbook pics. Looking back on them can induce a real cringe factor if you're not careful.

- **What about color?** If you've worn black every day for the last five years, a white dress may not be your thing. Brides *have* been seen wearing black from time to time, but do remember that to many people black signifies death and mourning. You may also wish to wear a color that's symbolic in your own or another culture. For instance, Chinese brides wear red, which is the color of celebration; and for hundreds of years Irish brides wore blue on their wedding day. In addition, for African-American brides, Afro-centric attire in bold colors, fabrics, and patterns is growing in popularity.

- **What's your wedding style?** If your wedding is to be held in an unconventional location, such as the beach or a ski slope, a formal white ball gown may not fit the bill. More appropriate for a beach wedding may be a white silk sarong and tank top. For the slopes, white ski pants and a ski jacket—or a white skirt with a colorful Nordic sweater—may be just the thing.

- **What do you feel comfortable in?** Few brides truly feel immediately comfortable in a big white ball dress, only because dressing this way is so foreign to most women. But it does feel more natural as the day goes on, and remember that this is one of the only occasions during which you'll have the opportunity to dress this way. Keeping this in mind, you may still wish to wear something more simple—but still elegant—such as a standard-cut dress or suit.

ALERT!

If you're having a religious ceremony, be sure to check with your officiant as to whether there are any parameters on attire—*before* you invest in that white leather miniskirt.

Variations on the Classic

There are some unique ways to find—or create—variations on the classic wedding gown. For instance, if you live in a small town and your choice of dresses is limited, search for dresses online. You will have access to countless styles and prices from designers all over the country—and the world.

If you like the idea of a formal wedding gown but want something a little different, try shopping at vintage shops, at thrift stores, or even on Ebay.com online (an auction site) for an antique gown. It may take a while to find just the dress (and size) you're looking for, so be sure to give yourself plenty of time.

You may also consider wearing your mother's wedding dress—or at least using it as the basis for yours. If it's not the right size or style, you may want to use the elements that fit—or that you like—as part of a newly designed dress. For instance, if you love your mother's full tulle skirt, ask a dress designer or seamstress to design a new top to attach to it. Or use the sleeves, lace, or other elements in a custom-designed dress, or as part of a headpiece, bridal purse, or garter.

Of course, you can also have a dress custom designed from scratch. This may be a particularly good option if you've searched and just can't find what you want, or if you'd like to create a completely original gown you won't see anywhere else. As stated previously, you can take the elements you love from many styles you've seen—say, the long flowing sleeves of one dress, with the empire waist of another, with the beading of a third—and ask a seamstress to incorporate them into one dress. The result of a custom-made dress is a perfect fit and style, which may not necessarily be any more expensive than a store-bought style (and may be less, depending upon the materials used and the dressmaker's rates).

QUESTION?

How long will it take to have a dress custom made?
You'll probably need to allow at least four to six months for the entire process, possibly longer depending on how elaborate the dress is.

Finally, you can get creative with your accessories. Accessorized differently, the same basic dress can look completely unique. For your wedding day, your accessories may include jewelry, headpiece, veil, gloves, purse, and shoes. So, even if you'd like to wear a traditional white wedding gown, you can still make a unique statement with your accessories.

When accessorizing, look to various sources for creative inspiration. These may be cultural influences—for instance, jewelry styles are reflective of various cultures. They may be individual interests, such as a sport or hobby (think shoes). Or they may be family inspired, such as with a hand-me-down headpiece, veil, or piece of jewelry.

Dramatic and different looks may include a beautiful arm bracelet worn on the upper arm; distinctive, colorful jewelry such as turquoise or jade; a head wreath of flowers in place of a headpiece and veil; a turban-style headpiece; embroidered or even colored gloves; and creative footwear in any style you choose (cowboy boots, sneakers, Doc Martens, sandals, ballet slippers, vintage mules, etc.).

Is the Groom Stuck in a Tux?

Men's clothing choices are a bit more limited for the groom's wedding day. However, the groom, too, can add some creative touches so that he's not just another guy in a monkey suit.

Speaking of the monkey suit—even though they're very popular, there's no rule forcing a groom to don a tuxedo on his wedding day. If you're looking for a dressy style but don't want a tux, try a quality, well-cut suit and tie. It's something that may be a better investment if you plan to purchase, rather than rent, your wedding attire.

Brides—consider giving your groom a pair of special cuff links as a wedding gift, especially if he owns his own tux or is purchasing one for the wedding, or if you attend a lot of dressy events.

If you do wish to wear a tux, however, there are plenty of styles and accessories to help you stand out from the pack. First, start with the tuxedo cut—there's a cut to suit your taste and body type. Single- or double-breasted jackets, tailcoats, and cutaway coats are a few of the styles available to grooms—all of which have a very different effect. In addition, grooms have a wider choice than ever with shirt styles (wing-collar, banded-collar, laydown collar), as well as ties (traditional bow tie, four-in-hand tie, or ascot).

Probably the widest variety comes with the vest, which can really be a stand-out piece for the groom. Vests are available in many colors, patterns, and styles, including high-cut—six- or seven-button styles—and low-cut—three-button style. Or the groom may choose a cummerbund or formal suspenders to finish his look.

Another area for the groom to show off his individuality is with additional accessories, such as button covers, studs, and cuff links. Whimsical and/or classic looks are readily available to reflect the groom's distinct personality.

The more creative or offbeat groom may also wish to search out some more unusual attire. Vintage-style tuxedos or suits from the 1930s, 1940s, and 1950s can offer exceptional panache in a more classic cut and style. For the really courageous, many tux shops also have stock from the 1960s and 1970s on hand—check them out to achieve your own Austin Powers or Dance Fever look.

The (Dreaded?) Bridesmaid Dress

In recent years the bridesmaid's dress has become one of the most maligned pieces of attire ever designed, sewn, and worn. Entire books are devoted to recycling that bridesmaid's dress once it's done its duty (because, of course, most women wouldn't think of wearing it again). It's no wonder styles are slowly becoming more wearable, flattering, and practical for future use—however, they still have a long way to go on all three counts.

For some brides, the bridesmaid's dress is a necessary evil. You've bought countless style-challenged dresses for your girlfriends' weddings—now it's payback time. However, consider taking the higher ground. There are definitely creative ways to get around the traditional, expensive, one-time-only bridesmaid's dress.

The first way is to allow your bridesmaids to choose their own dresses. If you crave some uniformity, choose a color and/or length, and let them shop from there. Choose a color that's easy to match (avoid difficult or unusual shades with trendy names—"moss," "melon," "loden"—and stick with the classics—black or navy are probably the easiest). This will allow your bridesmaids to choose a style they feel comfortable and look great in.

If you can't quite give up that much control, consider choosing a dress style that isn't specifically designed for bridesmaids. Pick a nicer retailer such as Ann Taylor, J. Crew, Banana Republic, or a large department store and choose a style that your bridesmaids could actually wear again (for real). Or choose a skirt-and-sweater set that looks classic and dressy and will be comfortable for your bridesmaids.

A final option is to have dresses custom made. If you just can't find something you and your bridesmaids like, custom-made dresses can be a welcome alternative. This could be a money-saving option as well, depending on the material and the dressmaker.

Of course, if you're throwing a theme wedding, your bridesmaids' dresses may be a bit more defined. Costume rental shops, vintage and thrift stores, the World Wide Web, and/or dress designers will probably be the way to go for period theme weddings such as a 1920s wedding, a medieval wedding, or a Victorian wedding.

All the Groom's Men

You can always go with the typical black tux rental for your groomsmen. Or you can add a touch of creativity to your groomsmen's attire, in similar ways that you would to the groom's. Choose creative or unusual accessories, including vests, suspenders, cummerbunds, studs, button covers, or top hats and canes; choose a slightly offbeat style such as tails or cutaway coats; or allow your groomsmen to show their individuality with footwear (but be prepared for some wacky stuff). Obviously, if you're throwing a theme wedding such as in a Western style, you'll probably want to accessorize with cowboy boots and hats; if it's a disco wedding, you may want your groomsmen in leisure suits.

QUESTION?

Do the mothers of the bride and groom really need to coordinate outfits?
Traditionally, the mothers have coordinated their attire to ensure that their styles are similar in formality and the colors don't clash. The motivating factor is typically photography, as the two mothers will not be attached at the hip for any length of time at the wedding.

Not Your Mother's Church Basement

Forty years ago the typical, middle-class wedding was often characterized by a religious ceremony followed by a huge reception in the church or temple basement or banquet room. The idea was to include as much family and as many friends as possible in the most cost-effective way.

Today, the "typical" wedding takes place in a religious or other setting, followed by a reception that is often at a separate site, such as a banquet facility or hall. As with ceremony sites outlined previously (see Chapter 15), there are countless options as to the setting for your reception site. In fact, most of the unusual and creative ceremony sites already outlined apply to reception sites as well—refer to pages 198–202 for ideas.

Remember, an unusual or out-of-the-ordinary reception site may require unusual or out-of-the-ordinary planning strategies and permissions. Do not begin planning your site-specific reception until you are absolutely sure you will be able to have it there. Also, unlike a banquet facility or restaurant, more unusual sites may not have everything you need, such as silverware, linens, tables and chairs, serving dishes, utensils, tents, a bar setup, and dance floor. You may have to rent these individually, which can increase costs (and details that need tracking) significantly.

Flowers That Set the Scene

Fresh flowers can be a major part of your wedding day budget. As such, they better say "bloomin' beautiful" rather than "wallflower." There are many creative ways to include flowers in your bouquets and for your attendants and special guests. There are also many ways to include alternatives to the areas traditionally filled with fresh blooms. These areas include bouquets, decorations, and centerpieces.

Everything's Coming Up Roses

When you think of the bridal bouquet, what comes to mind? Huge sprays and elaborate arrangements that take months of weight training to carry all the way down the aisle? While a large bouquet may be just your thing, there are many beautiful, creative alternatives that don't break the bank—or your back. Some of these include the following:

- **A single blossom**. Choose a dramatic flower, such as a sunflower or calla lily, and carry it down the aisle simply and elegantly. The florist may wrap it with a single beautiful ribbon or bow to dress it up. This works beautifully if you have an elaborate dress or outfit and don't need anything extra competing with it.
- **Silk flowers.** Depending on the quality and quantity, they may not be any less expensive than fresh flowers, but they can be equally beautiful, especially when certain blooms are difficult to come by. They're also something you'll be able to keep forever in their full splendor.
- **Dried flowers.** These can provide a unique, creative look for your bouquet—as well as your bridesmaids' bouquets. Again, you won't have to worry about what's in season or whether your florist will be able to get a particular bloom at the time of your wedding.

If you're fiancé has given you flowers over the months or years you've been dating, and you've had the foresight to dry and save them, you may also use these as a very personal addition to your bridal bouquet.

- **Wildflowers**. Those tight, sculptured-look bouquets so popular now are not for everyone. Wildflowers provide a looser, more free-flowing feel that may be ideal for your particular wedding style. Gather them with a beautiful ribbon and let the stems show. Wildflowers can also be significantly less expensive than cultivated blossoms such as roses or tulips.
- **Do-it-yourself bouquets**. Proud of your garden—or have a close family member or friend whose garden grows . . . and grows and grows? Create personalized bouquets you can carry with pride, with blossoms from your own garden. Set aside enough time the day of the wedding to arrange your bouquets—or have a creative family member or friend do the honors for you. Be sure to have plenty of ribbons or flower holders on hand to work with. This is also the least expensive route to creating gorgeous flower bouquets.

You may also choose specific blossoms to express a particular sentiment. Various flowers have a meaning all their own **(SEE TABLE 16-1)**. If you chose blossoms based on their symbolism, include their meaning in your program so that all your guests will understand their relevance as well.

Table 16-1 Flowers and Their Meanings

Flower	What It Symbolizes
Daisy	Innocence, loyal love
Hydrangea	Understanding
Carnation (pink)	Boldness
Carnation (red)	Love
Carnation (white)	Talent
Chrysanthemum	Wealth, abundance, truth
Calla lily	Beauty
Ivy	Wedded love, fidelity
Lily of the valley	Completeness, contentedness
Daffodil	Regard
Gardenia	Purity, joy
White rose	Innocence and secrecy
Stock	Bonds of affection
Tulip	Perfect lover
Freesia	Innocence
Stephanotis	Happiness in marriage
Lilac	Love's first emotions
Magnolia	Love of nature
Orchid	Love
Iris	Friendship

FACT

The Anti-flower Bouquet

Of course, you don't have to carry flowers down the aisle. There's nothing stopping you from carrying something else (or nothing at all). A particular item could hold sentimental value for you—say, a picture of a departed loved one—or may be part of the ceremony, such as a book of verses or poetry. Other items you may decide to carry in place of a traditional bouquet include candles, a love letter, a prayer book wrapped with a ribbon, an heirloom rosary or other religious piece, an embroidered or lace hanky from your mother or grandmother, a beautiful bridal purse (some purses actually made from flowers have been spotted among trendy brides), your dog leash (attached to your dog, of course), or your child.

Even if you carry a flower bouquet, you can still hold onto a sentimental item as well. To keep a lost friend or relative close, you may also tuck a picture or memento from them into your bouquet. Ask your florist to add it when designing your bouquet.

Creative Centerpieces

From flowers to flower alternatives, reception centerpieces can be more creative than ever. Rather than simply choosing a familiar and homogenous floral centerpiece for each table, brides are feeling freer to express their individuality—and personality—through the reception décor.

If you would like to use flowers, but would like them to look different than the standard large, centrally located centerpiece, try some of these ideas:

- **The individual touch.** Include small vases of flowers at each place setting, which can also double as wedding favors. Flowers may be small, beautiful wildflowers, or a single, beautiful bloom.

- **More is better.** Instead of including one large arrangement centrally on your guests' tables, have your florist design a cluster of smaller containers or vases on the table. Low blooms work best for a cluster effect, and once again, these can also double as wedding favors—one per couple.
- **Love in bloom.** As an added touch for a centerpiece—or in place of a traditional one—include a single bloom, such as a rose or tulip, tucked into each placecard holder.
- **Wreath of flowers.** Ask your florist to design a wreath of flowers to cover the center of the table. For some height, include candles or another item (such as tree ornaments at Christmas time, or seashells for a tropical-themed wedding).
- **Living color.** Instead of—or in addition to—blooms, consider using other items in your traditional centerpieces. One growing trend is to include colorful fruit or vegetables in your centerpiece, such as lemons, limes, grapes, berries, pears, peaches, asparagus, gourds, squashes, zucchinis, and pumpkins.
- **Forgo symmetry.** You don't have to have twenty matching centerpieces for twenty matching tables. Mixing it up a bit can add an interesting element to reception décor. For instance, instead of using the same tall crystal vases on each table, try using varying pieces from table to table, such as tin-look vases mixed with crystal or glass vases mixed with white ceramic containers. Or use unconventional flower holders, such as mason jars; antique water pitchers; and bowls in china, glass, and metal. The different height, color, and texture, as well as the uniqueness, of each flower holder will add up to a more interesting look for the room as a whole. If you'd like to remain somewhat consistent, use similar blooms or a similar-colored flower in the various containers.
- **The non-flower centerpiece.** There are also countless ways of decorating your tables that don't include flowers—but that can be just as beautiful and creative. Choose items that express your individual style, or that add whimsy or curiosity to your celebration. These items may include the following.
- Balloon arrangements
- Antique or contemporary candelabras

- Aromatherapy candle arrangements
- Tea lights at each place setting
- Glass bowls with floating, lit candles
- Fishbowls with live fish
- Seashells
- Soothing mini waterfalls
- Bonsai trees
- Sculpture
- A photo collection in beautiful, matched frames (with different photos on each table)
- Items that match your theme (cowboy hat, mini jukeboxes, miniature cars, etc.)

Chapter 17

Unforgettable Receptions

The difference between a great wedding and a forgettable one usually has nothing to do with cost or extravagance. A menu, a bar, and music that are creative and reflective of your personalities will keep things lively, interesting, and most importantly, fun. Consider infusing your own style into each of these areas to create a party that's unforgettable.

Memorable Menus

To some guests, the food is the single most important factor for enjoying a wedding. It's surprising, then, that so many weddings continue to go with the safe old standards—chicken and beef prepared in familiar ways. To be fair, many brides and grooms choose to err on the side of caution, serving time-tested crowd pleasers. However, if you think you have particularly open-minded diners or more sophisticated palates on your guest list (or you'd like to give guests a new experience), you can make a statement with your menu that goes way beyond traditional wedding fare.

Hors d'Oeuvres

Even if you plan to serve a traditional dinner or luncheon, hors d'oeuvres present the perfect opportunity to mix in exotic, unfamiliar, or extravagant vittles. Before you decide upon specific items, though, you should first decide upon your presentation. The way in which hors d'oeuvres are served can be as interesting as the food itself; they can be served in an elegant butler-passed style; at a large, central spread; or at stations placed throughout the reception site.

If you choose to have butler-passed hors d'oeuvres, consider serving the standard favorites mixed in with the more unusual or exotic. In other words, serve stuffed mushrooms, but don't be afraid to offer Thai chicken satay or mini egg rolls. Butler-passed hors d'oeuvres are becoming freer in nature, with new and ever-growing choices like skewered meats and vegetables accompanied by hot dips, oyster shooters, and even soup shooters like gazpacho and bisques.

If you decide to have a large, centrally located spread or stations during cocktail hour, consider theming them—for instance, if you plan to include a raw bar with clams, oysters, shrimp, and crab legs, decorate your table with a nautical theme (add a life buoy, seashells, fish netting, or even wooden sailboats to the table). If it's a sushi bar, include Japanese-inspired décor such as paper lanterns, rice paper, or a Japanese table covering.

Your reception doesn't have to be a traditional sit-down meal or buffet. Try an upscale barbecue with great cuts of meat and marinated vegetables, or a giant clam bake with all sorts of sumptuous seafood.

Food stations—during your cocktail hour or as the primary menu for a cocktail-style reception—are a somewhat newfangled take on the old buffet. Food stations are generally set up on the perimeter of the reception site, with supervision of each station by a chef or member of the kitchen staff. Food stations are usually a bit more creative in presentation than standard buffet food, however, with choices such as a potato bar with a selection of savory toppings; a Mexican taco or burrito station; a Thai food or Chinese food station; a hibachi-style Japanese station; a traditional meat carving station with tenderloin, turkey, or ham; or even a soup or salad station.

Reflections of You

There are many ways you can get personal when it comes to designing your menu, from your hors d'oeuvres to your main meal. By reflecting the personalities or experiences of you and your groom, you'll add an unforgettable special touch—and a more meaningful menu for all. But how will you do that?

Start with a trip down memory lane. Consider some favorite moments from your relationship—an unforgettable vacation, the place where the two of you met, the restaurant where he proposed—and use it for inspiration for your menu. Did you vacation in Maine? Serve lobster bisque or fresh whole lobsters. Did you meet during your semester in France? Serve a rich French feast. First say "I love you" in Philly? Serve tiny steak hoagies as hors d'oeuvres. Did he propose at your favorite Indian restaurant? Include your favorite curry dishes on the menu. Mix and match food items based on your shared history and experiences to create an entire menu that's based on you.

You may also wish to take your inspiration from the future—the very near future. That means using your honeymoon destination as your culinary guide. Going to Japan? Serve sushi and other Japanese-inspired dishes, or "fusion" cuisine, where East meets West. Honeymooning in Hawaii? Serve a pig roast with other Hawaiian delicacies. Is Jamaica your destination? Serve jerk chicken or other Caribbean-style dishes.

Can't choose between two great-sounding entrees? Serve both in slightly smaller portions, such as a steak with fish, or chicken with a pasta dish. Guests will appreciate the choice, especially if they have dietary restrictions.

A final way to personalize your menu is to use geography as your guide. This is an especially great idea if you hail from two different regions and you're having your wedding in a third, neutral location, or if the wedding is in one of your hometowns and you'd like to include the spirit of the other. You can personalize your wedding this way by including menu items your home region is famous for, such as Maryland crab, Maine lobster, Buffalo wings, Boston clam chowder, Wisconsin cheese, Georgia peanuts, or Florida oranges.

No matter how you personalize your menu, be sure to let your guests know why certain menu items where chosen. To do this, you can include creative menu cards at each place setting, outlining each course and what it symbolizes. It's a great memento of your shared experiences or backgrounds, and it's another way to help guests feel included in your celebration.

Presentation

Unique food presentation is another way to add creativity to your reception menu. One way to "wow" your guests is with the artistry of food preparation, by taking the kitchen into the reception area. Employ a hibachi chef (à la Benihana style) to serve up hibachi-style hors d'oeuvres at a dramatic Japanese food station. Guests will enjoy watching the slicing, dicing, and flipping. Or ask the sushi chef if he will prepare items where guests can watch. A particularly agile omelet maker or French crepe maker can also be an interesting addition. Unusual or exotic dishes are perfect for displaying the artistry of the chef. Talk to your caterer about specifics.

FACT

A brunch can be an elegant alternative to the traditional dinner reception, with rich, classic dishes such as quiche, smoked salmon, carved meats, and other upscale breakfast dishes. Include Belgian waffle and omelet stations for fun and variety.

Another way to incorporate creative presentation is in the serving of the food itself. Talk to your caterer about introducing unusual presentation methods, such as appetizers served in chilled martini glasses, soups served in bread bowls or hollowed out pumpkins or gourds, sorbet served in melon shells, or any other creative serving methods they may have. These can range from the elegant to the whimsical.

Ethnic Influence

Personalize your menu by reflecting your ethnic heritage. This is growing more and more popular among brides and grooms who wish to honor their cultures and backgrounds. You'll definitely please your parents and their contemporaries, and it's a great way to introduce your guests to ethnic fare they may have never before sampled. Whatever your background—Thai, Chinese, Japanese, Indian, Moroccan, Mexican, South American, Greek, Italian, Polish—you may choose to include an entire menu based on classic dishes, or to introduce a few items into your menu as an accompaniment to traditional Western dishes.

Creative Extras

The food doesn't have to end with the serving of your wedding cake. Consider including after-hours treats to keep the party rolling, such as a dessert spread of pastries, éclairs, petit fours, and tarts; a make-your-own ice cream sundae station with various flavor ice creams, sauces, and sprinkles; a coffee bar with cappuccino, espresso, and a variety of coffee flavorings; or even a late-evening or midnight buffet (to absorb the alcohol or re-energize dancers) with finger foods such as cold cuts and cheeses, mini quiches, egg rolls, or chicken wings and pizza.

What Are You Drinking?

Unlike your college friends who still consider Rolling Rock to be the drink of choice, bar snobs or serious drinkers will notice what you're serving.. If you've got top-shelf taste but a bottom-shelf budget, there are creative ways to serve the good stuff without breaking the bank (or even worse—including a cash bar). Plus, you can incorporate creative and unusual touches into your bar for some more frivolity and fun at your reception.

More Than Beer and Wine?

As with your menu, there are lots of ways to get creative with your reception bar that are personal and symbolic—or just a lot of fun. In addition to the basics—beer, wine, and hard liquor—consider adding some whimsy to your bar choices. Include a separate martini-only bar, where guests can order martinis in all the latest flavors—melon, lemon, lime, chocolate, and, of course, cosmos.

You may also wish to consider serving other "spotlight" drinks from the main bar or with a separate bar setup, such as a frozen drink station. These spotlight drinks might include the bartender's secret-recipe sangria (a mix of wine and liquors), frozen or on-the-rocks margaritas, flavored daiquiris, or piña coladas (these choices are especially great for an outdoor reception, beach reception, or tropical-theme wedding). Or spotlight seasonal favorites with pre-made pitchers of, say, gin and tonic and sloe gin fizz for summer; hard cider for fall; or eggnog for winter. If you're having a brunch reception, include killer Bloody Marys, mimosas, screwdrivers, and champagne.

You may also wish to include choices that reflect your ethnic heritage (or your honeymoon destination), such as a selection of Irish beers like Guinness and Bass Ale, Mexican beers like Dos Equis or Corona, Jamaican Red Stripe beer, Belgian beers, Russian or Polish vodka, Italian grappa or wine, or Japanese sake.

You may also wish to incorporate a wine-tasting event. This can be especially appropriate if you're having your reception at a vineyard or near wine country (or if you have a special connection to a particular winery). (See Chapter 10 for some specific ideas on including a wine-tasting event at your wedding.)

FACT

Don't forget the after-dinner liqueurs and drinks, such as port wine, sherry, dessert wines, or coffee drinks, which can provide an elegant and welcome end to a tasty dinner.

Bar on a Budget

Alcohol can be one of the most expensive elements of your wedding. If your caterer is providing it, it's generally the area in which he/she makes the majority of the profits. There are creative ways, however, to include a great bar that's still affordable.

The least expensive way to serve alcohol at your wedding is to do it yourself. Because many reception sites may not allow this (restaurants and halls with caterers onsite, in particular), be sure to check in advance before you begin stockpiling cases of liquor. If you are permitted to, however, it may provide a real financial advantage. Setting up your own bar will avoid a significant markup that a caterer includes, and you will only need to pay for what's been consumed—the fee-per-person-per-hour pay schedule can often end up being much costlier than what was actually imbibed. Return unopened bottles to the store where you purchased them, or keep them as a housewarming for your own home bar. Of course, remember there will be the additional costs of shipping the liquor to the site, setting up the bar, rental of glasses and bar ware, and a bartender's fee. Be sure to factor in these additional costs if you're planning to do it yourself.

Other strategies for keeping costs down include serving only beer and wine (though expect a few grumbles from liquor-only drinkers), limiting the hours that the bar is open (try closing the bar during dinner or ending the bar service before the band stops playing), or eliminating wine service during dinner. You may want to consider either keeping the bar open or including dinner wine service, so guests aren't completely without a cocktail for any length of time. These strategies may also free up the bucks to put toward serving higher-quality liquors or wines that would have otherwise been cost prohibitive.

Delicious Cakes

Today's wedding cakes can range in cost from hundreds to even thousands of dollars. The good news about today's cakes is that cake designers are getting much more creative, and couples are taking advantage of the deviations from the standard white, over-the-top creation with fountains, lots of frosting, and the requisite ceramic cake topper. And while wedding cakes have also historically been given a bad rap on the flavor front, today's bakers are ensuring their cakes are just as delicious as they are well designed.

You may know just what you want your wedding cake to look like, or you may simply know you want something a little different. As you begin consulting with cake designers to find the best one for you, here are some creative cake ideas you may wish to consider. Not all cake designers will (or can) do all things, so be sure the one you choose has the requisite capabilities before putting down a deposit.

- **Color.** Your wedding cake is definitely no longer limited to white. Bright and whimsical designs are popping up all over, with stacked cakes in different colors and patterns ranging from plaids to polka dots. Whether it's Wedgwood blue or tickled pink, color can make the most classic cake design look bold, fresh, and exciting. You may wish to incorporate your wedding colors, or just your favorite color into the wedding cake—most designers can include any color you wish. Or liven up a white cake with color, such as stacks of bright red or purple flowers between tiers of cake; bright flower petals strewn atop the cake; or ribbons and bows (actual or made of edible gum paste) in your favorite colors.
- **Shape.** While classic and beautiful, the shape of your cake does not have to be stacked tiers of round cakes, decreasing in size as you go

upward. The right cake designer can make a cake of any shape and size to reflect your individual style or personal interests. If you're having a medieval or fairy-tale theme, for instance, you might adore the idea of a cake shaped like a castle; at Christmas time you might want a cake that's shaped like a wrapped gift, Christmas tree, or Christmas ornament. Whatever your interest, your cake can reflect it— a tennis racquet, a musical instrument, a sailboat, a flower blossom, a bicycle—anything goes. It's just a matter of finding a cake designer who's willing—and able—to shape your vision.

FACT

In ancient Roman times, small, biscuit-like cakes were prepared and thrown at the bride on her wedding day. This practice was thought to bring fertility and was later amended so that the cakes were crumbled over the bride's head rather than pegged at her.

- **Flavor.** Why stick to plain old vanilla? Most cake designers and bakers have a wider variety than ever to choose from, such as carrot cake, mud cake, cheesecake, spice cake, coffee cake, pound cake, chocolate mousse—even ice cream cakes. If you're having a traditional tiered cake, you can also create variety by including a different flavor for each tier. Honor your mom, dad, or grandparents by including the flavor you know is their favorite; some bakers will even use a family favorite cake recipe if you request it.

- **Variety.** Instead of one large cake, create your own wedding dessert tradition by serving tiny, individual-sized wedding cakes to each guest. Or include a small cake among an extensive table of pastries, chocolates, cookies, tarts, éclairs, and other fancy desserts for guests to choose from. You may also choose to commission a cake for each table, which can double as a centerpiece—after dinner, you and the groom can cut the first slice of each cake at each table, giving you a chance to visit all your guests as you go.

- **Dress it up.** In addition to the cake, don't forget to get creative with all the accoutrements, such as the cake stand or pedestal, cake plate, and cake knife. Use family heirlooms, shop for something in an unusual color or style, or if you have the time and inclination, create your own from pottery, ceramic, or metal. And don't forget your cake table—decorate it with flowers, flower petals, balloons, candles, or a collection of framed family photos.

- **Little extras.** You may also choose to include other creative elements with your cake, such as an unusual cake topper—there are many variations that reflect couples' interests, such as animal figurines and sports- or hobby-related toppers. You can even have an artist custom make a cake topper to resemble you and the groom.

Name That Tune

At any gathering, music can make or break the party. Lack of music can make a party feel lifeless and sterile; bad music can have even worse consequences. Complicating the issue of music at your reception is a cross section of people you wouldn't normally find listening to the same radio stations or attending the same concerts—while Mom's at the Neil Diamond show, Junior's moshing at Blink 182. Needless to say, finding that happy medium is no small feat.

ALERT!

Beware of cheesy DJs and band emcees who make *themselves* the center of attention at *your* wedding. Be sure to get a solid recommendation or to see them in action at another wedding before you commit.

Presumably that's why many couples choose to go with a DJ or a "wedding" band who can play favorites from the last fifty years, in styles ranging from James Brown to James Taylor.

But what about the couple who wants something a little different? Do you have to please all the people, all the time? As long as your band or DJ is good, it shouldn't matter. Introducing a different style of music at your wedding can be an invigorating change of pace among the wedding guest circuit, particularly if it's music that gets your guests on the dance floor. The following are some ideas.

- **A Caribbean-style or steel drum band**. Bring the feel of the tropics to your wedding with a reggae beat. Guests will instantly go into vacation mode.
- **A jazz quartet**. A quality jazz band can be unusual wedding fare, providing toe-tapping, finger-snapping entertainment.
- **Disco cover band**. Guests of all ages won't be able to stay off the dance floor with a great 1970s disco band playing all the familiar favorites.
- **R&B band**. Find a group that can play R & B favorites, both old and new, and watch your guests fill the dance floor.
- **Country or bluegrass band**. Hire a dance coach for your reception who can teach all the latest line dances—you'll have all your guests on the dance floor in no time.
- **Elvis impersonator**. There's one in every region. Find yours and let the fun ensue.
- **Swing band**. Guests of all ages will appreciate these classic favorites and will welcome the chance to show off all those swing dance lessons.
- **Celebrity DJ**. Be prepared for very current, very hot club favorites.

Can't decide on the song for your first dance? Let your guests decide. At the rehearsal dinner, give them a list of song possibilities, then take a vote—the song with the most votes wins. This can be a fun way to add spontaneity and have wedding guests feel included.

Capturing It All on Film

The best wedding photographer is the one you barely know is there, catching your special moments without actually becoming part of the special moments. And some photographic artistry doesn't hurt either. Photography is innately creative and highly personal. Different photographers will offer you different photographic styles. For that reason, it's worth doing some research before deciding on your final choice, in order to find the style and look that suits your taste.

Growing in popularity—and a creative choice for your wedding—is the photojournalistic style of shooting weddings. Rather than ending up with a stack of posed, staged shots, photojournalism style aims to catch its subjects in the moment, with lots of candid and unstructured shots. The results of this style of photography are often priceless, with the real emotions of joy, surprise, melancholy, and contentment caught on film permanently. It's also a great style to use if you don't have the patience to pose for a lot of photos. Do be sure, however, to pose for a formal portrait or two of you as bride and groom, and to include photos of your immediate families and wedding party.

Ask your parents and grandparents in advance what their wedding songs are—then have the emcee or DJ announce and play them at your wedding for a sentimental touch.

Another choice growing in popularity is the use of black-and-white film. Black-and-white film adds a timeless quality to photos and can be an artistic and beautiful addition to your album. Or go with all black-and-white photos if you don't want any color at all. Your photographer can also manipulate black-and-white prints to have a sepia tone—that antiquey, golden glow of old photos. Your photographer can also simulate the look of old-fashioned tinted photos by taking a black-and-white image and tinting a small but integral portion of it, such as the bridal bouquet, boutonniere, centerpieces, or cake flowers.

Alternative Photos

In addition to professional photography, there are alternative methods to capturing your day on film. You've undoubtedly seen the idea of disposable cameras on each guest table in action. This practice gives the bride and groom another set of photos from completely unique perspectives. A variation of this practice would be to give certain key guests a disposable, digital, or traditional camera for an assigned period of time, whereby they'd photograph the events during that time period only. In other words, assign five or six friends or family members an hour each during the reception to get additional posed shots and/or candids. This can ensure you'll get photos of different wedding events ranging from cocktail hour to the last dance.

FACT

Ensure you get a snapshot of all your guests by placing a Polaroid instant camera next to your guest book. Ask guests to tape a photo of themselves next to what they've written. Be sure to include tape and extra film nearby.

Use of a digital camera, as well, can be a great tool for sharing photos instantly over the Internet right when the wedding is over. Ask someone to take some key shots throughout the wedding to upload to a special Web site or to e-mail loved ones who were unable to attend from afar. Your guests, too, will enjoy reliving the festivities.

Another fun idea would be to rent an old-fashioned photo booth and place it somewhere in your reception area. Rig it so it's free for guests, and allow them to take that classic old strip of four black-and-white photos home with them, or to leave them with you in a special book or poster designed for the occasion.

Storage and Gifts

There are many creative ways to store and give away your wedding photos that fall outside the traditional white album with silver lettering. Today's savvy scrapbookers are lovingly creating their own wedding albums, with colorful paper, stickers, old-fashioned photo corners, and written captions to preserve names, faces, and events of the day. Your region is sure to have a craft store that carries all the essentials to create a unique album full of personal expression and presentation.

If you don't have the time or inclination to make your own, there are people who'll do it for you, such as your photographer. Ask him or her about photo storage alternatives, such as old-fashioned-style photo albums with black pages and photo corners, which would look terrific with black-and-white and sepia-toned photos, or more contemporary looks such as black board-mounted photos stored in a funky photo box.

Your photographer will probably also carry many alternatives for framing and small albums for friends and family.

You may also consider inserting a photo of you and the groom in your thank-you cards. This can be an especially appropriate idea if you've given picture frames as wedding favors—your guests will have a perfectly-sized photo to insert. The same goes for your groomsmen and bridesmaids. If you've given them a nice frame, for instance, as a thank-you gift, why not give them a nice 8×10 or 5×7 photograph after the wedding to fit inside?

Videography

As with your photographer, the biggest factor influencing your final video will be your choice of videographer. Different videographers will charge difference prices and have different styles—some you'll like, some you may not. So, before making your final decision, be sure to look at some of the videographer's prior work to be sure your choices of style match. Beyond that, it will generally be your videographer's vision driving the look, music, editing, and pacing of the video.

For great video footage at your reception, set up a special "video station" in a set location where guests can speak directly to the camera. You'll get lots of well-thought-out private footage—kind of like the "confessional" in the *Real World*.

As mentioned previously, one thing you may choose to do is to purchase the full, unedited video footage rather than a final, cut, abridged version. This will allow you to have all your video intact and as it was filmed—keep in mind, however, that it may include lulls as well. Or ask your videographer if you can have both—the unedited video as well as a stylized edited one. This way you can always manipulate the unedited video later if you'd like.

Getting Guests Involved

Don't forget that your wedding is what you make of it. Aside from the great traditions like dancing, toasts, cake cutting, and more, you can also add any traditions or activities you like. For example, brides and grooms are finding creative alternatives to the old "clinking glasses," whereby wedding guests would clink their wine or water glasses during dinner in order to elicit a kiss from the bride and groom. Let your guests know before dinner that more than just clinking glasses will be required for the honors this time around. For instance, have guests come together as a table to sing a song with the word "love" in it. Or reward whoever comes to the mike to tell a joke with a kiss. Or you might try tying a couple of balloons to each table—guests can break the balloon and do what the message inside says, such as "tell a funny story about the bride and groom."

You can also have guests do an activity at their table—answer a questionnaire about the bride and groom, for example, or solve a puzzle. Once they've completed their task, they can bring it up to the bride and groom in exchange for a kiss. (This can also be a great ice breaker among tables at which guests don't know each other.)

You may also try turning the tides on your guests. Whenever guests start clinking glasses, have the emcee break a balloon—inside will be the names of a couple attending the wedding (set this up in advance and include the names of all your guests). Instead of the bride and groom kissing, the couple chosen will have to.

Chapter 18

It's the Little Things

By now you've probably gathered that great weddings are often the result of a real connection between the guests and the wedding couple. And there's really no end to the possibilities that will help you foster that connection. This chapter outlines some of the ways you can further personalize the proceedings, through invitations, favors, placecards, and transportation.

Setting the Tone with Invitations

Invitations are your first opportunity to communicate with your guests, set the tone for the party, and create excitement for your big day. As such, they're a very important element—and also an opportune way to show some creativity. While the classic wedding invitation has been quite standard over the years—heavy white and ivory stock engraved with familiar, formal wording—brides and grooms are taking the opportunity to get much more creative with this "window" into the impending nuptials.

So what can you do differently? Anything, really. From the materials to the script to the wording, your invitation is open for reinterpretation.

Medium

While the classic invitation has typically appeared on heavy white or ivory stock, the medium for your announcement is very much up to you. Talk with your stationer about paper alternatives, such as recycled paper, heavy colored paper, parchment, corrugated paper, vellum, foiled papers, shiny, smooth stocks, or even fabric. Paper alone can set your invitation apart but still provide as formal a tone as traditional-style invitations. Or if you're looking for something more casual, the creative use of paper can give you more flexibility in design. Of course, you may even choose to use paper alternatives, such as fabric, wood, or another material, depending upon your concept and the look and feel you're trying to achieve.

Font

There are many fonts you can choose from that go beyond traditional formal script. Fonts provide another forum with which to set your tone, such as the clean, contemporary look of Arial; an old-fashioned, medieval look such as Charlesworth or Sherwood; an Art Deco-y look like Bernhard Fashion; or even the whimsical feel of Bazooka or Jester. Designers and printers work with countless fonts, and more are designed every day. Very specialized fonts—such as a Frank Lloyd Wright, Bauhaus, Art Nouveau, or the Monet look—can be researched online and/or purchased from a design firm such as P22 Type Foundry, a company that creates typefaces inspired by historical artists, movements, and time periods.

Wording

There are many books and resources that dictate the proper wording of invitations based upon criteria such as divorced parents, deceased parents, stepparents, and who is hosting. And while these guides can be a good start leading you in a standardized direction for any number of familial situations, you may prefer to create your own invitation wording if these lines don't meet your needs. This is perfectly acceptable and will allow you to personalize your invitation to reflect your own unique gathering. After all, no one tells you how to word invitations for any other party you've thrown—why should your wedding be any different?

If you'd like a very different look or themed invitation, have your invitations custom designed and made by a graphic designer or artist—or make them yourselves.

With your wording, just remember to include the important facts—the who, what, when, and where—the "why" is up to you. You may consider including a poem, song lyrics, a quote from a well-known figure, a quote from one of you, a line from a book, etc. This creative addition may be included on a separate card, or on the page facing your invitation information if it's a folded piece. Whatever you choose to include, it can reflect your feelings about marriage, commitment, trust, or love. Tell the story of how you met, explain why you've chosen to get married, or communicate any other story or message you'd like your guests to be included in.

Embellishments

Your invitation can also take on other creative elements. Perhaps each one is hand painted or stamped with a uniquely created design; maybe each is a tasteful collage of old family photos, newspaper clippings, or other mementos. Feel free to make creative configurations with paper, ribbons, buttons, bows, lace, or other materials in order to create just the look you want. Commission an artist or graphic designer to create the final look—or do it yourself for an even more personal touch.

Use heirlooms, such as your grandmother's damaged but still salvageable lace tablecloth, or your mother's wedding dress (if she doesn't mind it in pieces, that is) as materials.

Three-Dimensional Design

A three-dimensional mailer—a box or a tube, for instance, with something inside—can be an eye-catching and attention-getting way to announce your wedding to friends and family. With a three-dimensional mailer you can include an item that's symbolic of your union, such as a plant seedling, a small "unity" candle, a tied "knot," or LEGOs (to symbolize joining together). Or you can tailor the item to your season or wedding theme—send suntan lotion for a beach wedding, dreidels for a Hanukkah wedding, or Easter eggs for an Easter wedding. You may also wish to incorporate your own talents into your invitation, such as an invitation carved into wood, or a hand-sewn piece. Or include half of a pair of items, of which guests will receive the other half at the wedding; pairs might include a pen and journal, a bookmark and a book, a water bottle and bandanna, a wine glass and mini bottle of wine, or a salt and pepper shaker. Then you won't have to think about what to give as favors!

QUESTION?

Can we e-mail our invitations?
Most etiquette books still advise against e-mailing invitations, but obviously it's up to you. Remember, though, that not everyone has an e-mail address or feels comfortable on the Internet, and e-mail will appear much more casual and informal than a mailed invitation.

Clever Favors

Favors are one of the most creative parts of your wedding. These little gifts for your guests can range from the romantic to the seasonal to the just plain fun, providing the opportunity to personalize your wedding in a way your guests will remember.

The most traditional Western favors, probably, are candied almonds—they have become de rigueur among many cultures including Italians,

Greeks, and, now, Americans. Usually tied in a pretty net, tulle, or fabric bag, the candied-almond tradition originated in the old country, when wedding guests would throw them at the bride and groom for good luck. Today, fortunately, they're eaten before they can be thrown.

Brides and grooms today are finding new ways to express their gratitude to guests, with wedding favors that reflect their individuality and personalities, as well as their wedding themes. The following ideas are offered to inspire you and get you thinking—and to provide some specific suggestions that you can incorporate yourself.

Create do-it-yourself favors inspired by your shopping. If you see pre-made candy favors that are boxed and wrapped, for instance, instead of buying them, purchase each item yourself—chocolates or candies, boxes, wrap, and bows—and make them just the way you want. You'll undoubtedly cut costs this way as well.

Geography

Your wedding favors can reflect your geographic area in a number of ways. One idea includes giving guests a snow globe, picture postcards, or mini replicas of a landmark in your area; this is a particularly nice idea if you're having many out-of-town guests. Or you can use your vacations together as inspiration—have each guest table represent one of your destinations, and include edible or other treats that symbolize that location. For example, include coffee on the Seattle table, tea on the London table, chocolate on the Swiss table (or San Francisco table), and maple syrup on the Canadian table. You can also tailor your centerpieces to reflect each destination, which can be as simple as framed postcards mixed in with flowers, candles, or other items.

Food

Food items are always a welcome—and practical—gift. Try these:

- Chocolates, lemon drops, or hard candies or mints enclosed in a small, pretty box

- A miniature candy apple
- A box or bag of quality nuts
- A small jar of honey
- Herbs or spices in a pretty package
- Gourmet jelly beans
- Candy canes
- Lollipops
- Hot sauce with a personalized label (do it yourself or find a vendor who will)
- A personalized chocolate bar
- Bubble gum
- Cotton candy
- A tin of cookies
- A small bottle of wine or champagne (with a personalized label)
- Ethnic favorites, such as cannoli, baklava, or Irish soda bread
- A small bag of Hershey's Kisses

Hobbies and Activities

On a more personal note, you can give a favor that will reflect your interests or hobbies. Consider your favorite activities, and get creative from there. These items might include the following:

- A golf ball monogrammed with both your names or initials
- A water bottle with your names and the date, or with your wedding colors
- A bookmark with a pretty design or commitment-minded message
- A blank book or journal
- A tree sapling, packet of seeds, or flower bulbs, if you love to garden
- Stationary tied with a ribbon
- A small bag of seashells or sea glass
- Paint and/or paint brushes
- A comic book
- A recipe book
- A fun kitchen utensil with a poem attached

Pretty Mementos

You may also use wedding favors to help decorate your tables. Here are some ideas:

- A pretty silver picture frame at each place setting
- A tiny vase with one bloom
- Goldfish in a little bowl
- A wind chime
- A sake cup
- An aromatherapy candle
- Potpourri
- Mini soaps in your wedding colors
- A keepsake wine glass
- A small "trinket" box
- A key chain (silver or leather)
- A music box
- A tiny bunch of herbs, such as lavender
- A little stuffed animal

A Light Touch

You may also want to include a fun favor that will amuse your guests or remind them of something from their past (think retro toys and games). Consider items such as these:

- Weeble Wobbles
- A pet rock
- Silly putty
- A deck of cards
- Jacks
- A baseball cap with a special logo or your initials
- A T-shirt with a saying like "I survived the Smith-Jones wedding"
- A lottery ticket or scratch-off
- A magic eight ball
- A kazoo

- A matchbox car
- A harmonica
- A mini flashlight ("We've finally seen the light")
- A Post-it notepad printed with a saying or your initials
- A jigsaw puzzle (have one made with your engagement photo)
- An eye pillow
- A kaleidoscope
- Marbles in a leather pouch

Think of a way to tie the item into your special day, and add a tag that explains the symbolism, such as "We'd lose our marbles if we couldn't be together."

Contain It

There are many items you can use to contain favor items. Try small boxes wrapped with a ribbon, bags of velvet or fabric wrapped with a leather or fabric strap, tulle wrapped in a bow, small tins, glassine bags, tissue paper, or small wooden boxes. Search the Internet and your local craft store for specifics.

Placecard Art

Placecards can be much more than a practical way of assigning guests to tables; even the most simple placecards with calligraphy provide a beautiful addition to your wedding décor. However, there is much more than simple fold-over cards to individualize your placecard display. You can incorporate your wedding favors into your placecard display or just kick placecards up a notch with added accoutrements.

Placecards are great if you'd like to make guests comfortable with specific seating for a sit-down meal. However, if you're having a more casual wedding or a cocktail-style reception, you probably will have open seating without placecards, which is a great style for groups who like to mingle.

For example, instead of using plain cards, why not attach each card to a colorful piece of fruit with a simple, pretty stickpin? Use green or red apples, pears, lemons or limes, or other fruits to create an unusual and eye-catching display for guests as they walk in.

Or attach cards to tiny flower pots containing a single bloom, herbs, or wheat grass. You may also choose to insert cards into pretty frames set on display; or attach them to popular items made just for placecards, such as small porcelain or pewter chairs, ceramic figurines, tiny flower pots, little vases and bells, or sachets.

Transportation Worth Talking About

Coming and going in style is always fun, and there's no better time to spoil yourself than on your wedding day. Aside from the traditional limousine service, there are plenty of ways to reach your destination in style—and depart with a flourish.

Get Me to the Church on Time

On your wedding day, you may be planning to get ready in relative solitude at your parents' house—or you may be surrounded by bridesmaids and family members prior to your trip to the ceremony. Or you and your groom may be traveling to the ceremony together. No matter what your circumstances, the most important factors about your transportation to your ceremony are reliability and comfort. That means even if you plan to ride off into the sunset on horses *after* your ceremony, you may want to use the traditional limo on the way there, to ensure there are no problems such as torn dresses or—worse—broken bones.

If your ceremony and reception locations are different, it's generally the transportation after the ceremony that will provide the most novelty. Before deciding on your mode of transportation, first decide who you'll be riding with: Will it be just you and the groom? The entire wedding party? You, the groom, and both sets of parents? If your idea is to start celebrating as soon as the ceremony's over, consider renting a large-capacity vehicle. These might include an extra-long limousine; a customized bus with seats that all face inward, so everyone can face each other; a trolley; a "Hummer" limo or stretch Hum-V; or a Lincoln Navigator limo. With your whole wedding party present, you can break out the bubbly and start celebrating with your nearest and dearest. Plus, the vehicle can take you all to any additional photo sites you'd like to take advantage of, such as a historical building, a botanical garden, or a pretty park, on your way to the reception.

Of course, if it's just going to be you and the groom transported from one site to the next, your options are even greater. You might rent your dream car (a Jaguar or other high-end sports car) and drive yourselves, rent an antique car and hire a driver, or commission a horse-drawn carriage.

Be sure to choose a reputable vendor for your transportation needs. No matter how great or creative the vehicle is, if it doesn't show up, you'll have a logistical nightmare.

If your ceremony and reception sites are near one another, you may also consider an old-style wedding walk, whereby the bride, groom, wedding party, and guests all walk together to the reception site. This is a particularly nice idea for low-traffic areas or cities with ample sidewalks—you may even consider having musical accompaniment for your walk, such as a bagpiper, a school band, or a flautist or trumpeter heralding the way. Wedding walks were once very common in European towns and cities, where passersby would clap and wave to wish the new couple good luck.

If your ceremony and reception sites aren't close enough to walk to, but you'd still like to transport all your guests there (a good idea in cities where most people use public transportation, like New York), consider renting a double-decker bus, a trolley, or a customized bus to accommodate everyone. This will ensure all your guests will get to your reception in one piece—without worrying about cab shortages, bad weather, or unreliable public transportation.

Dramatic Send-Offs

It's never easy to end your reception. But if you do it with some excitement, it can be more sweet than bitter. The send-off is a somewhat old-fashioned practice that's coming back into vogue, whereby couples make a dramatic exit as their guests cheer them on.

Some ideas for great exits include the following:

- In a hot air balloon
- In a dogsled
- In a horse-drawn sleigh
- In a horse-drawn carriage
- On horseback (after you change into your bridal britches)
- In a boat or a yacht
- On jet-skis
- In a motorcycle with a sidecar
- On a bicycle built for two
- In a trolley
- On "chariot"-style bike—the kind where someone else does the peddling and you do the sitting
- In a small plane or a helicopter
- In an antique or upscale car, such as a Mercedes, BMW, Jaguar, or Lexus
- In a convertible
- In a rugged jeep
- On foot
- On inline skates
- On skateboards

Of course, there's always the classic "Just Married" car, which groomsmen decorate with a big sign, streamers, balloons, and tin cans. If this is your preferred exit, drop some well-placed hints so that groomsmen know about it and can plan ahead of time.

Child-Friendly Receptions

More and more of today's weddings have become "adult-only" affairs, if only because the expense of adding children to the mix can really add up. However, if you couldn't bear to be without your favorite nieces, nephews, and cousins on your wedding day, you can include some creative touches so that children will be amused and entertained—and their parents will be able to kick back and relax as well.

Day Care

You may wish to consider a care provider or sitter for very young children and babies. If you think your guests may have trouble finding a sitter (an out-of-town wedding can present a particular challenge), or if you have a number of friends or family members who are breastfeeding young children, employing a day- (or evening-) care provider may be the way to go. Ask a trusted neighbor, a friend's or family's nanny, or a guest's teenage child if they'd like to do childcare duty during the reception. If your wedding is at a hotel, rent a suite for the evening so children have room to play and move; or set up an alternative site nearby such as a family member's home. This way, parents can check up on children during the reception and barely miss a beat.

Diversions

If your reception will include many children, consider hiring special kids-only entertainment to keep them occupied. Employ a clown, a face painter, or a tattooist specializing in temporary tattoos to give kids something to do. If your reception is outdoors in a wide-open space, consider including kid-friendly attractions like an inflatable jumping cage, badminton, ping pong, or volleyball. If it's near water, rent a few paddleboats, rafts, or inner tubes (and hire a lifeguard to supervise). If your reception is indoors, set aside a special kids' area with toys, games, and activities for kids.

Tailor Adult Activities

In addition to furnishing kids with entertainment all their own, you may also wish to tailor some of the adult activities to appeal to kids, too. For example, in addition to your wedding cake, have a kids' cake made, and have a contest to see which kid gets to cut it first. Include kid-friendly dances like the hokey pokey or the chicken dance. Set up kids-only tables at dinner, to give parents a break and allow kids to play and mingle. Have a kids' first dance that follows the couples' first dance or the father/bride dance, where kids are specifically invited onto the dance floor. The overall idea is to think of how children will fit into traditionally adult activities at your wedding, and to make special concessions for them.

Kids' Favors

You should also consider giving children their own special wedding favors. This can be a variation of adult favors—such as a children's CD to mirror the adults' CD; a coloring book to match the adult's journal; or a set of crayons or markers if you've given adults a nice pen. You may also wish to give kids activity-based favors, such as a book of puzzles, kids' videos, or DVDs (see if your caterer can set up a video-viewing area), sports equipment like a Nerf game (if your reception is outdoors), or other keep-busy items. This will help keep children occupied as the day or evening wears on.

Chapter 19

Taking the
Road Less Traveled

After all those months of intense wedding planning piled onto your already hectic lifestyle, there's no better time to get away from it all. Your honeymoon offers the perfect chance to get creative and plan the trip you've always dreamed of—the possibilities are as endless as your imagination.

Creative Planning

One of the most user-friendly, practical resources to come out of the advent of the World Wide Web is travel planning. There's probably no easier (or cheaper) way to check out unfamiliar destinations; research travel deals; and find unusual travel packages to destinations around the world. If you have a general idea of where you want to go, the Internet can help you narrow down your search even further to discern which region or city you'd like to visit, based on your interests and travel style. You might also try unconventional travel guides such as the Dog Lover's Companion Series (which outlines dog-friendly destinations and establishments) for ideas.

Employing a travel agent is a very good idea. To find a reputable one, ask family and friends for recommendations, use your corporate travel agent, or interview a few and use the one you feel comfortable with. A travel agent can be especially helpful if you're traveling out of the country, to ensure complicated travel plans are confirmed and that you have all the correct identification and/or supplies before you leave.

Like to live on the wild side? Wait until a week or so before your wedding and take advantage of last-minute travel deals offered on Internet sites like ✍ *www.lastminutetravel.com*, or on Yahoo!'s popular travel section. These sites cover everything from cruises to spas to golf vacations, plus airfare, hotels, and rental cars.

Adventure Trip

For some, sitting on a beach for ten days sounds like the perfect vacation. For others, it sounds like torture—where's the action? What's there to do? Action mongers need to keep going on their honeymoons, and for them relaxing means more time to do the activities they love, like cycling, running, hiking, kayaking, mountain climbing, or skiing. Luckily, there are many vacation packages that cater to the active traveler in every corner of the world.

Cycling

A cycling trip package perfectly combines activity and sightseeing into one amazing vacation. If you like biking, a cycling trip offers many options—mountain biking or traditional road cycling; varying levels of difficulty based upon daily elevation totals; different levels of accommodations ranging from four-star luxury to outdoor camping; and the entire gamut of destinations that include domestic and international routes from Louisiana to Vermont to Alaska, and from Ireland to the Mediterranean Coast to Vietnam.

ALERT!

In today's uncertain travel climate, it's especially smart to purchase travel insurance in case of unforeseen events at home or at your destination, such as weather, tourist alerts, or other hindrances. It's usually not very expensive and well worth the price if you have to cancel.

Bike tour companies will establish a route and itinerary for the group—all you need to do is show up and pedal. These trips include daily rides along the most scenic routes, a "tour bus" that furnishes meals and drinks and helps out riders along the route, and evening accommodations including dinner. Tours are often flexible, offering riders mileage options on a daily basis—shorter or longer routes based on mood or ability. Shuttles often pick up riders along more difficult or challenging portions of a route, dropping them off beyond it.

Many cycling tour companies also combine cycling with other interests, such as gourmet cooking lessons through a bike tour of Tuscany or a museum bike tour through France. A great resource for cycling tour packages around the world is ✐ *www.backroads.com.*

Climbing

If mountain climbing is your passion, consider a climbing, trekking, or mountaineering trip for your honeymoon. Obviously, some experience is necessary, but like cycling tours, mountain climbing trips range from the moderate to the extremely challenging. Experienced guides can lead you to destinations all over the world, from the Himalayas, Mt. Everest, Mt. Kilimanjaro, Mt. Vinson in Antarctica, Mt. Elbrus in Russia, and the mountains of Central America to home in the Rockies. Some resources to begin planning your mountaineering expedition include ✐ *www.mountain guides.com* and ✐ *www.mountainmadness.com.*

Can't get enough of the water? Why not charter a sailboat for a week or two? Many charters come with a captain and a gourmet cook who'll sail the boat and prepare meals according to your specifications. Or fly to your dream destination and travel "bareboat"—meaning you charter and sail the boat yourselves.

Wildlife Safari

There are a countless number of places to choose from when planning your safari—from the northern reaches of Egypt to the southern tip of South Africa to the island of Madagascar, along with the traditional East African destinations. Safari packages to destinations including India, Sri Lanka, Argentina, Ecuador, and the Amazon rain forest also ensure your safari is not limited to Africa. You can plan a wildlife observation trip just about anywhere.

Before choosing any tour operator, be sure to check them out with the Better Business Bureau or go with recommendations of friends and family who've used them before.

A Range of Options

Like any vacation, safaris can range from absolute luxury to the down and dirty. What may come as a surprise, however, are the many options and packages that are available when planning your safari. There are many safari styles that go beyond the standard four-wheel-drive caravan through the wild. These include alternative forms of transportation as well as activities that are tailored specifically to your interests. The following are some options:

- **Canoe safari.** View unfamiliar creatures—elephants, buffalo, hippos, zebras, and crocodiles—at close range as you canoe down the rivers and streams of the African jungle. Canoe tours may also include fishing.
- **Elephant-back safari.** Forgo modern-day mechanics and travel the natural way—on the back of an elephant—through the jungle. Specially designed saddles make elephant travel more comfortable than you might expect. You may also choose to travel on horseback or camelback.
- **Train travel.** With a bit more distance between you and the wild, traveling by train may be the option for you. The famous "Blue Train" in South Africa will take you through areas ranging from the jungle to the winelands to the thirstlands, and through the diamond mines of Kimberley to cosmopolitan Cape Town. With deluxe accommodations and meals, you'll experience the best of both worlds.
- **Sailing safari.** Whether you're a beginning sailor or an expert, you can spend your honeymoon sailing the channels on a catamaran, accompanied by a larger guide boat. Your guide will provide sailing lessons, provide information on the terrain, and prepare meals. After every full day you'll sleep under the stars in your own private catamaran.
- **Camping safari.** While many walking and driving safaris provide guides who will set up camp, prepare meals, and break camp the next day, there are also tours that allow travelers to rough it as well. This type of safari will give you the responsibility of setting up your own tent, helping prepare all meals, and packing the vehicle the next day. Often these tours will offer a guide to help you navigate the best route.
- **Do-it-yourself safari.** Want to wing it in the wild with just you and your honey? Go on your own safari for two. All you need is a U.S. driver's license to rent a four-wheel-drive vehicle, a map, and some supplies—but be sure you are well prepared for all contingencies.
- **Bird-watcher's safari.** There are also tours available that focus specifically on spotting birds.
- **Gorilla-trekking safari.** This safari is tailored specifically to observing gorillas. Tour operators offer very controlled access in order to protect animals in their environment.

Archeological Trip

Longing for the adventure of Indiana Jones but don't want to get an archaeology degree? Your honeymoon is the perfect time to fulfill your archaeological fantasy, whether it's a guided tour of recently uncovered ancient worlds, or an actual archeological dig in which you participate— and even keep—what you find!

See and Do

In just about any area of the world there are archeological artifacts that you can observe—as well as a host of guided tours. There are also countless places around the world where you can experience the wonder of history's preserved artifacts in their natural environments, be it in Central America, South America, or Europe. There are also many sites in North America, including areas in Canada, Mexico, and the United States. In fact, in the United States there are tours of archeological interest as well as the chance to excavate for yourself.

Before planning your honeymoon to your chosen destination, be sure to research whether there are any U.S. State Department travel warnings for that area.

One of these U.S. sites is in Monticello, Utah, where for a fee you can excavate on a designated dig led by trained archeologists. The fee is rather steep: For $2,500 a day you can dig and keep any artifacts you find, such as arrowheads, pottery, or jars, and for $1,500 you can pay for the experience and have your findings preserved in a museum. For more information, visit ✍ *www.anasazi-digs.com.*

Another site in Arizona offers a similar experience, with hands-on excavation in small groups led by a professional archeologist. You can help record and document any artifacts found in the state's historical records. This adventure consists of a day's worth of excavating, with meals provided. For more information on this group, visit ✍ *www.archaeologicadventures.com.*

There are also tour groups that provide archeological adventures internationally, such as ArchaoExpeditions, a company out of Ottawa, Ontario, Canada. This company provides one- to two-week trips (some go longer) that include fieldwork in various locations—previous sites have included Antigua, Belize, Russia, Tibet, Turkey, and Quebec.

Volunteer Work Trip

You've just shared one of the happiest, loving days of your life—why not share that love with others who might benefit from your youth, health, and positive energy? A volunteer trip will allow you to travel somewhere exotic and do good for others at the same time—starting your marriage off on a giving note sure to last a lifetime.

Habitat for Humanity

Most people are familiar with Habitat for Humanity, the Christian-based organization that builds (and renovates) houses for low-income families. Habitat for Humanity also offers its International Global Village Program, which allows volunteers an "educational and spiritual experience within a cross-cultural environment." Participants travel to destinations around the world—including Africa, Asia, South America, Central America, the Caribbean, and Europe—for an experience that's as much about education as it is about helping others. Itineraries are more loosely structured than many volunteer tour work groups, and include work, rest, and free time, as well as time to visit local cultural landmarks. Don't expect four-star accommodations—most likely your lodging will be quite primitive, and your meals will follow local customs. The cost of this trip can range from $1,800 to $4,000 per person, depending upon the destination; it includes airfare, room and board, travel insurance, and a donation to the local program affiliate. Many participants raise funds to make the trip. You may even consider a honeymoon bridal registry for this trip in lieu of traditional wedding gifts. For more information, visit ✐ *www.habitat.org*.

Don't forget your passport! If you don't have one already and plan to leave the country for your honeymoon, give yourselves plenty of time to get one—the U.S. Department of State advises that you apply for one several months before your scheduled departure date.

Other Volunteer Work Trips

There are countless other volunteer experiences you can take advantage of at home or abroad. Speak to your church or synagogue about specific opportunities that may also provide a valuable spiritual or religious experience. Or search online for the many opportunities available. Different tour operators offer different trip features. For example, some volunteer groups run on charitable contributions from others, which means you will be charged only a nominal fee for your trip. One such organization is Volunteers for Peace at *www.vfp.org*, which runs international work camps in eighty countries ranging from Australia to Nepal to Romania. This group provides volunteer trips in the $200 to $400 range, which is much more affordable than many of the other groups that rely on contributions from individual volunteers to fund trips.

Before sending any volunteer organization a cash deposit or down payment on a trip, be sure to thoroughly check them out (or go only with organizations that come personally recommended). Ask around, call the Better Business Bureau, and get as many references as possible before booking your trip.

Another group offering volunteer opportunities is Cross-Cultural Solutions, at *www.crossculturalsolutions.org*. This group provides short-term volunteer trips to counties including Brazil, China, Russia, Thailand, and Costa Rica, for which volunteers pay their own travel, lodging, and meal expenses. Volunteers with no experience are welcome, as are volunteers with special skills. Work on these trips includes teaching English, sports participation, art instruction, day care, helping people with disabilities, geriatric care, AIDS prevention education, physical therapy, assisting teachers, and much more.

Another organization offers environmentally conscious volunteers the opportunity to help out in international locations. In addition to traditional work projects such as teaching English as a foreign language, (i-to-i) offers the opportunity to be involved in the historical preservation and conservation efforts in Ireland and the reforestation efforts in the rain forest in Ecuador. For more information on these and other potential volunteer trips, visit ✍ *www.i-to-i.com.*

Special Events

Another different and memorable way to celebrate your honeymoon is to plan your trip to coincide with an exciting worldwide event. Maybe there's something you've always wanted to experience live—like World Cup Soccer, the Stanley Cup, or some other sporting or cultural event. Why not plan your wedding and/or honeymoon around this long-anticipated event? Keep in mind that if you're looking for quiet and seclusion, these are probably not the ideal type of places to go. But if you crave excitement and lots of people, consider the following:

- **The Fiesta of San Fermin, Pamplona, Spain** (also known as the Running of the Bulls). Every year this famous event takes place from July 6 to 14. Basically, this is a week-long party highlighted by the daily morning running of the bulls, followed by bullfights in the afternoon. This three-minute run has taken its toll historically with many a brave runner gored or even killed. For a week there is nonstop partying and revelry in the streets, restaurants, and drinking establishments. So if excitement and action are what you crave, this is the right place for you.
- **Wimbledon** (or one of the other Grand Slam tennis events, including the Australian Open, French Open, and U.S. Open). Wimbledon is the oldest of the four Grand Slam events (it began in 1877), and its grounds and atmosphere are still steeped in much tradition and history. Held at the All England Croquet and Lawn Tennis Club in

Wimbledon, England, this event is annually held at the end of June and beginning of July and provides the world's best tennis.

- **Mardi Gras, New Orleans, Louisiana.** Like the Running of the Bulls, this is a frenzied few weeks of partying and revelry that overruns the city of New Orleans, Louisiana. Every year Mardi Gras takes place on Fat Tuesday, or the day before Lent begins (Ash Wednesday), typically in late February or early March. However, there is plenty of fun to be had well before that date—the three weeks preceding Mardi Gras are filled with parades, parties, and countless tourists. If you're looking for excitement and action, this is the place. If you're looking to relax and unwind, find somewhere else—far, far away.

- **The Olympics.** To enjoy the traditional Summer Olympics, from cycling to baseball, tennis to tae kwon do, and, of course, the ever-popular gymnastics, why not schedule your honeymoon to coincide with the Olympics? Or if your wedding is in winter, take a trip to the Winter Olympics.

- **Superbowl.** Are you both big football fans? Plan to get tickets—whatever way you can—to enjoy the spectacle and excitement of the Superbowl. Chances are it'll be a warm climate, so plan to enjoy the surroundings before and after the game.

- **Fantasy Fest.** Another week-long opportunity to party and celebrate, Fantasy Fest in Key West is almost as outrageous as Mardi Gras. Typically held the last week in October, this festival features parades, costumes, parties, and some of the best-looking cross-dressers you'll ever see. Plus there's that gorgeous Key West sun to soak up your daily hangovers. Ⓔ

Chapter 20

Making the Most of Anniversaries

After the wedding is over and the excitement of the day has waned, you've got the memories (and the pictures) to remind you of that special day. And your anniversary celebrations can be as creative as your wedding plans. This chapter covers creative methods to keeping your romance alive and kicking, from your first anniversary to your fiftieth.

What's Next?

Months after your wedding, friends and family are *still* talking about it, which means your creativity, individuality, and attention to detail have made you a huge success. Well, you're in luck. Because the same qualities that made for a unique, unforgettable wedding are the qualities that make for a harmonious, productive marriage. Just as a wedding can't plan itself, neither can a marriage sustain itself—without a little effort, that is. It takes constant work—albeit fun work, in most cases—to maintain a successful, happy marriage.

Annual Celebrations

There's no argument that people remember their wedding day as one of the most exciting and important days of their lives. Too easily we forget the anticipation and joy of our wedding day when life's daily stresses take over. After all, when the baby's crying, you're paying bills, and your mother-in-law is driving you crazy, who recalls the euphoria of one's wedding day? As these stresses take over, however, you may both eventually feel that something is lacking—and then wonder how you got to this point. That's why it's so important to infuse some of the romance and excitement of the early days—and your wedding day—into your everyday life.

Nothing says "I love you" quite like a specially prepared meal. From comfort foods to luxurious gourmet meals, cooking for your spouse is a great way to celebrate your anniversary (especially if you're the out-to-eat type). Try including foods popularly known as aphrodisiacs, such as oysters, dishes prepared with exotic spices like cumin and curry, and, of course, some good wine.

There's no better time to re-create the excitement of your wedding day than on your anniversary. And while anniversaries are a great excuse for flowers or an elegant dinner on the town, there are also ways that can help you get past the daily grind to celebrate the day as it should be celebrated—by truly connecting and sharing your love for each other.

How can we do this, you might ask? Well, all you need to do is to tap into that creative spirit utilized so well during your wedding planning to create anniversary celebrations that are equally unforgettable.

Create Your Own Traditions

Adopt an activity that you'll do together on your anniversary from year to year. The activity can be as involved as planning a trip to as simple as taking the day off together. Other ideas include the following:

- Watching your wedding video
- Looking through your wedding photos
- Conference calling your best man and maid of honor to chat, no matter where they may be
- Enjoying dinner (or lunch or brunch) at the restaurant/hotel where your reception was held
- Buying a cake in the flavor of your wedding cake and indulging
- Playing your wedding song and sharing a dance in the living room (or at a supper club)
- Throwing a party with friends and family to celebrate another year of wedded bliss

Anniversaries are a wonderful time for reflection and renewal. Instead of just going to dinner and a movie, why not infuse some meaning and symbolism into your anniversary? After all, you're celebrating another full year of marriage—why not celebrate in a way that honors the previous year? For example, you could each spend some time reflecting on the last year and present to one another the five favorite moments that occurred with your spouse (these might consist of a vacation taken together, a special walk in the park, the moment you found out you were pregnant, a party you attended together, the time he made you breakfast in bed, etc.). Or look to the future, and name three things you'd like to accomplish together over the following year. Not only will this activity help you bring back fond memories, it's also a great form of communicating exactly what makes you happy—a good reminder for future happiness.

Relive your honeymoon. Start a tradition of enjoying a yearly escape—out of town. You may wish to revisit your honeymoon locale every year, or you may take the opportunity to test the waters somewhere new. Either way, take time for just the two of you, even if it's for just a few days.

You might also try doing an activity together every anniversary (and involve kids, too, if you have them) such as taking all the previous year's photos and making a photo album. This activity will allow you to reflect upon the last year as well as accomplish a task you've probably been meaning to do. Or if your creative juices are really flowing, write a poem, paint a watercolor, or express your feelings about the last year through an artistic piece of your choosing. You can even use each anniversary as inspiration for a long-term project, such as a quilt—prepare a new square every year based on what happened the previous year (for example, stitch a house design if you've bought a house or baby booties if you've had a child). Then you'll have an anniversary quilt to pass on to future generations.

Afraid your spouse won't remember your anniversary? There's nothing wrong with dropping hints a few weeks before, to ensure there's no disappointment—or planning a special occasion for the two of you yourself.

Theme Anniversaries

So you pulled out all the stops and had a theme wedding? Why not celebrate a theme anniversary? For example, if you had a Renaissance wedding, prepare a medieval feast for the two of you to enjoy—or invite family and friends as well. A Halloween wedding? Throw an annual Halloween party and use some of the decorations you had for your wedding. A beach wedding? Find another beach to have a picnic on, or return to the same one for a romantic lunch—or a raucous party. A destination wedding? Go back and indulge yourselves. No matter what your theme, you can recreate it to bring back the excitement and celebration of your wedding day.

Say It with a Gift

Somewhere along the way, each anniversary year had a gift type assigned to it. Table 20-1 shows the traditional gift categories (rather than the modern updates), which allow for more creative interpretation than the modern ones. Create an anniversary tradition that keeps your spouse wondering just how you'll interpret this year's gift tradition.

Table 20-1 Traditional Anniversary Gifts

Anniversary	Gift
First	Paper
Second	Cotton
Third	Leather
Fourth	Linen
Fifth	Wood
Sixth	Iron
Seventh	Wool
Eighth	Bronze
Ninth	Pottery
Tenth	Tin, aluminum
Eleventh	Steel
Twelfth	Silk
Thirteenth	Lace
Fourteenth	Ivory
Fifteenth	Crystal
Twentieth	China
Twenty-fifth	Silver
Thirtieth	Pearl

Table 20-1 Traditional Anniversary Gifts	
Thirty-fifth	Coral, jade
Fortieth	Ruby
Forty-fifth	Sapphire
Fiftieth	Gold
Fifty-fifth	Emerald
Sixtieth	Diamond

FACT

Anniversary gifts also have "modern" alternatives. For example, instead of fourth anniversary linens, electric appliances are the accepted modern gift interpretation; instead of steel, "fashion jewelry" is appropriate for the eleventh year.

Ideas for creative gifts include the following:

- **Paper.** A special signed or first-edition book by his/her favorite author; fine art or photo prints; a photo album or framed picture; beautiful, high-quality writing paper or stationery set; cookbooks; sports tickets; fine cigars; a love letter; life insurance
- **Cotton.** Bed linens; table linens; monogrammed towels; a tapestry from a faraway culture; a throw rug; an article of clothing
- **Leather.** A beautiful leather-band watch; a high-quality leather belt; leather boots; a nice (or designer) handbag; a wallet; a desk set; a leather jacket or pants
- **Linen.** Beautiful table linens; place mats; bed linens; a scarf; linen clothing
- **Wood.** A workbench; a wood carving or sculpture; new hardwood floors; a table or other piece of furniture; wooden kitchen bowls; a bookcase; a tree
- **Iron.** Cast iron cookware; iron furniture; sculpture or artwork made of iron; garden sculpture
- **Wool.** A beautiful Nordic ski sweater; a coat; a hand-knitted sweater, socks, or blanket
- **Bronze.** A bowl; a sculpture; bookends; a mirror
- **Pottery.** Decorative pottery; serving pieces; kitchen canisters; antique pottery

- **Tin/aluminum.** A mountain or street bicycle; a boat; jewelry; a tin mirror; bakeware or cookware; outdoor furniture; a wok
- **Steel.** A car; cookware; a watch; exercise equipment
- **Silk.** A designer scarf; lingerie; a beautiful blouse; a tie; curtains; upholstery; wall coverings; silk sheets; silk flowers
- **Lace.** An antique tablecloth; an article of clothing; place mats; lingerie; a handkerchief
- **Ivory.** An ivory elephant carving (for good luck); a piece of jewelry; furniture with ivory inlays; a bowl, vase, or sculpture, anything ivory colored
- **Crystal.** A beautiful bowl or vase; wine glasses; champagne glasses; salt and pepper shakers; a crystal clock
- **China.** A bowl; an antique set of dishes; a vase; a trip to China
- **Silver.** A silver serving platter; a silver bowl; silver jewelry; a silver-colored automobile; a silver-hued motorcycle; picture frames; belt buckle; a trip to Mexico
- **Pearl.** A pearl necklace, earrings, or bracelet; cuff links or a tie tack
- **Coral/jade.** A trip to the Great Barrier Reef (or anywhere where coral reefs exist); jewelry or cuff links; a pendant
- **Ruby.** Jewelry; glassware; a red sports car
- **Sapphire.** Jewelry; a trip to a seaside resort (as in, sapphire-colored sea)
- **Gold.** A necklace or other jewelry; antique gold coins; a gold-leaf frame; a gold nugget; a trip to San Francisco (gold rush town)
- **Emerald.** Jewelry; a first edition copy of *The Wizard of Oz*
- **Diamond.** Jewelry; a trip to the World Series; a trip to South Africa (where diamonds are mined)

Why not create your own gift categories prior to your first anniversary? Come up with categories that demand creative interpretation. Instead of linens, china, and gold, use categories like "fun," "getaway," "hobbies," and "pets" and see what ensues.

Reaffirming Your Vows

Reaffirming your vows offers a very direct way of reigniting that spark from your wedding day. Many couples choose to reaffirm their vows on a significant anniversary (the tenth, fifteenth, twentieth, or twenty-fifth), following a life-altering event (an illness, marriage difficulties), or if they've eloped or never had the chance to enjoy a big wedding ceremony or reception. Or some couples simply wish to recommit themselves to one another—no other reason necessary. Either way, your reaffirmation ceremony can be as intimate or as public as you wish, involving just the two of you or a huge gathering of family and friends.

If you do plan to share your reaffirmation with family and friends, you may follow traditional wedding practices as a loose guideline. Use whatever vows you like—your original vows, a poem, a literary passage, or self-written vows—whatever works in expressing your feelings to one another. (See Chapter 15 for ideas on self-written vows.) You may also wish to exchange rings—your current rings or "updated" rings are both appropriate.

FACT

Because your reaffirmation ceremony is not legally binding, you can choose any "officiant" you like. Ask your best man or maid of honor, your child, or your parent to oversee the proceedings. You may also choose to have a religious ceremony. Speak to a clergy member at your church or synagogue for details.

As far as attire, you may decide to wear you original wedding dress (who says you can only wear it once?) or take advantage of the occasion to buy a beautiful evening gown, suit, or whatever outfit you like. A large wedding party probably isn't necessary, but you may wish to include your original bridesmaids and groomsmen in a special way—asking them to do a special reading, honoring them with a little gift, original wedding photo, or remembrance. If you have children, you can also include them in the reaffirmation ceremony with their own special vows or in nonspeaking roles, such as lighting a unity candle.

Feel free to follow your ceremony with a reception or party. Once again, this is open to interpretation. It might consist of a brunch for twenty or a formal dinner for two hundred. Obviously, your reaffirmation ceremony and reception is not an opportunity for more "wedding" gifts, so make this clear on your invitation—and by all means, do NOT register for gifts.

Appendices

Appendix A
Useful Internet Sites

Appendix B
A Thumbnail Guide to
Five Outrageous Weddings

Appendix C
Expense Worksheet

Appendix A
Useful Internet Sites

Wedding Attire

- *www.tk-designs.com*—Maternity wedding gowns and ethnic wedding attire for men and women
- *www.renaissancecostumesclothing.com*—Renaissance costumes and bridal wear
- *www.renstyles.com*—Renaissance costumes and bridal wear
- *www.gypsymoon.com*—Unusual, gothic, "darkly romantic" dresses
- *http://tara1enchantedworld.com*—Costume-like, nontraditional, and sexy gowns
- *www.thefrock.com*—Well-preserved, unique gowns and accessories
- *www.bridal-orginals.co.uk*—Period gowns, custom-made all-original gowns
- *www.avintagewedding.com*—Gowns ranging from the 1900s to the 1980s
- *www.vintagewedding.com*—Vintage gowns from various time periods
- *www.vintagepimp.com*—Vintage street clothing specializing in 1960s', 1970s', and psychedelic styles
- *www.funkyboutique.com*—Very sexy clothing, including VERY racy wedding dresses and lingerie
- *www.lastminutebrides.com*—Discounted gowns available for immediate shipment
- *www.designerduplicates.com*—Designer knock-off dresses at lower prices
- *www.glamgal.com*—Wide array of headpieces, veils, jewelry, and gloves in traditional styles
- *www.bargainweddinggowns.com*—Wedding dress bargains in various styles and sizes

Wedding Invitations

- *www.wedding-stationery.com*—Unusual and unique designs in a spectrum of styles, with the option to customize
- *www.mvsweddinginvitations.com*—Great for theme weddings—reproductions of original artwork in various themes like beach, bicycling, etc.
- *www.invitesgalore.com*—Cool, unique designs in creative shapes and sizes
- *www.papermints.com*—Handmade papers in pretty designs
- *www.botanicalpaperworks.mb.ca*—Invitations embedded with seeds—paper is plantable and will yield wildflowers!

Wedding Favors

- *www.weddingfavorites.com*—A wide selection of traditional and unusual favorites
- *www.hansonellis.com*—A wide selection plus do-it-yourself options
- *www.wedthings.com*—Theme favors, containers, and more
- *www.weddinginspirations.com*—Traditional favor selection
- *www.botanicalpaperworks.mb.ca*—Offer paper favors that are "plantable"—yield wildflowers when planted in the ground

Vows

- *www.lovepoemsandquotes.com*
- *http://lovequote.com*
- *www.forbetterlife.org*—All three sites offer romantic quotes from various sources, including famous people, movies, songs, opera, and theater; useful for vows, wedding programs, etc.

Travel

- *www.incredible-adventures.com*—Offers extreme adventures like cosmonaut training, simulated space travel, shark adventures, and much more
- *www.austinlehman.com*—Offers adventure vacation packages in a full range of activities—cycling, kayaking, etc.—across the United States
- *www.adventureplanet.com*—Adventure vacations abroad and in the United States
- *www.geoex.com*—Offers exotic, worldwide adventures
- *www.backroads.com*—Great site with worldwide adventure packages for beginners through advanced athletes
- *www.archaeoexpeditions.com*—Archaeological experiences across the world
- *www.mountainguides.com*—Offer guided climbing trips worldwide
- *www.mountainmadeness.com*—Offer guided climbing trips worldwide
- *www.lastminutetravel.com*—Offers great deals on last-minute travel plans
- *http://travel.yahoo.com*—Comprehensive travel site with discounted packages and last-minute travel deals
- *www.habitat.org*—Habitat for Humanity site; outlines volunteer opportunities in the United States and abroad
- *www.crossculturalsolutions.org*—Volunteer work trips abroad
- *www.i-to-i.com*—Volunteer work trips abroad

Appendix B

A Thumbnail Guide to Five Outrageous Weddings

RENAISSANCE	DISCO	FAIRY TALE	PUPPY LOVE	UNDERWATER
Bridal Attire: Low bodice, full skirt, jewel-tone colors	Bridal Attire: Clingy, brightly hued, acrylic-blend Studio 54 party dress	Bridal Attire: Ultrafeminine whitegown with lots of lace, bows, and/or ruffles; "glass" slippers	Bridal Attire: Anything you don't plan on wearing again	Bridal Attire: Shimmery white bikini or white wetsuit
Location: Renaissance fairgrounds or old Gothic castle	Location: Cool retro night club	Location: Beautiful banquet hall or hotel ballroom	Location: Anywhere outdoors, with lots of room to run. . . er . . . dance	Location: Ocean, lake, pond, or pool
Reception Music: Bagpipes, flute, guitar, organ, harp, and mandolin	Reception Music: Blondie, Gloria Gaynor, and Sister Sledge	Reception Music: Classical waltzes	Reception Music: Snoop Doggy Dogg, Lil Bow Wow, Elvis's "Hound Dog"	Reception Music: Steel drum band
Transportation: On foot	Transportation: 1970s' vintage Corvette	Transportation: Horse and buggy	Transportation: Minivan, SUV, or station wagon	Transportation: Glass-bottom boat
Menu: Pig roast	Menu: Finger foods	Menu: Fancy multicourse feast	Menu: Casual barbecue, with plenty of dog biscuits	Menu: Clams, oysters, lobster, and other deep-sea delights
Alcohol: Ales, mead, and wine	Alcohol: Tab, champagne	Alcohol: Spiked punch	Alcohol: Beer and plenty of water dishes for the canines	Alcohol: Tropical and frozen drinks in little coconut cups
Favors: Blown glass, leatherwork, woodwork	Favors: Pet rock, seahorses, Abba CD	Favors: Exquisite chocolate truffles in an elaborately wrapped box	Favors: Poop-scoop	Favors: Swim goggles, sunscreen, sunglasses
Honeymoon: Museum and gallery tour Europe	Honeymoon: Ibiza	Honeymoon: The bridal suite at the Four Seasons in London	Honeymoon: Sailing trip (with Rover in tow, of course)	Honeymoon: Anywhere with soil

Appendix C
Expense Worksheet

This list/chart is intended to outline all possible wedding costs you may incur, including some of the "hidden" costs you may not automatically consider.

Expense Item	Budgeted Amount	Actual Amount Spent
WEDDING ATTIRE		
Bridal gown		
Alterations		
Veil		
Shoes		
Accessories (stockings, lingerie, purse, jewelry)		
Groom's attire		
Groom's accessories		
(tie, vest, shoes, cummerbund, cufflinks, studs)		
PRINTED ITEMS		
Invitations and envelopes		
Reception cards		
RSVP cards and envelopes		
Thank-you cards and envelopes		
Placecards—reception seating		
Wedding programs		
Guest book		
Calligrapher		
Postage		
CEREMONY		
Marriage license fee		
Ceremony site		
Officiant's fee		
Officiant's gratuity		
Decorations (pew bows, runner, flowers)		
Reception		
Site rental/room fee		

Expense Item	Budgeted Amount	Actual Amount Spent
Food		
Bar		
Wine		
Champagne		
Cake-cutting fee		
Corkage fee		
Gratuity		
Tent rental		
Table rental		
Chair rental		
Dishware rental		
Cutlery rental		
Linen rental		
Glassware rental		
Service professional fees (bartenders,servers)		
Equipment rental (bar, coffeemakers, chafing dishes, etc.)		
Dance floor rental		
Setup and takedown fees		

PHOTOGRAPHY/VIDEOGRAPHY

Expense Item	Budgeted Amount	Actual Amount Spent
Engagement photo		
Bridal portrait		
Photographer's fee		
Proofs fee		
Fee per print		
Album fee		
Photo negatives		
Videographer's fee		
Video duplicates		

MUSIC—CEREMONY

Expense Item	Budgeted Amount	Actual Amount Spent
Vocalist		
Organist or other musicians		

Expense Item	Budgeted Amount	Actual Amount Spent
MUSIC—RECEPTION		
Cocktail hour musician		
DJ		
Live band		
CAKE		
Wedding cake		
Cake topper		
Cake knife		
Groom's cake		
Delivery and/or setup		
FLORIST		
Bridal bouquet		
Bridesmaids' bouquets		
Corsages		
Boutonnieres		
Table centerpieces		
Cake flowers		
Other decorative flowers		
Decorations		
Toasting glasses		
Candles		
Guest favors		
Other		
GIFTS		
For the groom		
For the bride		
For the groomsmen		
For the bridesmaids		
For your parents		
"Goodie bags" for out-of-town guests		

Expense Item	Budgeted Amount	Actual Amount Spent
SALON		
Hair		
Makeup		
Waxing		
Manicure/pedicure		
Other		
TRANSPORTATION		
Limousine		
Driver's gratuity		
JEWELRY		
Bride's ring		
Groom's ring		
HONEYMOON		
Passports		
Flights		
Accommodations		
Rental car		
Going-away clothes		
Meals		
Activities		
Shopping		
WEDDING PARTIES		
Rehearsal dinner		
Bridesmaids' luncheon		
Bachelor party		
Bachelorette party		
MISCELLANEOUS		
Wedding consultant/planner		
Wedding night accommodations		
Insurance		
Legal fees (for prenuptial agreement)		

Index

THE EVERYTHING SERIES!

BUSINESS

Everything® **Business Planning Book**
Everything® **Coaching and Mentoring Book**
Everything® **Fundraising Book**
Everything® **Home-Based Business Book**
Everything® **Leadership Book**
Everything® **Managing People Book**
Everything® **Network Marketing Book**
Everything® **Online Business Book**
Everything® **Project Management Book**
Everything® **Selling Book**
Everything® **Start Your Own Business Book**
Everything® **Time Management Book**

COMPUTERS

Everything® **Build Your Own Home Page Book**
Everything® **Computer Book**
Everything® **Internet Book**
Everything® **Microsoft® Word 2000 Book**

COOKBOOKS

Everything® **Barbecue Cookbook**
Everything® **Bartender's Book, $9.95**
Everything® **Chinese Cookbook**
Everything® **Chocolate Cookbook**
Everything® **Cookbook**
Everything® **Dessert Cookbook**
Everything® **Diabetes Cookbook**
Everything® **Indian Cookbook**
Everything® **Low-Carb Cookbook**
Everything® **Low-Fat High-Flavor Cookbook**

Everything® **Low-Salt Cookbook**
Everything® **Mediterranean Cookbook**
Everything® **Mexican Cookbook**
Everything® **One-Pot Cookbook**
Everything® **Pasta Book**
Everything® **Quick Meals Cookbook**
Everything® **Slow Cooker Cookbook**
Everything® **Soup Cookbook**
Everything® **Thai Cookbook**
Everything® **Vegetarian Cookbook**
Everything® **Wine Book**

HEALTH

Everything® **Alzheimer's Book**
Everything® **Anti-Aging Book**
Everything® **Diabetes Book**
Everything® **Dieting Book**
Everything® **Herbal Remedies Book**
Everything® **Hypnosis Book**
Everything® **Massage Book**
Everything® **Menopause Book**
Everything® **Nutrition Book**
Everything® **Reflexology Book**
Everything® **Reiki Book**
Everything® **Stress Management Book**
Everything® **Vitamins, Minerals, and Nutritional Supplements Book**

HISTORY

Everything® **American Government Book**
Everything® **American History Book**
Everything® **Civil War Book**
Everything® **Irish History & Heritage Book**

Everything® **Mafia Book**
Everything® **Middle East Book**
Everything® **World War II Book**

HOBBIES & GAMES

Everything® **Bridge Book**
Everything® **Candlemaking Book**
Everything® **Casino Gambling Book**
Everything® **Chess Basics Book**
Everything® **Collectibles Book**
Everything® **Crossword and Puzzle Book**
Everything® **Digital Photography Book**
Everything® **Easy Crosswords Book**
Everything® **Family Tree Book**
Everything® **Games Book**
Everything® **Knitting Book**
Everything® **Magic Book**
Everything® **Motorcycle Book**
Everything® **Online Genealogy Book**
Everything® **Photography Book**
Everything® **Pool & Billiards Book**
Everything® **Quilting Book**
Everything® **Scrapbooking Book**
Everything® **Sewing Book**
Everything® **Soapmaking Book**

HOME IMPROVEMENT

Everything® **Feng Shui Book**
Everything® **Feng Shui Decluttering Book, $9.95 ($15.95 CAN)**
Everything® **Fix-It Book**
Everything® **Gardening Book**
Everything® **Homebuilding Book**

All Everything® books are priced at $12.95 or $14.95, unless otherwise stated. Prices subject to change without notice.
Canadian prices range from $11.95–$31.95, and are subject to change without notice.

Everything® **Home Decorating Book**
Everything® **Landscaping Book**
Everything® **Lawn Care Book**
Everything® **Organize Your Home Book**

EVERYTHING® KIDS' BOOKS

All titles are $6.95

Everything® **Kids' Baseball Book, 3rd Ed.** ($10.95 CAN)
Everything® **Kids' Bible Trivia Book** ($10.95 CAN)
Everything® **Kids' Bugs Book** ($10.95 CAN)
Everything® **Kids' Christmas Puzzle & Activity Book** ($10.95 CAN)
Everything® **Kids' Cookbook** ($10.95 CAN)
Everything® **Kids' Halloween Puzzle & Activity Book** ($10.95 CAN)
Everything® **Kids' Joke Book** ($10.95 CAN)
Everything® **Kids' Math Puzzles Book** ($10.95 CAN)
Everything® **Kids' Mazes Book** ($10.95 CAN)
Everything® **Kids' Money Book** ($11.95 CAN)
Everything® **Kids' Monsters Book** ($10.95 CAN)
Everything® **Kids' Nature Book** ($11.95 CAN)
Everything® **Kids' Puzzle Book** ($10.95 CAN)
Everything® **Kids' Riddles & Brain Teasers Book** ($10.95 CAN)
Everything® **Kids' Science Experiments Book** ($10.95 CAN)
Everything® **Kids' Soccer Book** ($10.95 CAN)
Everything® **Kids' Travel Activity Book** ($10.95 CAN)

KIDS' STORY BOOKS

Everything® **Bedtime Story Book**
Everything® **Bible Stories Book**
Everything® **Fairy Tales Book**
Everything® **Mother Goose Book**

LANGUAGE

Everything® **Inglés Book**
Everything® **Learning French Book**
Everything® **Learning German Book**
Everything® **Learning Italian Book**
Everything® **Learning Latin Book**
Everything® **Learning Spanish Book**
Everything® **Sign Language Book**
Everything® **Spanish Phrase Book,** $9.95 ($15.95 CAN)

MUSIC

Everything® **Drums Book (with CD),** $19.95 ($31.95 CAN)
Everything® **Guitar Book**
Everything® **Playing Piano and Keyboards Book**
Everything® **Rock & Blues Guitar Book (with CD),** $19.95 ($31.95 CAN)
Everything® **Songwriting Book**

NEW AGE

Everything® **Astrology Book**
Everything® **Divining the Future Book**
Everything® **Dreams Book**
Everything® **Ghost Book**
Everything® **Love Signs Book,** $9.95 ($15.95 CAN)
Everything® **Meditation Book**
Everything® **Numerology Book**
Everything® **Palmistry Book**
Everything® **Psychic Book**
Everything® **Spells & Charms Book**
Everything® **Tarot Book**
Everything® **Wicca and Witchcraft Book**

PARENTING

Everything® **Baby Names Book**
Everything® **Baby Shower Book**
Everything® **Baby's First Food Book**
Everything® **Baby's First Year Book**
Everything® **Breastfeeding Book**

Everything® **Father-to-Be Book**
Everything® **Get Ready for Baby Book**
Everything® **Getting Pregnant Book**
Everything® **Homeschooling Book**
Everything® **Parent's Guide to Children with Autism**
Everything® **Parent's Guide to Positive Discipline**
Everything® **Parent's Guide to Raising a Successful Child**
Everything® **Parenting a Teenager Book**
Everything® **Potty Training Book,** $9.95 ($15.95 CAN)
Everything® **Pregnancy Book, 2nd Ed.**
Everything® **Pregnancy Fitness Book**
Everything® **Pregnancy Organizer,** $15.00 ($22.95 CAN)
Everything® **Toddler Book**
Everything® **Tween Book**

PERSONAL FINANCE

Everything® **Budgeting Book**
Everything® **Get Out of Debt Book**
Everything® **Get Rich Book**
Everything® **Homebuying Book, 2nd Ed.**
Everything® **Homeselling Book**
Everything® **Investing Book**
Everything® **Money Book**
Everything® **Mutual Funds Book**
Everything® **Online Investing Book**
Everything® **Personal Finance Book**
Everything® **Personal Finance in Your 20s & 30s Book**
Everything® **Wills & Estate Planning Book**

PETS

Everything® **Cat Book**
Everything® **Dog Book**
Everything® **Dog Training and Tricks Book**
Everything® **Golden Retriever Book**
Everything® **Horse Book**
Everything® **Labrador Retriever Book**
Everything® **Puppy Book**
Everything® **Tropical Fish Book**

All Everything® books are priced at $12.95 or $14.95, unless otherwise stated. Prices subject to change without notice.
Canadian prices range from $11.95–$31.95, and are subject to change without notice.

REFERENCE

Everything® **Astronomy Book**
Everything® **Car Care Book**
Everything® **Christmas Book, $15.00**
  ($21.95 CAN)
Everything® **Classical Mythology Book**
Everything® **Einstein Book**
Everything® **Etiquette Book**
Everything® **Great Thinkers Book**
Everything® **Philosophy Book**
Everything® **Psychology Book**
Everything® **Shakespeare Book**
Everything® **Tall Tales, Legends, &**
  Other Outrageous
  Lies Book
Everything® **Toasts Book**
Everything® **Trivia Book**
Everything® **Weather Book**

RELIGION

Everything® **Angels Book**
Everything® **Bible Book**
Everything® **Buddhism Book**
Everything® **Catholicism Book**
Everything® **Christianity Book**
Everything® **Jewish History &**
  Heritage Book
Everything® **Judaism Book**
Everything® **Prayer Book**
Everything® **Saints Book**
Everything® **Understanding Islam**
  Book
Everything® **World's Religions Book**
Everything® **Zen Book**

SCHOOL & CAREERS

Everything® **After College Book**
Everything® **Alternative Careers Book**
Everything® **College Survival Book**
Everything® **Cover Letter Book**
Everything® **Get-a-Job Book**
Everything® **Hot Careers Book**

Everything® **Job Interview Book**
Everything® **New Teacher Book**
Everything® **Online Job Search Book**
Everything® **Resume Book, 2nd Ed.**
Everything® **Study Book**

SELF-HELP/ RELATIONSHIPS

Everything® **Dating Book**
Everything® **Divorce Book**
Everything® **Great Marriage Book**
Everything® **Great Sex Book**
Everything® **Kama Sutra Book**
Everything® **Romance Book**
Everything® **Self-Esteem Book**
Everything® **Success Book**

SPORTS & FITNESS

Everything® **Body Shaping Book**
Everything® **Fishing Book**
Everything® **Fly-Fishing Book**
Everything® **Golf Book**
Everything® **Golf Instruction Book**
Everything® **Knots Book**
Everything® **Pilates Book**
Everything® **Running Book**
Everything® **Sailing Book, 2nd Ed.**
Everything® **T'ai Chi and QiGong Book**
Everything® **Total Fitness Book**
Everything® **Weight Training Book**
Everything® **Yoga Book**

TRAVEL

Everything® **Family Guide to Hawaii**
Everything® **Guide to Las Vegas**
Everything® **Guide to New England**
Everything® **Guide to New York City**
Everything® **Guide to Washington D.C.**
Everything® **Travel Guide to The**
  Disneyland Resort®,
  California Adventure®,

Universal Studios®, and
the Anaheim Area
Everything® **Travel Guide to the Walt**
  Disney World Resort®,
  Universal Studios®, and
  Greater Orlando, 3rd Ed.

WEDDINGS

Everything® **Bachelorette Party Book,**
  $9.95 ($15.95 CAN)
Everything® **Bridesmaid Book, $9.95**
  ($15.95 CAN)
Everything® **Creative Wedding Ideas**
  Book
Everything® **Elopement Book, $9.95**
  ($15.95 CAN)
Everything® **Groom Book**
Everything® **Jewish Wedding Book**
Everything® **Wedding Book, 2nd Ed.**
Everything® **Wedding Checklist,**
  $7.95 ($11.95 CAN)
Everything® **Wedding Etiquette Book,**
  $7.95 ($11.95 CAN)
Everything® **Wedding Organizer,**
  $15.00 ($22.95 CAN)
Everything® **Wedding Shower Book,**
  $7.95 ($12.95 CAN)
Everything® **Wedding Vows Book,**
  $7.95 ($11.95 CAN)
Everything® **Weddings on a Budget**
  Book, $9.95 ($15.95 CAN)

WRITING

Everything® **Creative Writing Book**
Everything® **Get Published Book**
Everything® **Grammar and Style Book**
Everything® **Grant Writing Book**
Everything® **Guide to Writing**
  Children's Books
Everything® **Screenwriting Book**
Everything® **Writing Well Book**

Available wherever books are sold!
To order, call 800-872-5627, or visit us at everything.com

Everything® and everything.com® are registered trademarks of F+W Publications, Inc.